The New City-State

The New City-State

Change and Renewal in America's Cities

by Tom McEnery
Foreword by Richard Daley, Jr.
Mayor of Chicago

ROBERTS RINEHART PUBLISHERS

For Ben, Katie, Margaret, Dolores and
all the other travellers who came to
a valley and built a city.

Copyright © 1994 by Tom McEnery
Published by Roberts Rinehart Publishers
Post Office Box 666, Niwot, Colorado 80544
International Standard Book Number 1-879373-40-8
Library of Congress Catalog Card Number 94-66090
Printed in the United States of America

Distributed in the U.S. and Canada
by Publishers Group West

Table of Contents

The future belongs to
those who can imagine it.

Luis Valdez

Great Countries Need Great Cities

Mayor Richard M. Daley,
City of Chicago

The transformation of America from a nation of farms and cities to a country predominated by suburbs has brought on a wave of city-bashing that seems to grow stronger each year. People tend to blame cities for all kinds of national problems, such as rising crime, failing schools, a declining industrial base, and pollution. This viewpoint is not only patently untrue and unfair, it also ignores the central role that cities have played, and continue to play, in our nation's economy and our national identity.

History has shown us that all great countries had great cities that defined their societies and embodied their boldest and most profound aspirations. This is no more apparent than in Tom McEnery's San Jose, which proudly anchors the remarkable city-state known as Silicon Valley. Cities are the center of commerce and culture—the fertile meeting grounds of ideas and actions that have advanced civilization over the centuries. Humankind's boundless ingenuity thrives in cities where people are brought together in pursuit of common goals and interests.

In the city of Chicago, where I have lived and worked all my life, our greatest assets are a product of the vision, forethought, and insight of our predecessors. They preserved Chicago's lakefront for recreation. They laid out our city to foster easy travel and movement between communities. They capitalized on our geographically central location by turning Chicago into the crossroads of the nation for trucks, trains, ships, and planes.

My predecessors' mission was to build a city of the future with all the conveniences and attributes a truly modern city should have. Our mission today is to build a future for our city, by enhancing our strengths as an international destination for conventions and tourism, by restoring our beautiful tree-lined streets and neighborhoods, and by attracting growing industries like health care and finance.

The challenge, of course, is to reinvest in our city at a pace and a price that will not hasten our decline. Every mayor would like a major infusion of money to give his or her city a facelift, to double the size of the police force, and to spend more on education and to launch a range of economic incentives that can bring jobs. In the real world, however, mayors must work within their means. Raising taxes only drives people, businesses, and jobs away. In *The New City-State*, Tom McEnery wisely scolds his colleagues in many cities for their dependence on federal aid, citing the efforts of several big cities (Chicago and his own San Jose among them) to work more closely with private enterprise in pointing their communities toward the twenty-first century.

Like Tom McEnery, I look positively on the future of cities across America. They can be saved and they should be saved—not only for the benefit of the minority of Americans who live in cities—but for the majority who do not as well. It is in our national interest to keep our cities alive and thriving, because cities are the economic engines of America; when cities decline, the surrounding suburbs decline as well.

While it may be true that the problems of crime, unemployment, and infrastructure decay are more acute in older cities like Chicago, Detroit, or Philadelphia, it is also true that we are further ahead than non-urban America in solving those problems. We have already begun to deal with the kinds of crime problems that many suburbs and rural areas are only now starting to experience. We're leading the fight against crime, with innovative new projects like community policing. We have already begun recycling abandoned industrial areas, while many non-urban communities continue to develop virgin farmland, blithely assuming they will never run out of space. We have already found new, cost-effective ways to rebuild 100-year-old sewer and water systems; new communities would do well to learn from our mistakes and our achievements in these and other areas.

Perhaps, most important of all, cities in America have learned what it takes to build and maintain strong communities, which are the foundation of our society. In one sense, now that we have tamed the wilderness cities represent the new frontiers of society, Today, the most compelling threat to our nation's growth and progress is not some external enemy or some overwhelming and mysterious force of nature. It is right here on our own doorstep, in struggling communities that have lost jobs and succumbed to crime, decay and despair. We cannot simply turn our backs on these communities, and believe that America will always be strong despite these failures. We must bring the same sense of urgency and a commitment to meeting these challenges as we have brought to every other challenge America has faced.

If, as a nation, we come to recognize the vital role our cities play in defining our economic and social identity, then we can build on that understanding to reshape our national priorities toward renewal instead of expansion—toward the issues that unite us instead of those that divide us—toward a culture of diversity instead a diversity of cultures. I share Tom McEnery's view that cities can—and must—be renewed through a combination of vision, leadership, and commitment. I emphasize, moreover, that in doing so, we not only guarantee a stronger nation in the century ahead, but we help fulfill the timeless promise of America as a nation of infinite possibilities that offers hope and opportunities to everyone.

Acknowledgments

The first time I wrote a book, I was fleet of pen. Before I entered public office, I wrote a fictionalized history of an early pioneer, Captain Thomas Fallon. After some lengthy research, I completed the short manuscript in about two weeks. It was intense; it was quick.

This book was to prove a different experience. I had been thinking about the essential thesis of *The New City-State* for most of my last year in office. I was very fortunate to have the help, thoughts, and friendship of a very talented and unusual public servant, Lewis Shepherd, in the genesis and evolution of this effort. As I made the transition from mayor to chairman of a nonprofit youth foundation, Lewis and I discussed and refined the ideas and the central message. Over four years, we have worked side by side on many wonderful projects designed to reform the politics and education of one corner of the world. This book is a result of that collaboration.

I was afforded the opportunity to test and clarify the theme with some of the finest young minds in America as a lecturer at the Graduate School of Business at Stanford University and for two years as the first Presidential Fellow at my alma mater, Santa Clara University. For the latter appointment, I wish to thank President Fr. Paul Locatelli and Academic Vice-President Fr. Steve Privett; I hope that this work can help improve and inspire young minds in the Jesuit tradition of service to others.

I made good use of the excellent resources at Stanford University's

Green Library, Orradre Library at Santa Clara, and the California Room at the Martin Luther King Jr. Main Library in San Jose. Lewis Shepherd and I did the primary research and analysis, but we were aided by a talented assistant in Emily Jones. In the first year of the project, Sarah Labouisse joined us after receiving an advanced degree in American history from Stanford, and she did some extraordinary research on trends in urban history.

Old friends and co-workers reviewed the work in progress and offered many good suggestions. I wish to thank David Pandori, Greg Larson, Frank Taylor, and Kathryn Ballentine for a great deal of effort and counsel with early drafts. In addition, friends who make their living as editors, Rob Elder and Allan Wylde, submitted many valuable ideas and modifications and added simple tact to some of my blunter assessments. (I could not bear omitting those that remain.) Mike Malone, a talented social critic and chronicler of technology, gave me a great deal of advice and encouragement at the inception of my efforts to describe and explain Silicon Valley, a task he does well himself.

A select group of current and former mayors from around the country submitted helpful advice and anecdotes for the final work; I should particularly thank New York's David Dinkins, Chicago's Richie Daley, and San Diego's Roger Hedgecock for their input. Ed Koch gave me an acute if unintended description of my "unremarkable" city. Former mayor Terry Goddard of Phoenix was, as always, a great source of ideas and assistance. He proves that talent and humor can go together well in the business of government.

The most talented of the recent Irish historians and a good friend, Tim Pat Coogan, was the fortuitous link with my publishers, Rick Rinehart and Jack Van Zandt. Without the encouragement and good humor of Rick, bringing this hybrid and somewhat unorthodox book to market would have been a near impossibility.

Most of all, I give my thanks and love to Jill and to Sarah, Erin, and Molly, the ultimate source of all that is valuable to me. They also served as true assistants on this book. The remainder of my inspiration came, as always, from the people of San Jose. They honored me with the chance to be their mayor and, for a brief but beautiful time, to imagine the future.

Introduction: Saving Your City

I had never lost $60 million before.

It can happen in one particular job, in the flickering of an eye. I have the scars and the headlines to prove it. That is what it is like to be a mayor in America today. I persevered, though, and so did our city, and we did so confident in our future.

That day had begun fairly unmemorably—it was going to be just another ordinary, hectic day. I had been in office a little over a year, twelve months calm and productive enough to get me named, in an editorial in the *San Jose Mercury News*, "Rookie of the Year" among my colleagues. It seemed to be clear sailing ahead with only the usual reefs to negotiate . . . until I received that fateful message: Gerald Newfarmer, my city manager, needed to speak to me urgently. I called him. In his clipped speaking style, he mentioned that we had a significant problem with our investment portfolio and that we should meet immediately. I sensed trouble, big trouble. After some quick questions that were parried deftly but disturbingly, we agreed to meet at the San Jose Athletic Club, across from old St. James Park in the historic section of the downtown.

On my way, I passed through the park. It was here in 1933 that the last lynching occurred in a major American city. A mob of well-known citizens and ne'er-do-wells meted out their form of justice to the two kidnappers and murderers of the scion of the local department store magnate. There is little to remember the event by, no historic marker. I had heard the story many times from old-timers, replete with many gory details of bludgeoning and cigarette burns. It was something I always thought of when I passed the fateful spot.

The noon rush was over. It was a very warm May afternoon, and my anxiety was tempered by the reality of just another "crisis" for this week. I entered the athletic club bar and ordered a beer. (San Jose may be larger than Boston or Washington, D.C., but a mayor here can still sneak away for a drink without causing a stir.) The bar was empty except for a few lawyer types trying to impress the cocktail waitress. Shortly Newfarmer joined me. Jerry had an air of authority and command that was always part of his standard demeanor, only today it seemed to trail a few feet behind, like a tired aide-de-camp.

I soon knew why. Our city was on the brink of bankruptcy.

Jerry outlined our predicament sketchily but ominously, in simple declarative sentences. Midlevel bureaucrats had been playing numbers games with city bonds. They had recklessly, almost insanely, borrowed the limit and beyond. Their supervisors had gambled that no one would notice, that good times would stave off the red ink. Suddenly, the house of cards was collapsing all around us, like an old masonry wall in a California quake. My career was almost finished before it had begun.

It was the worst day of my political life. The bond-loss issue, as it became known, would eventually end the careers of a number of high officials; a half dozen top administrators were fired. I had survived days that were almost as bad, and I managed to survive this one as well. My handling of San Jose's most grievous fiscal crisis, a story I tell in this book, was judged by the voters who reelected me to a second term. Still, I often look back on the traumatic and frightening few days of that late springtime of 1984. It was the single most catastrophic event of my near decade as mayor, and clearly the most instructional. I was responsible.

There were, of course, naysayers; you do make an occasional enemy in the job. I wasn't, after all, a member of Congress, trying to hide, working on reelection every two years, and remembering the name of the most obscure acquaintance. My father used to say that if you failed to make any enemies, you must not be on the side of the angels.

The job of mayor is the hardest job in government today—bar none, top to bottom, the all-out toughest. It is almost impossible to do correctly and to survive. Mayors do not have the luxury of a president's Air Force One to whisk them out of town after a bad speech or a bloody riot or away from a crowd protesting a police shooting or demanding the defeat of a housing proposal. Sitting behind that city hall desk is the most challenging assignment we give to any elected official in modern America. It is gut-wrenching, in a manner more immediate and quite apart from the job of president or governor, certainly more so than any legislator. Unlike the legislator, you are not a mere observer of things, great and gruesome. You must do, or you will certainly die.

Yet the time is also rewarding, immensely so, and offers the greatest chance for change and innovation in our democratic system. There are few jobs where you can imagine the future and actually build it: a museum, a cohort of police officers, a park, a youth service program. Mayors, at their best, can be catalysts for change and improvement, for the lessening of people's burdens, the protection of their families, the inspiration of their young. The job is at once sobering and exhilarating.

This is not an autobiography, and if it were, it would run only a chapter and a half. It is a challenge to those who care about what this nation is, where it is going, and the road it is not choosing.

When I was elected mayor in 1982, I was given a rare opportunity to change the city I love. San Jose, the eleventh-largest city in the United States, was in the grip of a dark force, suffering an identity crisis it could not answer. We had endured a period of uninspired leadership, and the dragon's teeth of apathy and decline were taking root. Some politicians run for office because they believe in the superior value of their own ideas. Others run to climb higher on the ladder of career politics or to establish one-member cults. My motivation, at least at first, was anger. I wanted things to be better than they were. I was elected first to the city council and, by age thirty-six, found myself propelled into a race for mayor by my aggressive challenge to what I enthusiastically referred to as "the sewer lobby, a coalition of ignorance, apathy, and greed." We had seen entrenched interests snuff the life out of our downtown, the heart and soul of our city, in their willy-nilly quest to become bigger than Los Angeles (and coincidentally to make a few small fortunes in the process). Through the Sixties and Seventies, San Jose had grown bigger and bigger, almost exponentially, but certainly not better. The growth was part conspiracy, part something so haphazard and disorganized that calling it a conspiracy would be giving legitimate plots a bad name.

Those of us on the sidelines during that period, in small businesses and in the neighborhoods, could only watch in amazement and disgust as the city core was suffocated, rampant abuses of power and influence were winked at, and minor corruption was tolerated. Just before the dawn of the Reagan era, I had had enough. Rashly, perhaps, I decided I could make a difference. I really wanted to climb into what Teddy Roosevelt called the arena, get some sweat and blood on me, and try to harness growth. If only we could tie the center together in ever-expanding concentric circles to our neighborhoods, chain the centrifugal forces, "the demons," and redirect them to drag San Jose, kicking and screaming if necessary, into the twenty-first century.

We had a measure of success. As the Nineties matured and beckoned toward the new century, I was able to leave office with great pride in how far San Jose had traveled. Today San Jose has a functioning downtown, described by the *Chicago Tribune* as "a manmade sight as majestic as the snow-capped peaks and potentially as lucrative as the rich farm soil that sustained the region for nearly two centuries—a downtown skyline." A bit hyperbolic, certainly, but I like it, and its verisimilitude is as solid as the fact that our industrial parks, comprising thousands of acres, are crammed with the greatest entrepreneurs and thinkers since the Industrial Revolution: the wizards of Silicon Valley. Combine that with the lowest crime rate of any of the top fifty cities in the country, and you have an enviable combination.

We have been called California's city of the future, the city on the cutting edge, the city where dreams come true. In the words of a *Washington Post* writer, we are "the model of the good life in America." Like all good things, it came with a high price tag, for this metamorphosis was painful and punishing. I was mayor, and the buck, the blame, and some of the accolades arrived on my doorstep like uninvited relatives at Christmas.

I also had something much more significant: I was allowed to dream and to watch dreams come true. I have seen parents and teachers take back a neighborhood school all but lost to drugs and those forces of darkness. I have seen that same school selected as one of the 200 best in the nation twenty months later. I have watched a local enterprise zone energize and revitalize large areas of our old downtown core. I have visited and been amazed by ten-year-olds at our new Tech Museum of Innovation becoming one with a personal computer and bursting forth with a poem, a portrait, or their idea for a redesigned city center.

The American city can be saved, and with it two centuries of accumulated progress, innovation, and achievement. I believe that the shared values of our nation, values so intertwined with our cities, make regeneration a moral imperative. This salvation will not be the result of more federal largesse or another "save urban America" plan from Congress. It will come through the initiative and creativity and hard work of those closest to the problem. San Jose and other cities have pioneered innovative approaches to some age-old problems and waged a battle against some new and pernicious plagues.

In all of these challenges, the most important ingredient is leadership. No other factor, natural or economic, so affects the success of a city's endeavors as that single, indispensable quality of leadership. As Oscar Wilde noted in judging literature, there are no moral or immoral books, only those well written or poorly written. The modern city is like the modern company; it is either well led or poorly led, inspired or adrift. Despite the hand-wringing and gnashing of teeth from politicians and pundits alike, bemoaning declining revenues, federal apathy, or even cosmic forces, there is no substitute for leadership. In a community's rare confluence of leadership and imagination, alchemy can result.

Citizens can judge for themselves the quality of their city-state's leaders. They do, every day in the streets and cafés and cabs. They can also make that judgment, do not forget, on Election Day.

Part One

THE IDEA

1
THE NEW CITY-STATE

A city-state is not a mere society, having a common place.
It exists for the sake of noble actions.
—*Aristotle*

A big-city mayor thinks big. He sits behind a big desk and thinks of massive projects, tall skyscrapers. There are heavy responsibilities but enormous opportunities, and it helps to have a can-do attitude. "Our obstacles are surmountable" is the standard rhetorical flair in any mayor's State of the City speech.

In sharp contrast, most Americans outside city hall see the typical American city today as anemic, embattled, besieged. We lament "the dying city," threatened on all sides.

The most dramatic demonstration I have ever seen of the vulnerability of a city was on October 17, 1989, when the tremendous Loma Prieta earthquake struck the Bay Area. At 5:04 P.M., just as city employees were packing up to head home, I was in my top-floor office in city hall. I felt a shake like no other, and its length and strength let me know that "the big one" was finally here. Instead of doing the sensible thing, the practiced duck-and-cover, I went to the window. I watched as the nearby county government high-rise swayed from side to side.

San Jose, though much closer to the epicenter than San Francisco or Oakland, fared much better than those cities—no loss of life, few injuries, but widespread property damage. Our coastal neighbor to the south, though, Santa Cruz, was cursed with a nineteenth-century downtown sitting five miles from the epicenter of that 7.1 quake. After a day of securing our own citizens and harnessing our emergency resources, I decided I would go to Santa Cruz to lend a hand. We had a cohort of police officers there already, helping the besieged local force. The dead and injured toll was climbing as victims were pulled from the rubble of destroyed buildings, and I wanted to offer help.

I had read the phrase before: "The smell of death was in the air." Nothing prepared me, though, for my sunny noontime walk through Santa Cruz's downtown, or what was left of it. My mind flashed on newsreel images of wartime London just after a V-bomb had smashed into a neighborhood, raining death and destruction. In 1991, we would see these images on CNN from Saudi Arabia and Israel, the results of Iraqi Scud missiles. But I didn't need metaphors. On my own doorstep, in a town I had visited hundreds of times, here was the literal dying city. The faces of those whose homes were destroyed, whose businesses and life's work lay in ruins after a few seconds of shaking, or whose relatives were being pulled, alive or dead, from heaps of rubble showed me nothing but despair and hopelessness. It was the most horrible sight I have ever seen.

Forty months later, the rebuilt downtown of Santa Cruz opened with fanfare and hoopla, a well-deserved celebration for a city whose citizens put their shoulders to the wheel and worked together.* Local government had a lot to do with the success. It was redevelopment in a microcosm.

Not every American city suffers an earthquake or a devastating hurricane or flood, but the challenges every city faces are dramatic and historic in fundamental ways. New economic, social, and political burdens land on the mayor's desk each day. The good news is, some cities with spunk and determination are responding. What I see in vibrant metropolises around the country, and what we have experienced in San Jose, is a strong rebuff to the trendy assessment that cities are archaic relics, doomed to fail.

What Is a City?

It is a commonplace to say that as America's cities go, so goes the nation. But when we speak of our cities, we need to have clearly fixed in our minds what these places are. Urban areas have developed far beyond what the Irish writer Brendan Behan once described: "A city is a place

_____

*We established a San Jose Earthquake Relief Fund, which contributed some $820,000 to Santa Cruz, Los Gatos, Watsonville, and other towns most affected by the 1989 quake.

where you are least likely to be bitten by a wild sheep!" That sparse definition does not capture the size, reality, color, and excitement of the modern American city.

The Census Bureau long ago defined an "urban place" as having a population over 2,500 people. In 1910, policy wonks of the day began using the horrible phrase "Standard Metropolitan Statistical Area" for research purposes, and, like most appalling bureaucratic labels, it stuck. By 1961, some of these SMSAs had grown so massive and crowded that urban scholar Jean Gottman used the term "megalopolis" (actually, the name of a small town in Greece) to describe the modern large city.

Malthusian Metropolis

By the early 1990s, global population had surpassed 5 billion people. Adding some 90 million people a year will take us to 6 billion by the year 2000. Some 45 percent of the world's inhabitants now live in urban areas, and because most new population growth is in cities, that ratio will increase to 58 percent by the turn of the century. At the higher end of the scale, the United States already has some 77 percent of its population in cities.

Three out of four Americans today live in cities or their nearby suburbs. The top ten cities in the country have populations over 1 million, and the eleventh largest, my own San Jose, will crack that club by the turn of the century. Just a century and a half ago, New York City was the only city in the United States to hit the 250,000 mark, but by 1900, there were a dozen, three with over 1 million people. Speaking today of the nation's "big cities" casts a wide net: by 1993, we had more than 220 cities with over 100,000 people.[1]

No area of the country has escaped urbanization. When the 1990 census defined "urban" as central cities of 50,000 or more and their suburbs, even the bucolic South counted 69 percent of its population as urban. Western states are 86 percent urban, and the Northeast crowds in at 79 percent. Trendsetting California leads the nation with 93 percent of its population in cities.[2]

Talking about national policy today in almost any field is becoming more and more synonymous with urban policy. Any nation is defined by, represented by, judged by its cities.

Observers judge our cities harshly, in a spirit of crisis that so powerfully paints the urban picture in American minds today. I have lived in a city all my life and can understand the fatalism of Aleksandr Solzhenitsyn, who concluded years ago that "urban life is utterly unnatural. . . . The cities of today are cancerous tumors."[3] (Solzhenitsyn spent his years in exile in the backwoods of Vermont before his 1994 return to Russia.) After 1992's Chicago flood and Los Angeles riots, after all the other calamities that have afflicted our cities, liberal social critics and curmudgeonly conservatives alike seem united in their judgment. "Are Cities Obsolete?" *Newsweek* magazine asked in a 1992 cover story. "Is the American City Obsolete?" echoed the *New York Times* in a high-profile Sunday piece.

Cities fell to a low point in self-esteem during the 1992 presidential campaign, when it seemed that establishment mayors gave up any hope of solving their problems themselves. While average citizens were cheering Ross Perot's assault on billion-dollar federal sinkholes, some mayors took on the demeanor of welfare recipients, incapable of independent action and dependent on federal assistance for survival. Ray Flynn of Boston, in his capacity as president of the U.S. Conference of Mayors, charged at the beginning of the campaign that the federal government had shown a "callous indifference" toward America's cities and blamed "the whole Washington bureaucracy, and that includes the White House, the Congress, Democrats as well as Republicans. There has been no policy whatsoever."[4] Old-line mayors around the country first courted Bill Clinton and proposed massive, traditionally-Democratic spending programs, releasing a $35 billion "seven-point program to revitalize the nation's cities." When Clinton instead campaigned as a "new kind of Democrat," they turned in frustration to Perot and ended up being burned by the ambivalent billionaire. In June of that year, a group of big-city mayors trooped to Perot headquarters in Dallas. Boston's Flynn revealingly answered the question of why they were there: "Mr. Perot is a hot item in America today. . . . If there's a tone of frustration in our voice today that brings us here to Dallas, Texas, it's because nobody is listening to us." Alongside Flynn were the mayors of Cleveland, Newark, and Miami. Rounding out the group was San Diego's Maureen O'Connor, who had indicated her political judgment by endorsing Jerry Brown in the California primary over Bill Clinton—Brown's expected "Klingon vote" never materialized. Perot told the mayors, as they dejectedly reported afterward, that he would be "a fool" to endorse their $35 billion plan without studying it first.[5] No more was heard of Perot's stand on cities, and the old-line mayors returned to the Democratic fold. As Willie Sutton said of banks, they believed that's where the money is.

A liberal Washington think tank, the Economic Policy Institute, issued a report in the midst of the 1992 presidential campaign, trumpeting the buzzword "infrastructure" and demanding $60 billion to $125 billion in increased federal spending on cities annually. The National Urban League renewed its call for a "Marshall Plan for America," proposing $50 billion more to cities per year for ten years. "Cost is not the issue," the league's director said in proposing the plan.[6] But cost is an issue, and an even more important issue is effectiveness. The question most observers would ask before committing more dollars is, aren't there better ways to help the cities than pumping in more federal money? That question remains unanswered, and new plans abound. David Dinkins, then mayor of New York City, delivered a twenty-four-page letter to President-elect Clinton the day after his election. The letter was a plea for billions more in federal funding for housing, roads, schools, bridges, police, and job training directed into the cities.

Such top-down plans for urban renewal have been tested over the past three decades, and the result of the simple test alone has been a resounding failure. The main federal welfare program, Aid to Families with Dependent Children (AFDC), is widely viewed as terribly flawed, spawning generations of families shackled to the government dole and with little incentive to get jobs. President Clinton and Congress dueled in 1994 with competing welfare reform programs. The high-rise public housing projects of the 1950s and 1960s have been disastrous, winding up as breeding grounds for crime and despair. The urban "renewal" grants and highway program of the same period destroyed neighborhoods and encouraged abandonment of the cities. Billions of dollars in public works and job-training schemes have come and gone with little or no impact, except on the reelection of the often-cynical congressional incumbents who supported them.

Scholars in urban studies have begun to argue that traditional cities are anachronistic and that leaders must take account of global changes and opportunities to survive into the next century. The message has not filtered out to every local leader across the country, but more and more are realizing that a new era beckons. A city council member in New York publicly refused to participate in the Conference of Mayors' 1992 march on Washington for more federal funds, asking, "Can Washington really consider our city a good investment? Would you invest in a corporation run this poorly? I wouldn't."[7]

Rise of the New City-State

In May 1991, faced with yet another citywide fiscal crisis, the *New York Times* opened its Op-Ed page to two dozen short submissions on "saving New York City." The ideas came from New Yorkers high and low, businessman and pastor, social worker and poet. Proposed solutions ranged from the straightforward (cut spending) to the controversial (a youth curfew). Some were indignant: one respondent ordered New Yorkers to "Stop whining! Whining is not New York's style."

One contributor was blunt: the state superintendent of banks advised the city to "privatize most services, including education, but retain strict oversight of them. Provide vital services like public safety and water. Fund by local taxes."[8] That advice was lost among a page of utopian, draconian or brainless ideas. What readers did not learn is that entrepreneurial cities across the country are already taking those steps and more—much more.

In the final decade of the twentieth century, cities face the imperative of adopting the mantle and the modus operandi of the old mercantile and political centers of another time and place. The leading American cities of the 1990s are emerging as new city-states, more complex and ambitious than ever before, with autonomy and governmental scope reminiscent of Renaissance Italy or the Greek polis.

The new city-state is an entrepreneur. Strong and visionary mayors around the country are essentially forming their own departments of defense, commerce, even state, as they deal almost independently with violent crime, economic expansion, and international trade. Highly evolved police departments, forceful economic development offices, redevelopment and other funding mechanisms, sister-city and international trade relationships, all are found in the toolbox of innovative mayors. Today, local leaders with imagination and drive are inventing (not "reinventing") the American city-state as a powerful, independent actor in the nation and the world.

This successful new breed of mayors and local leaders have one thing in common: they see cities in a new way. They do so because they are forced to, as federal and state governments choose to balance budgets on the backs of the cities, and municipal governments face problems and challenges far more complicated than potholes. Look around and you see emerging a new kind of city, necessarily self-reliant and more independent in balancing resources to needs. Mayors today are blazing new trails, with imagination as important a tool as political acumen.

Imagination is critical to the future of the city. As town became city, and city became metropolis and megalopolis, there was no corresponding expansion in the vision—the picture of the future—used by local authorities to shape and lead their communities. The new city, aware of its profile in the world and the opportunities that can bring, is trying to recapture the sense of self-governing autonomy lost when modern technology began to break through city boundaries and break down city loyalties. The new technological and market forces that cities encounter are not beyond their control. Some American cities are harnessing those forces and shaping them to serve the human needs of their citizens.

The city-state prepares to prosper by gaining control over its own destiny. In the 1990s, major American cities will have the chance to serve as vital centers in a multipolar world, created by the end of the cold war and the transformation of the U.S. defense-oriented economy. The way a city presents itself to its region, to its state, to Washington, and to the outside world is now a primary concern, and the health of its finances and the safety of its streets are critical measures we will all use to judge the city-state. To exploit every opportunity for new partners and new priorities, the civic, political, and business leaders in each American city must rethink all their old approaches to economics, public safety, and even "foreign policy."

The City-State Economy

In 1815, Thomas Jefferson wrote to a friend about the revolutionary changes in Europe: "To me, they have been like the howlings of the winter storm over the battlements, while warm in my bed." Jefferson, then out of office, could view foreign affairs with a happy detachment. Bill

Clinton, who assumed during his 1992 campaign that in office he could concentrate on his domestic agenda, found in his first hundred days howling demands abroad, in the Balkans and the rest of the world, that rivaled the storms his predecessors had faced.

Fueling the President's new economic proposals in 1993 were the exploding demands of big spenders, pent-up and muffled for twelve years. Some were legitimate, thanks to the wrongheaded priorities of the Reagan-Bush era. Our cities desperately did need attention. Many such ideas, though, as Dorothy Parker once said in reviewing a book, should not be put down lightly—they should be hurled away with great force. I watched with concern as the nation's mayors trooped, top hats in hand, to the White House soon after the inauguration to lay a bill on the president's desk. I knew in my gut that the resulting "economic stimulus package" was doomed to failure.

Not that the mayors couldn't make a case for their billion-dollar wish list. Urban needs, which weren't met in the previous decade, are great. Teen mothers and crack babies, neighborhoods with crumbling schools and barbaric crime rates, all have bellowed the truth at our leaders. The statistics are frightening: in 1960, there was one felony for every three cops nationwide; in 1990, three felonies for every one police officer. Even more alarming is a societal snapshot: William Buckley correctly states that "the most readily identifiable tragedy of modern life is the illegitimate child." In 1970, the rate of illegitimacy hovered near 40 percent among blacks and a little over 5 percent for whites; two decades later, the rate among whites was 21.8 percent and among blacks 67.9 percent. Particularly in inner cities, we face households where there just may be no parents anymore.

Democrats blame Republican administrations for callous indifference; Republicans blame Democratic values and lifestyles. It was appealing in 1993, with a united White House and Congress, to expect an opened tap of Washington dollars to flow into city coffers and solve urban problems.

The cities were genuinely hurting. In the decade from 1980 to 1990, federal funds to cities were cut by more than half. What had been $47.2 billion in federal aid had fallen to $21.7 billion. Mass transit funds were cut in half, and one major subsidized-housing program was cut by 70 percent.[9] The federal government (as well as government at the state level) has been asking local city halls to do more and giving them less support to do it with. Examples abound in areas such as housing. In New York and Chicago, low-income families who need to apply for public housing today put on waiting lists of two or three *years* before they are assigned public housing. In 1992 alone, the Los Angeles Housing Authority's waiting list of applicants for public housing grew from 12,000 to over 20,000 for rare openings in the fewer than 9,000 units in the city projects. And that list is considered a last resort; it was compiled only after a waiting list of 50,000 applicants for federal rent-assistance housing units was closed.[10]

Yet cities continue trying to meet the demands of federal and state mandates and guidelines on housing, as they do on so many other issues. Robert Isaac, mayor of Colorado Springs, has criticized the explosion of mandated programs: "Congress makes many promises and passes many laws and can't fund them anymore, but that doesn't stop them. We're going to have to start electing magicians at the local level."

Too many mayors have essentially thrown up their hands in final dismay. In the aftermath of the 1992 riots in South Central and other depressed Los Angeles neighborhoods, Tom Bradley ducked the blame. Not for him Harry Truman's "The buck stops here." For Bradley, the buck was passed via airmail, 3,000 miles: "The underlying alienation is due to the fact that since 1980 there has been a tremendous reduction of federal funds and of interest in the cities of the nation." Bradley deflected any responsibility, saying that poverty cannot "be corrected by a mayor or all of City Hall put together."[11] (Governor Pete Wilson, a former mayor of San Diego himself, took a similar don't-blame-me attitude, offering only to tour the area by helicopter.)

In that spirit came the Clinton administration's first economic bill, the infamous $19.5 billion "stimulus package." The proposal was based on a list, provided by the U.S. Conference of Mayors, "ready-to-go" construction projects. The original list of 7,000 projects was politically correct: it included over 500 cities and claimed to create 400,000 jobs. But it was nothing more than a wish list, and a mighty expensive one at that. Presenting it to Henry Cisneros, incoming secretary of Housing and Urban Development, and Federico Peña, the new secretary of transportation, who had, respectively, been mayors of San Antonio and Denver during the eighties, the mayors' conference executive director Tom Cochran said, "All we need is money."

I have worked with Cochran before and was surprised by the politically naive attitude, but not by the lack of judgment. I had a chance to make this point personally at a small Silicon Valley dinner in the San Jose suburb of Los Gatos in February 1993. In attendance were the newly inaugurated Bill Clinton and Al Gore and a handful of corporate heads. I warned the president against the wish list and suggested that federal money for cities would be better directed into education and public-private endeavors, à la Silicon Valley partnerships. In his most reassuring tones, Clinton responded, "Don't worry, Tom." He seemed in total agreement with me: America's cities should become less reliant, not more, on aid from Washington if they are ever to climb out of the recession's cellar. However, all the president's men continued to push the package. The administration ignored the mixed signals at its peril. The bill died in the U.S. Senate, and the president received a black eye in his first legislative foray.

As most Americans suspect, and as many senators came to respect, the solution isn't as easy as throwing more money at cities. Just as Washington needs to care again about cities, mayors need to recognize the fundamental changes that have occurred in the national economy and the very fabric of metropolitan life. Successful cities today, and those marked successful in the next century, are those responding to challenges by recognizing a new era of opportunities. They find new sources of revenue in recycled industrial areas, beckoning economic relationships overseas and partnerships for those savvy enough to seek them.

We have followed that different path in San Jose. Just as America launched the Marshall Plan to rebuild a war-torn Europe after the cataclysm of World War II, we battled urban deterioration by priming the economic pump ourselves. In the capital of Silicon Valley, instead of debating enterprise zones for a decade, we enacted them in eight weeks. By waiving taxes initially to attract small and large businesses, we soon saw tax revenues flow into our coffers. We gave to get, and we got San Jose's new skyline, featuring a landmark Fairmont Hotel, office towers, a new convention center, three new museums, light-rail trolleys, and a city full of workers making good salaries and paying taxes to hire police and youth workers. To maintain the economic base underwriting all our efforts in building a safe community, we aggressively sought business partners among Valley firms, following the advice given in *Casablanca* by Claude Rains: we began to round up the usual suspects. An entrepreneurial city hall helped IBM, Hewlett-Packard, and dozens of others expand, while we recruited Fujitsu, Hitachi, and Sony to our industrial tax base, adding more revenue. Neal Peirce, a *Washington Post* columnist, called our approach "an amazing exercise in Robin Hood economics." Describing our redevelopment strategy to use industrial park revenues to finance a new attention to our decayed core, he approvingly wrote in 1987 that "for the first time anywhere, downtown is exploiting suburbia—not the reverse."[12] All this came with *no* federal redevelopment funds; those failed projects had been closed out years before.

Too often, observers point out the obstacles a city may face in attracting new business or keeping existing companies in town. A city's officials may bemoan the unattractive business climate of the inner city as if those conditions were static. Well, they are not static and immutable. An entrepreneurial city hall can grab the reins and make any number of changes for the better. Cities have an array of levers they can use and manipulate to encourage investment and industry, making their economic package more attractive. Public subsidies can be cautiously offered for land purchase or for environmental cleanup of old or polluted sites. General plans and zoning laws can be amended, not as a sop to special-interest developers but as a concerted effort at reform. Infrastructural requirements like sewer lines, roads, and communication links can all be enhanced by local government, and obstacles can be removed. The city-state needs to be as flexible as a successful entrepreneur in the private sector.

"Three Ps"—a Mantra for the City-State

During my second term, which began in 1987, as our entrepreneurial style took hold, our neighbor San Francisco was losing about 100 companies per year. Some were going to other states, but others were just relocating to communities in Silicon Valley. New companies settled into a new crop of buildings in the industrial parks we designed on land that had recently been orchards. They were doing the right thing for their shareholders, their customers, and certainly for the economy of new cities like San Jose.

There are thousands of attributes that one could ascribe to the well-run city-state, simply because city-states are flexible enough to employ different tactics for different circumstances. Overall, though, I see three strategic areas of concentration for successful cities. First, *professional management* is essential. Second, the city should operate with a culture of *public entrepreneurship*. Third, *political will* is the key that turns the lock on success, and without it, no mayor can hope to accomplish any good plan. To complete this discussion of city-state economics, we should examine the "Three Ps," strategic keys to success.

Professional Management. "Professional management" as a phrase carries the currency of a buzzword in government. Everyone knows the phrase, but no one does anything about it. In practice, it is largely unknown, an oxymoron like "military intelligence."

In too many cities, a nineteenth-century mayor or turn-of-the-century city manager could be brought back to life today and plopped into his old chair in city hall, and he would feel perfectly comfortable with the organizational structure and practices operating in the 1990s. The same strings would be attached to the same levers, which he would pull with the same impotent, self-deceiving air of control that his modern counterparts show. That is unacceptable. Change is endemic in the private sector, and top-notch municipal governments are learning that lesson as well. Cities need to search continually for more effective and efficient management practices, to sharpen their competitive edges and prevent major headaches down the road.

San Jose has scored well on annual rankings of the financial stability and fiscal management of the nation's thirty largest cities. In 1993, using measures of long-range planning, budgeting controls, accounting systems, and financial reporting, *Financial World* magazine ranked San Jose fourth in the country for the second straight year, and again we were listed with Dallas, Phoenix, and Portland as the only cities with A's. We ended up as the best-managed city in California; San Diego came in a distant nineteenth, and San Francisco was an embarrassing twenty-fifth out of thirty, with a C+ grade.

Management Grades for the
Thirty Largest American Cities

Dallas	A
Phoenix	A -
Portland	A -
San Jose	A -
Milwaukee	B +
Seattle	B +
San Antonio	B +
Austin	B +
Indianapolis	B +
Ft. Worth	B +
Denver	B
Oklahoma City	B
Boston	B
Baltimore	B

Memphis	B
El Paso	B
Cleveland	B
Los Angeles	B -
San Diego	B -
New York City	B -
Columbus	B -
Nashville	B -
Chicago	B -
Jacksonville	B -
San Francisco	C +
Houston	C +
Washington	C
New Orleans	C
Philadelphia	C -
Detroit	D +

Source: Financial World, March 1993

We receive such a ranking proudly, but it serves best as a pleasant affirmation of the controls we took after a 1984 bond-loss debacle, described in a later chapter. Heads rolled, practices were updated, and our administrative structure was revamped. Another benefit of placing value on professionalism is a more efficient staff. San Jose ranked first among the fifty largest cities in the country in a December 1991 study for the lowest ratio of city employees. San Jose's lean government has only 6.7 employees per 1,000 people, while Houston has 10.9, Chicago has 12.9, Philadelphia has 17, and New York has 20.8 per 1,000 people.[13]

A simple lesson in professional management we try to employ in our city is to allow creative people the freedom to pursue a good idea. The mayor is not always the best judge of whether or not their ideas are good; the people are. That element of risk taking, combined with good judgment and common sense, is the essence of entrepreneurship in city government. The ideas don't always work, but they don't have to every time. Experience keeps score, indicating eventually which avenues are promising and which to avoid. The key, though, is in the theme: managerial empowerment of creative, energetic professionals. It works.

A mayor with an oversized politician's ego learns this lesson reluctantly, but the results of good professional management always reflect well on the administration and the mayor's office anyway. Trying to avoid megalomania, I always allowed other bright stars to exist in my universe. Joe McNamara, my chief of police, always rivaled me for positive press attention, but then, he performed excellently in his job. So did many other stars on our team, such as City Manager Les White and council members Shirley Lewis, Judy Stabile, and Susan Hammer. Hammer followed me as mayor and was notably effective with programs for child care and neighborhood revitalization.

Start-up City

Silicon Valley programs often trace their birth to loose reins on professionals. One recent example originated as a summer research project by one of my students at Stanford University after I left the mayor's office. While teaching at the Graduate School of Business, I found that most first-year students were looking to the East Coast for summer jobs. I made a determined effort to get these bright M.B.A.s down to San Jose for a firsthand look at an entrepreneurial economy. One student, Sarah Daniels, took a summer position in our Office of Economic Development. After a week, she was still waiting for word from OED's director on what to do. My advice to her was simple: identify a project that looks worthwhile but isn't going anywhere, and take it over. Run with the ball.

She did. Sarah adopted the idea of a software design center to support the Valley's budding designers. The concept did not even exist on paper, only in office brainstorming. By the end of the summer, she had worked out a feasibility study and development plan and had even reached a verbal agreement with Novell Corporation to provide funding and personnel in a public-private partnership with the city. She was phenomenal.

Unfortunately, Sarah returned to complete her M.B.A., and the city took over the project. Measuring city productivity is too often like counting dog years—what takes one private-sector person can sometimes take seven city employees. Fifteen months later, San Jose opened a full-fledged Center for Software Innovation, offering space for individual designers and small companies to test their programming code on state-of-the-art computers. Had I still been mayor, I might have considered a less generic, more appropriate name for the facility: the Sarah Daniels Center.

As a postscript, in Sarah's second year at Stanford, while still pursuing her degree, she teamed up with another graduate student to form a start-up software company of her own. The company is growing steadily today. That is the spirit of the Valley.

The San Jose Metropolitan Area, or Silicon Valley, is home to more corporate headquarters and Fortune 500 companies than Los Angeles and twice as many as our neighbor and regional rival San Francisco. One of the most important lessons we have learned in the San Jose city-state comes from studying Silicon Valley's success. Cities of the future will be knowledge centers rather than manufacturing centers. Information will be the most valued premium in the economy of the next century, and our city-state's long-term viability will rest on our ability to nurture the way our citizens and our local companies acquire and use information. The professionalism of the city's management cadre is critical in remaining competitive with other cities and multinational corporations. As we keep finding in the high-tech industry, those corporations view themselves as world citizens selling in a global market, with no strong ties necessarily to a single community. Just as to most citizens, city-limit lines mean very little to a CEO. Mayors should think exactly the same way. The city-state must adapt to the changing realities of competition, and professional management should be a given.

Public Entrepreneurship: The Meek Inherit Nothing. On June 6, 1991, Mayor Mary Moran of Bridgeport, Connecticut, did something no other big city in America has done since the Great Depression. On behalf of her city, she filed for bankruptcy.

Bridgeport has over 140,000 people; it is the largest city in the state. It also happens to be located in one of the wealthiest counties in the country, but it faces social and economic ills familiar to every other city. Fifteen percent of its population was on welfare. That day in 1991, Bridgeport filed in federal bankruptcy court for protection under Chapter 9 of the bankruptcy laws, in a last attempt to escape the requirement of a balanced budget. Even after essential city services like street cleaning were eliminated, the required balanced budget could have been achieved only by raising the city's property taxes 20 percent. City officials saw no alternative.

Eventually, the city established a receivership, and without having to "go bankrupt," it achieved the same end. At the same time, not far away, officials in New York City were facing a $3.5 billion deficit. The country's largest city was forced to enact $2 billion in service and spending cuts, along with $1 billion in new taxes and fees—and the mayor still had to go to Albany and beg Governor Mario Cuomo for state assistance. All of that trauma occurred for a one-year fix, though. The deal failed to solve the long-term problem; in fact, it made it worse. The city had to raise money in May 1991 by selling $1.2 billion in high-yield notes, an unpalatable choice that simply passed the buck down the line to future Gracie Mansion residents. In 1992 and 1993, the sense of crisis returned like a bad penny. The anticipated gap for 1994 was $2.1 billion, which Mayor Dinkins hoped to resolve with service cuts, spending cuts, a $300 million tax increase and extra money from the state and federal government. In 1993, Dinkins was forced to campaign for reelection having raised taxes by more than a $1 billion over the previous three years to balance budgets.[14] He couldn't sell that to an angry electorate and became ex–Mayor Dinkins in a sound defeat by Rudy Giuliani.

By law, a city has to balance its budget every year. Unlike the federal government, it cannot run an annual deficit. Cities are therefore particularly vulnerable to recessions, when tax revenue plummets and demand on city services increases. In a survey published by the League of California Cities in 1992, a full 60 percent of the 330 cities in the state had dipped into fiscal reserves to balance their budgets, 66 percent had delayed construction projects, and 70 percent had raised taxes or fees. None of these were solutions oriented to the long term, though. Only 42 percent had cut staff positions, and barely 28 percent had actually reduced spending from the previous year. In those numbers lies little evidence of a creative, entrepreneurial approach to city-state economics.

Too many local officials find it more convenient to blame other parties for their problems. As state governments have suffered in the recession, they have passed along their losses to the cities and created a finger-pointing cycle with only one real result: it irks citizens to see their state and local officials playing the blame game. It annoys me as well.

New York State's estimated annual budget gaps in the past few years have reached as high as $40 billion, requiring a raft of "cost-sharing" measures in which cities took the short end. In 1992, Governor Lowell Weicker cut state aid to Connecticut cities by as much as 43 percent, holding back millions from already straining coffers in cities like Bridgeport. In 1993, California's governor Pete Wilson announced a draconian plan to hold back property tax revenues from cities and counties, potentially costing Oakland $22 million, San Francisco $25 million, and San Jose around $20 million dollars—cuts that California cities have vigorously and successfully fought. The meek inherit nothing in the world of mayors.

Beyond the blame game, there must be a better answer for cities. Richie Daley, mayor of Chicago, said in the wake of Bridgeport's hardship, "I'm a proponent of big cities going bankrupt—in many cases, it's the only way out." But Daley was speaking of short-term, back-to-the-wall situations. In his own city management, he has shown a remarkable ability to take the long-term view. In the long run, there are only two potential escape routes for cities fighting the contemporary budget-crunch epidemic.

The first route is the traditional one of relying on increased federal aid for cities. Bailing out our cities sounds good on a political platform in a mayoral campaign, even in a presidential race. Its track record as a strategy, though, is one of failure. Like a heroin junkie on methadone, or a welfare queen addicted to food stamps, cities have come to expect the bail-out and, in fact, now insist upon it as an American right. Even when it comes, cities have perpetually repeated the profligate errors that caused budget crunches in the first place. In 1992, as New York City suffered through yet another budget crisis, *New York* magazine pointed out that in the previous ten years the private sector of the city's economy had grown only 7 percent, while combined federal and state aid to New York City had increased by 78 percent, and the city's operating budgets exploded by 114 percent.[15]

The lesson of the 1990s is that our nation cannot possibly continue to subsidize local government at previous levels. Federal largesse, justified or not, is not a long-term solution to the economic challenges facing cities. It will not continue. The new city-state must find another way, and that route lies in developing a governmental culture of entrepreneurship, the only possible solution to current budget problems.

Philadelphia has begun to take that path. Throughout the 1980s, it deserved the nickname City of Brotherly Debt, running unlawful deficits in eight out of ten years. The state of Pennsylvania finally had to step in to create a new agency, the Pennsylvania Intergovernmental Cooperation Authority, to review and approve the city's budget plans as a condition for arranging state-guaranteed borrowing. To my mind, that is the worst of all fates that can befall a city, for it robs the citizens and their elected representatives of their direct authority. It was a sad day for the principle of self-reliance, and local resentment was bound to boil over.

In November 1991, the citizens finally stopped listening to empty promises from a can't-do political machine. Ed Rendell was elected mayor with a whopping 68 percent of the vote, on a tough platform of straight talk about the city's finances. He made no sweet promises, just presented a determined plan for a new fiscal integrity. I can testify how tempting it can be to slip and slide on the local campaign trail. Your advisors will tell you to shade a little on the positive side in projecting next year's growth figures or to trim a percentage point from expenses. It takes discipline, a strong gut, to keep your message honest and responsible.

Only a month into office, Rendell proposed a five-year budget plan detailing $1.1 billion in spending cuts, labor savings, streamlined management, and innovative new ways to increase revenues. The state's fiscal oversight board approved the plan, and since then Rendell has proven to be a model of pragmatic politics. He has privatized some sacred-cow programs like nursing homes and health centers and has balanced wage-freeze concessions from municipal unions with management staff layoffs. He has even begun replacing hundreds of stoplights with cheaper stop signs.[16] Best of all, Rendell has refused to portray the federal government as a scapegoat or a sugar daddy and has held back when other big-city mayors petitioned Bill Clinton for billions in new spending.

Cities do not, of course, have within their grasp every lever guiding their economic engine. Seattle, which benefited greatly from a regional economic boom right through the late 1980s into the early part of this decade, reacted with shock when Boeing, the region's largest employer, suddenly announced its intention to lay off thousands of workers. No major city in the country has been so dependent on a single employer; the aerospace giant provided at its 1990 peak 106,000 jobs in a metropolitan area of 2 million. The ripple effect of the layoffs is tremendously damaging to the city's economy.

But with an entrepreneurial attitude, the city-state can find many tools to attract and support business investment. Local business taxes are a key component. As a percentage of the average company's total tax bill (federal, state, and local business taxes), San Jose takes only a 5.5 percent bite, while San Francisco takes 6.3 percent, giving San Jose a small but meaningful comparative advantage. Meanwhile, some old-line Rust Belt cities burden companies even more heavily. New York City, which has seen many corporations leave for more hospitable venues, not coincidentally leads the list with 20.1 percent of a company's total tax bill going to the city and county. Detroit, Baltimore, and Chicago all grab more than 8 percent of the tax bill, while cities with very low business tax bills include activist Sun Belt communities like Phoenix, Jacksonville, Houston, and San Diego.[17]

Public Dogma: The Entrepreneur's Creed

The wave of entrepreneurial mayors in the 1980s, led by Terry Goddard in Phoenix, Henry Cisneros in San Antonio, and others, have been followed in the 1990s by leaders like Ed Rendell of Philadelphia and Dick Riordan in Los Angeles. Rudy Giuliani now offers even the nation's largest city, New York, a chance at innovation and energetic change. But Giuliani and others have learned from their predecessors.

Bill Hudnut was a minister before becoming mayor of Indianapolis in the late 1970s. In his secular role, he once outlined some principles for the creed of an entrepreneurial city. First, partnerships are created. Second, the city takes risks in return for tangible returns. Third, such a city uses and searches for more efficient and effective management methods to sharpen its competitive edge. Fourth, a city should treat its amenities as economic assets. Indianapolis proved that point with a cluster of successful major sports facilities, constructed in the past decade. Fifth and finally, the entrepreneurial city should attract urban reinvestment by relying not on Washington's money but on creative use of nontraditional resources on the home front—as in hard promotion of enterprise zones and other self-reliant methods.[18]

Downtown Indianapolis. Photo by Rob Banayote.

Our city government attempts to support the powerful economic engine of Silicon Valley by emulating the entrepreneurial spirit of the Valley's private sector. During the 1980s we invested $1.5 billion in the downtown redevelopment renaissance. All the while, we knew that our most important contributions would be made in conjunction with the private sector, and we worked in partnerships to leverage those funds. We identified some of those partnership opportunities through our Office of Economic Development, which provides a comprehensive program of services for private business ranging from economic tracking information, overseeing our enterprise zone and small-business loan program, to marketing the city and Silicon Valley to outside businesses. I hectored the office to become more activist and less academic.

Silicon Valley firms produce more than a quarter of all the nation's high-tech exports, and city hall makes certain to nurture that strength. Our local government has been globally minded for a long time, building on our many cultural links and a truly international population. Alongside the more established Mexican and European heritages, the Japanese, Chinese, Vietnamese, and other groups that have found new homes in San Jose provide local businesses with commercial and cultural networks. In 1990, San Jose opened the Center for International Trade and Development, to work along with the Office of Economic Development in identifying overseas prospects for investment in San Jose and to help local companies—particularly small ones—develop their export markets. The center has yet to become everything I wished it to be, and it may never. Yet it is a significant new approach for any city to begin.

The truth is, cities in the future will probably have no choice but to rely more on their own entrepreneurial efforts and less on the federal government. Cities will be necessarily self-starting and more independent in balancing resources to needs. Just as in large corporations or small businesses, if programs do not work, they should be "terminated with extreme prejudice"—a novel but valuable concept for government.

The federal government cannot by decree get us to the shining city on a hill, that ephemeral Reaganesque vision. That city must be built, as Bill Clinton says, by those of us down in the valley, but I don't think the vision has to be so dramatic in the economic sphere. Most people would settle, after all, for decent schools, a job, and physical safety. To provide the opportunity for those concrete benefits, mayors must work with their citizens in innovative programs and new partnerships, in the best American entrepreneurial tradition.

Political Will. Many mayors, some political cowards among them, do not follow the city-state path because of its liabilities. It can cost a politician a great deal in short-term political support to follow an entrepreneurial agenda. There are political minefields to be crossed in pushing a city toward accountability and activism. But there are many rewards.

Real leaders will recognize that they have little choice. The federal and state governments have no chance of becoming cash cows for cities. The private sector, meanwhile, operates on its own agenda and left alone will not independently make choices that a mayor or city manager would approve, to say nothing of voters. "Market equilibrium, as a guiding urban policy theory, sounds nice in the classroom, but it rarely plays well at City Hall," write economists Franklin James and Marshall Kaplan. "To ask a city to wait on the possibility that renewal will occur because people or firms will get tired of environmental or economic problems in their present locales and decide to relocate is asking much. . . . Waiting for market factors, or the like, to substitute for urban policies and programs is unlikely to satisfy people, businesses, and political leaders caught up in urban distress."[19]

Trying to satisfy every side is a strategy that, for politicians, can spell disaster or gridlock. For local government, it usually results in inaction and drift, a common fate for city leaders who lack courage. Better to stake a bold claim on the city's future, lay out a detailed vision of the community they want to see by the end of their term, and then implement, implement, implement. That approach requires *political will* most of all, the backbone, savvy, and stamina to push through a program against all odds.

Some areas on the city entrepreneur's agenda absolutely require political tenacity. An entire chapter later in the book deals with the hard game of politics that a leader must play as "Mr. Inside." For now, let's just examine one area as a good example. A growing number of mayors would testify with bruises and scars that the issue of privatization of city services requires the most political spine.

There are those who are dead set against privatization, foremost among them public-employee unions. An official with the Amalgamated Transit Union, criticizing cities that have put public transit services up for outside bid, charged that privatization "results in increased costs, financial and otherwise. It comes at the expense of safety and control over public service."[20] There can be a danger when services are handled by outside groups with insufficient oversight by those who are truly accountable—the city's leaders. Citizens want to know who will decide bus routing, or library hours, or street-sweeping schedules so that their voice can be heard if need be. Yet cities around the country are proving with concrete examples that spinning off public services can make great economic sense. Adam Smith's metaphor of the "invisible hand" alone guiding the free market may not satisfy everyone, but once a close analysis has determined that the city and its citizens would be better off with a privatized service, it falls to the political resolve of a mayor, or a manager or local school board, to sell the change on its overall benefits to the community.

One of America's better political implementers on the local level is the indefatigable Richie Daley, who learned the craft from his legendary father. Daley, fully cognizant of the political barriers he faces but determined to overcome them with good sense and hard dollar figures, has an ambitious program of privatization in Chicago. He offered New York City this advice: "City government should stick to basic services it provides very well and buy others. It matters little to the tax-paying public, which expects good service, who renders it."[21] Among Chicago's privatizing successes since Daley took office in 1989 is abandoned-car towing, which was costing the city millions of dollars when it had its own trucks doing the job. Now, neighborhood-based companies take on the job, able to respond quickly to local complaints, and they pay the city $25 a car for the privilege. In 1992, Chicago was pulling in $1.2 million annually from the program. The city also contracted out its substance-abuse programs to innovative private care providers rather than paying upkeep on crumbling city drug-rehab centers that were uneconomical and outmoded. Perhaps this kind of innovation could be extended to the troubled Chicago school system.

Other cities are experimenting with privatization slowly, testing the waters and locking down successes before fighting huge political battles. Los Angeles has successfully contracted out city bus services to private companies, with savings up to 56 percent on certain routes and better maintenance and fewer rider complaints. Jim McLaughlin, the city's chief of transit services, called the program "an unqualified success. Competition keeps the best people working at the best cost." A 1989 study by the National Commission for Employment Policy examined thirty-four cities around the country that were heavily engaged in privatized services and found that three-quarters of the local officials held "very favorable" impressions of the quality of service they were receiving from private companies. In Phoenix, my friend Terry Goddard's administration even used open bidding in the 1980s as a competitive spur to city departments, which responded to outside competition by overhauling organization and services, eventually winning back some city contracts.

Sometimes, a city or town may have no choice but to contract out services. Ecorse, Michigan, a small industrial suburb of Detroit, went broke in 1986, just one of several small Rust Belt towns that suffered during the recession. In the face of fiscal disaster and a comparatively huge $6 million deficit, local officials sent the city into receivership. A judge appointed a municipal finance consultant to oversee the town's budget. Louis Schimmel took on the mission with zeal, choosing to privatize city services. He shut down the public works department completely, selling its building and keeping only one employee to supervise the outside contractors hired to do the work of the department. Schimmel also farmed out trash collection, animal control services, even city ambulance billing to private-sector companies. Schimmel may not be a household name, but I like his spirit: "There's no end to what you could do with contracting. Had I been there longer, I would have gotten the city [involvement] down to nothing."[22]

Other levels of local government, like school boards, are feeling great pressure as well. More and more communities are gathering up the political will to take action when local school boards are swamped with infighting, turmoil, and financial crisis. Some boards have "chosen" to go bankrupt, letting their organization be tossed into public receivership in the vain hope that something better could come from such a roll of the dice. In Duluth, Minnesota, the board thought differently. After things got so bad that all extracurricular activities—sports, band, clubs—were eliminated and the superintendent abruptly quit, the school board shifted to a new way of thinking. As one board member, a small-business man, argued, "We need to act more like a business. We have a product—education. We have customers—the students and their parents. We have to be more accountable."[23] After considering and rejecting more traditional, short-term alternatives, the school board turned over control of the district to a private company—all twenty-six schools, 1,100 teachers, and 14,000 students. Education Alternatives, Inc., a consulting firm begun by former school administrators, stepped in and is now running the district under tighter financial controls and with greater streamlining and educational accountability.

In Chelsea, Massachusetts, the public schools have been run by Boston University since 1989 on a long-term contract after the traditional administrators proved fiscally irresponsible. In Cincinnati, the public school system is undergoing a massive restructuring, designed in 1991 by a business committee charged with streamlining a bloated administrative staff and overhauling the district's financial and educational systems.

It all certainly sounds good, and time (with close analysis) will tell. The important lesson for elected (and appointed) officials in the era of the city-state is to summon the political courage to bite the bullet on privatization and other new entrepreneurial economic programs. The costs may seem high and the benefits not immediately compelling, yet citizens deserve a long-term approach to city management. The independence and self-reliant style of the new city-state will require the political will to stay the course.

Self-Reliance

Bill Hudnut described the entrepreneurial approach as "a question of spirit, of mental attitude," and "acting as risk-takers, . . . becoming active competitors in the urban economic game."[24] Any successful mayor will agree with the need for cities to regain their momentum in the dynamic pitch of a new economic era. When speaking of the self-reliance cities must exercise, I don't like to use the buzzword "empower." That implies that city leadership awaits the bequest of powers by some other force before it may exercise them. Too many slackers are waiting for an Excalibur to be handed over by a watery maiden. I am a proponent of cities grabbing the sword themselves.

To lead the city-state to success requires what may be an ultimate sacrifice for politicians: public leaders will have to work together and put petty resentments aside for the good of the city. When this does not happen, disaster results. In the aftermath of the Los Angeles riots, Mayor Bradley revealed that he had not met face to face with Police Chief Darryl Gates in over a year. Acrimony and personal dislike took the place of professionalism, and neither man could place principle above personal pique. I was no fan of Gates; he was rarely concerned with more than his self-image as an icon of the right. But Tom Bradley's leadership style was just this side of quiescent. After South Central revealed its true state of economic neglect and despair, Bradley admitted to the *Los Angeles Times* his administration's impotence in finding solutions: "It was not a matter of calling on the heads of all city departments. They don't have any resources, any ability to affect that kind of a problem."[25] With that attitude, only a deus ex machina could provide any progress on urban problems. Don't look to such a city hall for leadership.

What Bradley finally did was appoint Peter Ueberroth to head a "Rebuild Los Angeles" committee, or RLA. Unfortunately, RLA quickly degenerated into window-dressing, with an eighty-member board appointed by quota that had no deep connections either to the ravaged African-American, Hispanic, and Asian communities or to the city's political administration. RLA was little more than an exercise in public relations. A full year after the riots, RLA was judged harshly for a lack of tangible results, either in rebuilding or in economic progress. Ueberroth resigned, leaving RLA in listless drift and the city no closer to a definition of shared values.

Networks of Responsibility

John Gardner, founder of Common Cause and one of the nation's most dedicated public servants, told me recently that his main hobby is the study of leadership in our country and that with the status of leadership now, it didn't take much of his time. After our encounter at a Stanford faculty get-together not long after the Los Angeles eruption, he sent along an essay he had perceptively titled "Constituents and Followers," in which he argued that America's fragmented society needs networks of leaders who accept responsibility for the larger concerns that society shares. He lamented the country's short memory, recalling that in the late 1960s he had presided over a national effort to create such networks in response to that decade's unprecedented urban riots. With sadness, he noted that these efforts of the Johnson administration had been forgotten as the sense of urgency dissipated. "Such networks form very swiftly in times of crisis," he wrote, citing New York City's response in the mid-1970s to a fiscal meltdown, but they remain temporary emergency reactions.

Gardner favors a more systematic collaboration of leaders from diverse segments of a community in what he calls "networks of responsibility," designed to overcome disparate or conflicting interests in behalf of the shared concerns of the community. He contends that such networks do not necessarily need to

have any official standing and that in fact they may be better off without it,
which would allow more flexibility and freedom of action. "Ultimately, of
course, leaders associated in such networks of responsibility will succeed or fail
depending upon the existence and strength of shared values within the commu-
nity," he notes. "There does not have to be agreement on everything or even
on most principles or shared aspirations, but there must be some common
ground."[26]

Like any politician, I looked for common ground in office. Sometimes, I found it. Rebuilding our downtown was a shared value, brought
to the fore with political leadership and the will of many. That shared
value underwrote our success and the rebirth of San Jose. Political will
helped us detect and amplify the common goal of nurturing Silicon Valley industry, for its economic engine provided good jobs at good wages
and provided the tax base for all our other city projects. Our tough approach to crime was bolstered by the recognition that the community
did in fact share a hope for a different future with safer streets, better
schools, and neighborhoods free of drug dealers. City government joined
with church groups, neighborhood associations, and just plain folks to
form a network of responsibility (we called it Project Crackdown), and
together, though we have not yet solved the problem, we have broken its
back with a common defense.

Mayors around the country, along with concerned individuals and organizations acting in concert, are forming networks mixing public and
private resources to combat shared enemies. In 1989, the Robert Wood
Johnson Foundation selected fifteen cities from among 330 applicants
across the country to take part in the "Fighting Back" planning project.
The immediate goal was to reduce demand for alcohol and illicit drugs,
but the larger vision was to enable communities to take charge of the
war on substance abuse and to learn how to engage in battle with homegrown partnerships. Participating cities in the two-year program included Little Rock, Milwaukee, San Antonio, New Haven, and San
Jose. These local networks of responsibility were encouraged to share information and strategies with one another, and the foundation supported
the free flow of ideas with its own health-care expertise.

The San Jose Fighting Back effort was modeled on our successful
Project Crackdown, coordinating police and community action to reduce crime and drug abuse in our hardest-hit neighborhoods. The Fighting Back Citizens' Task Force brought together for the first time

residents of the nine Project Crackdown neighborhoods, allowing residents to lead the meetings and provide their ideas to the mayor's office, city bureaucrats, the police department, and substance-abuse professionals. At the same time, as the network's chairman, I assembled a small strategy group of accomplished individuals from the private sector to provide a vision for Fighting Back's implementation.

Our local Fighting Back effort lasted only three years (the foundation money dried up), but the lessons we learned in bringing people together are being used in other ways and on other problems day after day.

The lesson of collaborative self-reliance should be taken to heart not just by city government but by every private organization concerned with a community's future. One good example to follow is the National Community Development Initiative, a joint venture among some of the leading philanthropic foundations in the country. In 1992, the Knight Foundation, the Pew Charitable Trusts, the Lilly Endowment, the Rockefeller Foundation, the John D. and Catherine T. MacArthur Foundation, and others joined in a cooperative funding strategy to distribute seed money to twenty of the most distressed urban areas in the country. They plan to leverage their $60 million with another $400 million from government grants and investment by banks and other lenders to finance construction of hundreds of thousands of low-income housing units. One of the benefits of cooperative national strategies like this one is that lessons learned can be shared quickly and effectively among cities trying to achieve the same ends.

In effect, city-states are joining in alliances as critical to American national security as NATO has been for fifty years. On the other side of our domestic iron curtain is a very real nightmare of urban hell, but in our persevering cold war victory lie lessons for the next generation of domestic leaders.

Cities' efforts should be small yet at the same time large. Any coalition to battle problems needs to be focused in a local effort but must in turn be broad and strategic, with a macro view of how the effort fits with all of the community's endeavors, public and private, to protect the quality of life. Walt Rostow, a national security adviser to Presidents Kennedy and Johnson, draws a negative lesson from a foreign policy debacle: "The way we fought the war in Vietnam reminds me of the way we are trying to deal with the cities, running after all the symptoms and putting Band-Aids on them instead of going for the cause."[27]

I will offer one final caveat, drawn from Silicon Valley, to cities that wish to benefit from alliance strategies, networks of responsibility, and public-private partnerships. Artificial alliances can be as dead-ended as sole public involvement. The high-tech industry witnessed a prominent failure with the Advanced Computing Environment (ACE), a high-profile consortium of computer hardware and software companies that banded together early in 1991 promising boldly to foster a "technology revolution" in the computer industry. The alliance fell apart later the same year amidst internal bickering, leaving an industry observer to note an expensive lesson: "Technology innovations still come from small groups of motivated engineers—not from industry committees. ACE, composed of dozens of members with frequently competing agendas, so far has proved too unwieldy."[28]

City-states must learn the same lesson that Silicon Valley companies are learning. Overly broad, unfocused alliances like RLA's initially flawed incarnation in Los Angeles are not the answer to the problems of the cities, nor are imposed federal solutions or wish lists. Progress and innovation come from below, from the motivated people on the urban front lines.

True Municipal Bonds

The legendary Richard Daley the Elder, mayor and kingmaker, once had a visit from George Moscone, mayor of San Francisco in the late 1970s. Daley told his visitor of the thousands of patronage jobs he controlled. Moscone thought a moment and said, "I think I have twenty-seven."

Too many modern mayors consider themselves powerless without patronage or the old perks. They content themselves with pulling levers behind a curtain like the Wizard of Oz, all the while grumbling that Washington or the state house bears the blame for all ills.

My thoughts on leading an American city are different, shaped by my own experience. The bottom line on my career and my city has been one of change, adaptation, and transformation, and the lesson can hold true anywhere. I went from a potentially fatal debacle in a $60 million bond loss to landslide reelection. In a similar metamorphosis over the past half century, San Jose went from a sleepy California town to become the Capital of Silicon Valley. The city's success had something to do with luck; it had more to do with a social compact. Leaders of cities can never forget on whose shoulders they stand. The most important feature of the new city-state is an acknowledged social and political compact, a bond between the citizens and those in power in local government. This contract is an agreement on ends and means, a common recognition of the way local society wants to be and the policies that will take it there. A community can reach such an alliance only if it shares a theme of pride, membership in something larger than oneself: a joint and common effort. Until we revive that compact on a national scale, citizens may feel more a part of their local government than our federal government.

Miracles can still happen at the local level, and cities are still the greatest platform for leadership in America. Five centuries ago, Machiavelli wrote, "It is not the welfare of individuals but the common welfare that makes cities great."[29] The American renaissance will not result from the brand of leadership we are used to from the federal level. A local government, a confident city-state, can assert and safeguard the common welfare more persuasively and more successfully than any other authority on earth.

2

HOW TO MURDER A CITY: LESSONS FROM THE PAST

> This way for the sorrowful city.
> —sign over entrance to hell, Dante's *Inferno*

Every American has in her head or etched in his mind a picture of the American city today. For many, the media provide the metaphor, like Tim Burton's "Gotham City," designed and portrayed so darkly in his *Batman* movies. That nightmare image, or the slick and faceless violence of the not-so-futuristic city in *Blade Runner,* sets for a lot of us a hackneyed mental portrait of modern urban life. For millions of others, the picture is a freeze-frame view of Los Angeles during the 1992 riots: the random beating of trucker Reginald Denny, live and in color in every living room in America; the replayed clubbing of Rodney King by swarms of police on a dark, ghoulish street; the long shots of the bleak Los Angeles skyline with entire city blocks ablaze and out of control.

All these images combine to provide us with our common national metaphor: the dying city. Many of us have occasion to see the metaphor made real, not least the 200 million Americans who live in our cities and daily confront the challenges of urban life—and death. The mayors of major American cities often feel they serve as doctors on final call with terminal patients, dutifully checking the weakening pulse and reading charts whose lines are going straight down. For America's big-city mayors, the Los Angeles riots and fires were no more than a TV mini-series, a condensed-for-television dramatization of everyday reality.

There can be a pall at the mere mention of the word "city," from Chelsea, Massachusetts, mired in bankruptcy, all the way to the tiny city of East Palo Alto, California, in the shadow of Stanford University but plagued by drugs and murder.

During the 1980s, America took a dark turn, reflected in our cities as dramatically as if we had turned off neighborhood streetlights, one by one, losing streets, blocks, and entire communities to violence and despair. San Jose has its drug-infested neighborhoods and violent outbursts reminiscent of New York and Los Angeles. The problems are everywhere and are mind-boggling, but we are wrong to speak of "our dying cities." The city is not dying. It is being murdered.

Decade Bookends

The Eighties began and ended for me with shocking cases of murder that seemed out of place in our city. A balmy summer night in 1980 encouraged San Joseans to linger outside, even as it approached midnight. On a moderately busy corner of a main downtown street, East Santa Clara, a young man stood quietly waiting for a bus. Returning from his Oakland job, Gregory Bickham was probably thankful to be almost home.

In movies and books, blades flash in the night, but I doubt it was so for young Greg. He probably didn't even see the knife; he was likely oblivious. He bled to death on the street shortly before midnight. Greg Bickham was just twenty-seven. His killer was only seventeen. Anthony Ruiz had been released four months before from jail on an armed-robbery conviction. Anthony pleaded guilty to the second-degree murder of Greg and received another sojourn in a correctional institution.

I was a city councilman, and the murder had occurred in my downtown district—my city, my neighborhood. I felt helpless, like most residents in the face of such random violence. I had often stood at that bus stop. I wondered if there was not more we could do to ensure the safety of our neighborhoods. I was sorry for the wasted life of Anthony Ruiz. I grieved for Greg Bickham.

H. L. Mencken cynically noted that for each difficult problem, there is an easy solution: simple, neat, and wrong. As a nation, we have found depressingly few answers over the past decade. For me, the Eighties ended as they began. In 1989, I welcomed a meek Japanese couple into my office for one of the most painful meetings I have ever held. They had flown to San Jose to collect the body of their sixteen-year-old daughter, Ai Toyoshima, a popular exchange student. Ai had been followed home on the bus by Gregory Calvin Smith, a thirty-year-old parolee who admitted at his trial that he had once again "helplessly" given in to the urge to rape, as he had thirty times before. Smith had confronted little Ai in a deserted school playground and had left her there raped, shot, dying.

Smith was given the death penalty, but as I write he still lives, on California's death row.

Ai Toyoshima was gone, and I had to struggle with her parents for words to explain. How, in a city as safe as San Jose, in a nation as wonderful as America, could one innocent girl lose her life like that? Why are so many of us the victims of acts of the most horrific violence? Answers lie in the gradual decline of the place where most of us live. For the answer, we must look to the city's past.

Daytime Nightmares

The historian in me sometimes reacts to portrayals of the American city as worse than it has ever been. I have studied the American West quite a bit and have ambled through European nineteenth-century and American twentieth-century history. There was no golden age in the city of the past.

New Yorkers were reminded of that ugly truth in the summer of 1991, when construction workers on a new federal courthouse site uncovered the long-buried Five Points neighborhood. More than a century ago, Five Points was the ultimate slum. A Columbia University history professor remembered it as "a brutal place in which to live and, just as likely, to die." Crime was rife, murders were frequent and unremarkable. Charles Dickens, after visiting New York in the middle of that century, was moved to write, "Let us go on again, and plunge into the Five Points. All that is loathsome, drooping and decayed is here."[30]

Five Points was flattened at the dawn of the twentieth century in a wave of reform, but there is much in common between the New York of Five Points and the Los Angeles of South Central today. Perhaps events like Ai Toyoshima's slaying or the L.A. riots simply serve as artificial archaeology, uncovering the darker roots of our urban reality. Stanley Cloud, former editor of the *Los Angeles Herald Examiner,* observed that the riots put "the real Los Angeles" on display to the world, as "wasted landscapes and hard people whose anger and alienation seemed for a while to know no bounds. . . . L.A. is what lies in store for everyone."[31]

What cannot be disputed is that we are no better than our predecessors at addressing those conditions and that we typically refuse to address them as problems in any realistic fashion. As residents and as community leaders, we act as if the distress and dysfunction around us are nothing more than a daytime nightmare, just the grabber on the nightly news. If we concentrate hard enough on avoiding it, turn our eyes away or shut them tightly, the nightmare will vanish. At the crux of our inability to save our cities is our persistent attempt to wish the bad dream away. Urban crisis management too often boils down to "This, too, shall pass."

Thirty years ago, the "urban crisis" led the nation's political agenda. Today, when problems are more severe and moral drift at its peak, public attention has diminished. Sadly, cities reach the front burner only when they are burning. The public's attention, shaped and reinforced by the media, surges after a major riot in Los Angeles but wanes again when the embers cool, just as the nation's attention span is revved up by a president's "drug war" or by the foreign villain-of-the-month: if it's Tuesday, it must be Qaddafi. Haiti's Cedras this month, Saddam Hussein the next. We can get the nation's attention only with a major catastrophe, as the Chicago flood proved in the spring of 1992, when the Chicago River burst through the tunnel system and pumped millions of gallons into downtown basements. Headlines followed: "200,000 Evacuated," "No Power for Days," "Mayor Daley Fumes as City Economy Takes Blow." Such events put "The Plight of the City" on the cover of newsmagazines. Yet come the weekend, our national agenda has changed, returned to what we inexplicably call normal.

Symptom _and_ Cause: The Terminal Dynamic

The wag says that city halls are places where officials sit overlooking the problems of others. Perhaps it's redundant for elected officials to admit that, yes, we often are removed from the real world.

I once bristled during a televised forum concerning transportation issues when Jerry Saunders, a powerful Silicon Valley CEO, acknowledged with a wispy smile the gridlock problems on our congested highways: "My chauffeur tells me the traffic is terrible." If we had had a studio audience, it might have stormed the stage. For one of the Valley's premier industrialists to display such flippant indifference to a crisis that affects so many in San Jose—and the viability of his own company—deserves the Marie Antoinette Award for Perspicacity.

Let's face up to reality: the problems don't fade away just because we choose to ignore them. Instead, we foster a negative cycle of problem avoidance, which itself ensures that a city slides further into the gutter. It is that *dynamic* aspect of the phenomenon that takes us from a mugging here and a murder there down the line to an abandoned city. Here's how the "terminal dynamic" works: First, the problems seem to grow to unmanageable levels. Second, naturally, the amount of money needed to address these problems mounts beyond our means. The politicians then get frustrated, deprived of the resources they crave, and begin to whine and gnash their teeth. The third stage of the cycle, then, is political gridlock. Fourth and finally, citizens recognize the inability of their local system to fix the problems. Those who can do so vote with their feet, and head for the suburbs. Others slip into apathy and self-pity, joining the victim class. These responses, of course, only encourage the cycle to continue, and continue it does. The cities are left with even fewer resources to deal with greater and greater problems.

This terminal dynamic begins in response to real dilemmas. They *are* real. Among the never-ending problems cities face are poverty, racial segregation, declining educational performance, welfare dependence, chronic unemployment, crime, fiscal calamity, drug addiction, teenage pregnancy, the AIDS epidemic, crumbling streets, inadequate housing. The disturbing list can divert our attention sometimes from the dynamic character of the phenomenon. A mayor has to address the items on the list, but he or she can never forget that the problems did not arise suddenly. If a city wants to reverse the circuit and revive itself, it first has to understand the downward spiral that abetted in this homicide.

Crime and Violence: Don't Count on the Dead Bolt

I noticed a grisly story in the papers a few years ago, about a New York taxi driver the tabloids were calling "the cadaver cabby." In three years driving a cab, the fellow had discovered five bodies and six heads (the heads came all at once, in a large cardboard box dumped in the gutter). Reporters asked for his reaction to his bad fortune, and his response sounded like a gallows-humor line from an Ed Koch TV commercial: "This never happened in Romania. New York is a crazy city."

Our cities are not very pleasant places at times. Some are safer than others. "Urban safety" can be an oxymoron, since every big city has experienced soaring crime in the last quarter century.[32] FBI figures show that violent crime across the country was up 33 percent in the decade from 1982 to 1992. Rural areas were not immune from this trend, but no one who has walked down a dark sidewalk in an American city can deny the particular feeling of imminent danger we accept as an urban given.

My feelings on crime came from a very basic and personal grounding. I have always lived in the inner city; I went to school there. My children have gone to elementary school there. In our neighborhood reside some of the most decent, hardworking citizens any community could have. There are young couples just starting out and octogenarians, Anglo and Hispanic and Asian. Some are recent immigrants, others descend from the original Irish land barons of the old Californian period when the state was in the Republic of Mexico.

Also in my neighborhood over the last few years have resided three men similar in one terrifying aspect: they were all mass murderers.

The accounts of their crimes, which in many homes were read at the breakfast table over coffee, took on a chilling immediacy for me: these were my neighbors. I encountered the first man, Donald Cummings, when my city council office began to receive complaints about a program for "nonviolent offenders" offered at San Jose State University. Some people feared that it was not being properly monitored. Knowing full well the inefficiency of the state parole bureaucracy, I suspected the worst as well. After analyzing the screening, or lack thereof, I called for the program's end. A host of apologists arose, citing the outstanding records of the participants and the competent administration. I was skeptical.

Shortly thereafter, Cummings was arrested after a particularly heinous sex crime. What we soon discovered shocked even the jaded homicide detectives and our chief of police, Joe McNamara, who thought himself inured to insanity by his experience as a beat cop in the Bronx's Fort Apache. Violent sex offender Cummings, in fact a repeat offender, had been admitted to the University Alternative Program and was maintaining excellent grades, but he had another job at night: prowling the downtown neighborhoods in search of prey. Cummings committed some of the most blood-curdling murders in the history of San Jose, one a brutal bludgeoning with a log. All this while he was on the honor roll!

The ACLU and other bleeding hearts were uncharacteristically silent when Cummings was arrested and the program abolished. A postscript worthy of a cheap Hollywood thriller was added when Cummings was inadvertently released from our local county jail in a prebooking snafu. (They got him back, and he is now serving life without parole.)

My second homicidal neighbor lived only three blocks away. Randomly pulled over in his van one night in 1989 by patrolling police officers, the mysterious Ferdinand Coto quickly shot his passenger, a "prisoner" he was transporting. He then turned the gun on himself. When detectives searched his home, trying to piece together the puzzling burst of violence, they discovered a small cubicle Coto used as his own private prison. This deeply disturbed man had probably been responsible for the torture deaths of at least three women.

As the mayor and as a father, these stories had a lasting effect on my thinking and on my public positions. My views about increasing the size of our police force were a direct result, along with a more aggressive determination for local government to make the urban environment safer.

The last of my neighbors to make a conspicuous entry into my mind and the nation's headlines gained his fifteen minutes of fame on a sunny afternoon in the fall of 1988, in the San Jose suburb of Sunnyvale. His name was Richard Wade Farley—as with many mass murderers, we now commonly remember him by all three names. Farley went to the headquarters of ESL, a Valley defense contractor and his former employer, with one singular obsession: killing Laura Black. In retrospect, it was all so very clear. Someone should have noticed, should have listened to co-worker Black's complaints about Farley's weird behavior. This bespectacled computer technician with a double chin had a full-blown obsession for the athletic young woman. He was a stalker.

Farley entered the corporate building weighed down with nearly one hundred pounds of weapons and began a shooting spree that ended only after a five-hour siege and the deaths of seven people. Laura Black was seriously wounded. Farley did not return home to "our" neighborhood that evening. We might not have noticed him if he had. Like any city's residents, we might simply have pulled our drapes and rammed home the dead bolt. (Sentenced to death, Farley now resides on San Quentin's death row.)

In America, we are breeding a terrible attitude to crime, an attitude summed up in a line at the end of a popular Jack Nicholson movie: "Forget it, Jake, it's Chinatown." Both officials and citizens seem to accept the coarsening and demise of the city as the way things have to be, and contemporary movies exalt the mindless violence with a casual, desensitizing attitude. Most films about the city do not have a Spike Lee moral or the redeeming worth of John Singleton's *Boyz N the Hood;* without them, a violent movie does great damage by never focusing a spotlight on solutions. In a more positive light in the 1930s, Louis B. Mayer and other East European refugees reflected an entirely different set of values: the Hollywood Dream. It was America the way it could be, populated by a host of wonderful characters, like Hank Fonda and Jimmy Stewart. The fairy tale they imagined and transmitted to the rest of us became as real for many people as the mythical Bedford Falls of Frank Capra's *It's a Wonderful Life*.

Today, Hollywood performs the same role, only creating a frightening and horrible view of the world and its seamier corners. That view reflects only one segment of the actual world beyond our dead-bolt locks. It is the only segment we are depicting today, and generations from here on out will have only that violent future as a reference point. Every day, we bring that future a little closer.

Drugs: An Escape Hatch

In my last two years as mayor, I spent a good deal of time exploring the parts of the city that my department heads rarely visited on their fixed-rail routes to and from city hall. One such excursion took me to the pediatric unit at Valley Medical Center. In that ward I came face to face with the indirect casualties of the vaunted war on drugs: children just a few days old dubbed crack babies. To see the difficulty and discomfort of their first hours of existence is to learn a good deal about the penalties of a drug-dependent life.

Alcohol and other substance abuse takes a staggering human toll in any city. The personal cost can be death, illness, or disability; costly health effects for the infants of drug-abusing parents; and the mental health consequences of destroyed lives. The cost to society is enormous: a workforce with diminished productivity; drug-related crime and violence; and increased demands on our health care, law enforcement, and judicial systems. National figures estimate the annual cost to American society of alcohol and other drug abuse at almost $230 billion.

There are a number of ways a mayor can choose to measure the extent of a substance-abuse problem in his or her community. I had all kinds of figures available to me, some based on hard data and some nothing more than guesstimates. Two sets of numbers struck me as most relevant. The first is perhaps the most direct measure of the *problems* substance abuse can cause a city: 59 percent of the individuals booked into our county jail in a recent six-month period tested positive for illegal drug or alcohol use. The second measure I note because of its import for a city's future. A 1992 study in our East Side Union high school district, with over 4,300 students participating, showed that 51 percent had used alcohol,

28 percent had used marijuana, and 12 percent had used cocaine or other stimulants.[33] A city's youths are its future leaders, the timeless cliché holds, and figures like those make you pause and consider the ability of future generations to answer society's problems.

Homelessness: Don't Talk about the Problem

As I walked the last seventy-five yards down a picturesque pathway, the pungent smell of urine assaulted my nostrils, and the occasional moan of a man wailed behind me. On an overcast day in 1989, I stood at the entrance to San Francisco City Hall, a building that rose like a phoenix out of the ashes of the 1906 earthquake, its dome a symbol of the collective will of the great city by the bay to survive. It was then a magnificent and statuesque monument, more befitting a state capital or an Italian piazza than a municipal structure. Times have changed.

Even with a police officer beside me, I felt distinctly uncomfortable as I waded through the human jetsam of Civic Center Plaza on my way to a meeting with San Francisco mayor Art Agnos. Ironically, the subject of the meeting was the homeless problem in the Bay Area and cooperative methods of addressing it. Also present were the mayors of Oakland, Berkeley, and Richmond. Art had called this mayor's summit to study the "comprehensive plan" he and his staff had devised.

It did not take a rocket scientist to know from the scene out front, which resembled a Depression-era Hooverville, that there was indeed much to learn from San Francisco.

The homeless issue was a 1980s and is now a 1990s story. I know of no city that can say it had a program dealing specifically with homelessness before 1980. Since then, of course, the problem has been on the national agenda as the number of people living on our streets, in our alleys and gutters, and on our grates has surged. They are the staple of every big city, a constant reminder, with their omnipresent shopping carts and out-stretched hands, of the fact that a rising tide does not lift all boats. Some are in the wake of a larger craft, some are scuttled, while others were perhaps never seaworthy at all. It is as if a medieval ship of fools ran aground in the center of each American city.

Where did they come from in such large numbers? In many ways, the general clichéd image of the homeless man babbling to himself insanely is correct and, more important, the root of the problem. Most mayors have now come to believe that the majority of homeless are not "people like you and me, a paycheck away from a normal life." Consider one striking trend of numbers: in 1950, there were almost 90,000 patients in New York State's mental hospitals; by 1987, there were 20,000, and just five years later, in 1992, there were only 11,000. As many scholars of the homeless problem have pointed out, this ominous decline is a result of federal and state policies to deinstitutionalize the mentally ill, particularly during the 1980s and the Reagan era.

The training ground for such policy had been California, the state that is the harbinger of most national trends, good or bad. With dizzying speed, and studied callousness, the center cities of California, San Jose included, were converted into institutions without walls during the 1960s and 1970s.

An Orwellian world was created, in a buck-passing technique that Governor Reagan would later raise to a fine art in his stay on the Potomac. The policy was cynical, dangerous, and, from a federal perspective, highly cost-efficient: dump the mentally ill in the city's lap, and let city officials and city dwellers deal with the consequences.

Unfortunately, in our largest cities, the past decade has also seen the emergence of cheap drugs like crack cocaine, producing what the *New York Times* called the "dangerous fusion of two trends" with frightening results: mentally ill patients who are addicted and therefore sentenced to acquiring drugs by any means.[34] Not all homeless individuals are addicts, or alcoholics, or even mentally ill. Some have indeed missed one paycheck too many in the middle of a recession. Others simply do not wish to work or live in the mainstream. The confluence of national factors gives cities a challenge for which they are nowhere near prepared.

Down for the Count

Numbers for the total homeless population are notoriously unreliable, and no mayor takes them at face value. For its 1990 tally, the Census Bureau conducted a much-ballyhooed "one-night count" of homeless people living on the street. On March 20, 1990, census takers made an express purpose of counting street people and came up with an estimate of 400,000 homeless people in the entire United States. Yet the methods used by the counters were severely flawed, and the U.S. Conference of Mayors sued the bureau over the count. That suit marks the midpoint in the downward spiral of the terminal dynamic implicated in the murder of a city. You might think a mayor would want to minimize the count of homeless in his or her city; if I could monkey with figures and make a problem appear less pressing on paper, I might be tempted. But the mayors of America are engaged in a political battle over the homeless count. In this battle, the winners are perhaps the biggest fools. Federal dollars for homeless programs are doled out according to census figures, and when federal dollars are at stake, most mayors scramble into action. It is one of the least salutary aspects of municipal government that mayors either lie outright or—almost as bad—"lie to themselves." The first is an error of ethics, the second an error of judgment. Both are contemptible, and both are part of the terminal dynamic that frustrates elected officials and their constituents, contributing to political gridlock.

Many cities have recognized the need to move beyond a reliance on federal assistance. Some have been forced into action, as New York City was in 1981 by a court order to provide beds to all who ask. In the next ten years, New York City built over 26,000 permanent housing units for the homeless (more than the federal government built nationwide). Yet an estimated 50,000 people still sleep on the streets of New York each and every night, and while the city has temporary beds for 23,000 in shelters, the accommodations are basically a cot and blanket, often in an armory hosting rampant drug abuse and violence.

Time for the D day Assault

The homeless issue is one that can often rouse cities to take action, attempt to interrupt a downward cycle of problem avoidance. In San Jose we tried a measured approach. We first moved to provide two new long-term shelters at a cost of $4 million; anyone who needed shelter in San Jose would receive it. Next we stressed an even more fundamental premise: we would not be a city where anyone would have to live in the streets or on a park bench or along the banks of our river. We would not tolerate encampments.

Recent figures in San Jose estimate that at any given time there may be as many as 2,100 homeless on the streets of San Jose. Our figures are comparable to other cities our size, perhaps a bit smaller. Early on, I recognized that addressing the problem of homeless with a full spectrum of shelters, food banks, and direct aid would require a high degree of public support; but support for helping the homeless would be jeopardized if the general public perceived the problem to be out of city hall's control. Such was the case in other cities, including our Bay Area neighbors. If encampments of people were allowed to monopolize our parks or other places of public assembly, such as the three-ring circus outside San Francisco City Hall, then our citizens would be rightly upset, even outraged. Enough was enough, they would shout.

Still shocked by what I had seen in San Francisco in 1989, I made the decision to clear out our own smaller camps, located in dilapidated areas along the Guadalupe River.

On my return to San Jose from the mayors' summit, the sometimes surprisingly efficient city apparatus swung into action. We used the department we had the most confidence in: the San Jose Police Department. The training and common sense of their men and women seldom disappointed me, and this was a very difficult task in which all their skill and diplomacy was needed. I also relied on the support of the city councilmember in that district, Susan Hammer. Even in the middle of a tough campaign to succeed me as mayor, she stood shoulder to shoulder with me.

As a first step in the operation, we coordinated with social service agencies to make sure we provided for people with special needs. In visit after visit to the encampments along the Guadalupe, we made it very clear that all were welcome in San Jose, but not in our public places or along our river. We notified them of the date, fourteen days hence, when the river banks would be cleared. They would all be leaving—that was nonnegotiable—but we were solicitous in informing them of the various shelters in which we could place them. Furthermore, if they needed help with drug problems or alcohol dependency, we would provide it. Counselors were available. We stood ready to offer them job training and transportation to a job site. We were prepared to help those with children get the necessary child care. In short, we were willing to treat them as human beings.

After two weeks of visits by me, the chief of police, and legions of alcohol and drug counselors of every type came D day. The police department and other emergency units swept the river area clean. As a community and as human beings, we were making a crystal-clear statement: we wanted to assist all those who wished our help. We valued them as fellow citizens. But we would not allow them to live like animals in our city. There would be no Hoovervilles in front of our city hall. Control of our city and community support was not forfeited on the altar of knee-jerk expediency. We nipped a burgeoning problem in the bud before it could explode.

Our actions were among the few successful strategic attacks against homelessness in the United States. Since that decision to take action in San Jose, I have followed with interest the efforts of other cities to remove the homeless from central public spaces. In New York City, David Dinkins attempted to roust the homeless from Tompkins Square Park in June 1991, announcing the raid by declaring, "This park is a park. It is not a place to live. I will not have it any other way." Because the city had let the problem fester for so long, the raid encountered violent resistance from the camping homeless, and blood was spilled in police confrontations. The only way after the raid's failure to keep the homeless away from the park was to barricade it for "renovation" at a cost of $2.3 million. The *New York Times* called that pretense "a costly excuse to close the park."

Other mayors have learned the same lesson of quick action we employed in 1989. San Diego's premier green spot, Balboa Park, was cleared promptly of a new homeless encampment in August 1992. One official said, "Once you let them believe they have a right to it, the city in effect loses control of the property. . . . [We've] seen what happened in New York." And even in Paris, the capital of European bohemian culture, Mayor Jacques Chirac took a hard line on the homeless in 1991, clearing large camps from the Bois de Boulogne and from a park near the Eiffel Tower. Chirac said they gave the city "a deplorable image."[35] It is not simply the municipal image that is injured in such situations, it is the fundamental confidence of residents that the city can provide a modicum of stability. It is the lesson of my afternoon stroll across Civic Center Plaza in San Francisco, and it is a lesson every public official should learn.

Money: Keep Your Credit Cards in Your Wallet

The Reagan administration made major cuts in federal aid to cities, reducing federal grants to local governments and giving back as much responsibility for urban programs as possible to state and local administrators. The administration did this without reducing tax payments to the federal government, thus straining severely the ability of local governments to maintain services at previous levels. The burden of city costs fell squarely on the shoulders of taxpayers. Effects of Reaganomics have been felt primarily by the urban poor and by working people.[36] Many costs were not immediately recognized, like the staggering cost of the criminal justice system and the exponentially increasing medical costs covered by local government.

The numbers are stark and speak for themselves. To paraphrase Everett Dirksen, once the Republican conscience of the Senate, a billion here and a billion there and pretty soon you're talking about real pain to the average citizen.

Federal Aid to Cities

| *Overall Drop* | 1980: | $47.2 billion |
| | 1990: | $21.7 billion |

Examples of Drop in Federal Dollars	*1981*	*1993*	*% Drop*
		billions	
General Revenue Sharing	$8.0	$0.0	-100%
Urban Development Action			
Grants (UDAGs)	0.6	0.0	-100%
Assisted Housing	26.8	8.9	-67%
Economic Development Administration	0.6	0.2	-67%
Mass Transit	6.9	3.5	-49%
Community Development Block Grants	6.3	4.0	-36.5%

All figures from the U.S. Conference of Mayors.

Murder most foul: empty lots of San Jose's past, circa 1971.

Since the 1970s, there has been an ongoing debate over the scale of economic decline in cities and what to do about it. The debate is, of course, tinged with ideology, both economic and political. One side has continuously argued that it is unwise to resist the logic of the market. Reflected in the supply-side policies of the Reagan era, this tough-minded laissez-faire approach paints uneven growth as simply an indication of economic adaptation to change. The supply-side principles must be obeyed, so the federal government lets cities sink or swim on their own. This approach was laid out at the beginning of the Reagan era and followed by three Reagan-Bush administrations. The other side, naturally, argues passionately against an abandonment of urban policy, often making the moral charge that politicians have a duty to save a declining city if possible. This Keynesian approach expects an interventionist federal role supporting local government, with government spending projects at all levels.

The debate is more than an academic exercise in counting ideological angels dancing on pinheads. The issue for many cities is one of survival. Older cities in the Midwest and the Northeast have suffered the most, of course. In Buffalo and St. Louis, jobs plummeted from 1960 right through the Reagan boom years. Newark, Detroit and Pittsburgh took true nose-dives. Michael Moore's film *Roger & Me*, about the decline and fall of Michigan's automobile-producing cities, is a darkly humorous, deeply depressing picture of urban bleakness, art imitating life in the Rust Belt.

Admittedly, by contrast, cities in the South, the West, and on the Pacific Rim have done well. Houston, San Jose, Phoenix, San Antonio, San Diego, Seattle, all have been major growth centers, at least until the downturn of the late Eighties and early Nineties. These differential growth rates, one set of cities moving down and the other arcing up, led urban scholar Ann Markusen and others to note that by the mid-1970s the "urban coalition" could no longer speak with one powerful voice. Cities were not all in the same condition and were not all represented by leaders with similar outlooks or even a shared basic philosophy.

Since the 1960s, the Frost Belt, or Rust Belt, has been characterized largely by knee-jerk Democratic local leadership, seeking interventionist policies from the federal government because of their declining populations, revenues, and aspirations. The Advisory Commission on Intergovernmental Relations in 1973 detailed the financial emergencies facing many cities. Worse off than New York City were Cleveland and Detroit, and others were in the same sorry league. The Sun Belt, meanwhile, has fostered local leadership featuring Republicans and nontraditional Democrats with business sympathies or with new ideas for invigorating the local economy, advocating laissez-faire policies from Washington, out of rational self-interest.

Too much has been made of the schism among cities, though. There is much to learn from the successes of the energetic leaders of Sun Belt cities. Many of the best ideas we put into practice in San Jose were products of our interchanges with other cities eager to experiment and change the old ways of governing. In some cases, we taught as well as learned. Most mayors of prosperous cities understand that if only a relatively few cities are prosperous and the others are reduced to municipal basket cases, that would be an unhealthy and ultimately destructive course for all concerned.

Urban Decay: Don't Watch the Paint Dry

Sometimes all the problems of a city are symbolized in a particular event uncovering the physical decay it is suffering, crystallizing the signs of decline for every citizen to see. In 1979, Chicago mayor Michael Bilandic lost his re-election bid. Bland Bilandic had succeeded Richard Daley père, Chicago's ma-

chine boss for two decades, after Daley's death in 1976. But the pretender was unable to hold the throne because the city had proven unable to deal with a major unexpected blizzard. The snowfall paralyzed the city administration, which failed to clear the streets or to deal with power failures. The city gridlocked, and voters revolted. Bilandic was overthrown, in a pure democratic reality check. When you fail to provide the simplest and most basic services, you can be assured of returning to a position among the "exalted masses of the citizenry," as Harry Truman used to say.

Of course, the people of Chicago then had to put up with Jane Byrne for four years, and I'm not sure Ol' Blandy looked too bad to them afterward. Years later, they had the opportunity to see what a Mayor Daley might have done in the snowstorm, when they watched Daley *fils* swing into action in response to the flood of 1992. Mayor Daley was able to get the city back on track, eventually, in the face of a major emergency. Passing that crisis-management test, though, did not lessen the lasting physical damage of the flood. It merely served to underscore the fact that our infrastructure is antiquated, our cities are crumbling, and we expect our mayors to perform miracles as patchwork engineers.

The Hemophiliac City

Admiral James Stockdale, a genuine American hero, was transformed into an hapless debate doormat in the 1992 presidential campaign when he was outmatched by Al Gore and Dan Quayle. Long before he gazed confusedly into the camera and uttered his single-word diagnosis of American politics, everyone in the viewing audience knew the truth of it: "gridlock."

All the problems afflicting cities are of human creation, and therefore, as humans, we should be able to address them. The political system our Founding Fathers gave us seems to provide us the tools we need. Yet we have managed to screw things up badly. Our political structure is rapidly becoming the moral equivalent of the mass collisions we see, horrifyingly, on California freeways. Fingers point and blame abounds, but Washington sees no destination. Politicians speed ahead, wrapped in a fog, oblivious to the carnage just down the road in urban America. Unifying the White House and Congress behind a single party banner does not appear to be the solution. Looking to Washington for help, let alone inspiration, has been a fruitless course of action for at least a decade. And when residents of a declining city can count on neither Washington nor their own city hall for solutions and leadership, they may seem to have no alternative but to jump ship. Depressingly often since the 1960s, they have voted with their feet, echoing Ronald Reagan's antigovernment, anti-city nihilism. Those who could get out, did.

We have spent three decades now looking on as established American cities suffer a particularly virulent form of hemophilia. At the slightest municipal bruise, the lifeblood—people—pours out. With a major blow, the flow streams out unstanched. The good old solid-American city of Cleveland, home of the Lake Erie waterfront, the football Browns, the baseball Indians, has suffered more than most. At least, that is what the population decline the city has suffered might testify. In 1950, Cleveland had 915,000 residents and was in the top ten of the nation's most populous cities. By 1990, the city's population had dwindled to barely 500,000, and was still heading down. There have been brave attempts to rally the city, notably led by former mayor and now governor George Voinovich, but those attempts have brought only limited successes.

Of course, Cleveland is not alone. Between 1960 and 1990, St. Louis lost nearly 50 percent of its population, Detroit lost more than 25 percent, and Philadelphia and New Orleans both fell by 21 percent. Population growth was limited to a few Sun Belt and Pacific Rim cities. Houston grew by nearly 75 percent in that same thirty-year period, while San Jose was earning the sobriquet of America's fastest-growing city.

During the late 1960s and early 1970s, in the Northeast and Midwest in particular, commerce and jobs followed the mostly-white middle class to suburbs. Cities tried to compensate by attracting services, tourism, and office employment into newly built downtowns, but these efforts didn't make up for lost employment in manufacturing and skilled trades. Even when businesses remained downtown, their employees often moved to the suburbs. Commuting into and out of the city decimated the tax base, but it also changed the city's social and political character. People cared less about the city, so crime, poverty, and unsuitable housing became more "tolerable"—or easier to ignore. It became someone else's problem.

It became the norm for surrounding towns to raid big cities for their businesses, affluent residents, sports teams, and political prowess. Cities became vulnerable to suburban lure and suburbs cared little, because they did not have to pay a price. These trends produced one irony noted by Bernard Frieden and Lynne Sagalyn: "While downtown jobs were changing, so were city populations. They were changing in opposite directions."[37] The jobs being created were for men and women good at speaking, writing, and managing, but those professionals now lived in the suburbs. Rebuilding a downtown with hotels, restaurants, and retail stores provided more jobs for city residents, but between 1970 and 1990, the U.S. economy lost nearly 2 million manufacturing jobs and gained 14 million in the service sector.

Eventually, the battle between suburb and city, have and have-not, became destructive. Neighborhoods reacted. Lines were drawn between established progrowth coalitions and neighborhood, populist antigrowth alliances. In poor cities, neighborhoods fought downtown for limited development funding. By 1992, fully half of the total $3.5 billion in federal Community Development Block Grants was going outside city centers. CDBGs began in the Nixon administration as a housing program for inner cities, but, as *Time* magazine put it, "money follows power." The magazine argued in 1992 that "the suburbs control the nation's political destiny. Voters there will punish any candidate who would have them transfer tax revenue back to the cities."[38] The 1992 presidential election was the first in which suburban voters were a majority of the total, up from 36 percent in 1968. A good friend of mine, novelist and social commentator James Houston, has defined the California dream as "ten acres at the end of a sewer line and an agreement to extend the line no further."

The line went a lot further, and now suburbs refuse to pay to solve city problems. From the mid-1960s on, American cities were immersed in racial conflict and were losing control of their economic base. Meanwhile, as Joel Garreau has pointed out in his book on so-called edge cities, suburbs emerged as competing centers of economic activity, and they weren't about to lose their winning edge.[39] Everyone trying to explain the Los Angeles explosion in 1992, scholar and statesman alike, cited the cultural divide between Simi Valley and inner-city South Central, the proverbial "hood." We were two different worlds, separate and unequal, just as the Kerner Commission cautioned in the 1960s. It was a very one-sided rivalry.

Abandon Ship

In one of the oddest and funniest chapters in the annals of crazed ship skippers, a few years ago Captain Yiannis Avranas of the sunken cruise liner *Oceanus* explained why he headed off board before any of his passengers reached their lifeboats. "When I give the order to abandon ship, it doesn't matter what time I leave. If some people want to stay, they can stay."

As the remaining residents of old cities scramble for lifeboats, the battles have begun among them: battles over spoils, battles over what's left. There is also the ongoing dispute over who is responsible for the wreck.

It would be bad politics and, I am told, bad social science to identify just who pulled a trigger, firing the shot that murdered the American city. Looking back decades can be more disturbing than enlightening. Reading the work of urban historians over the past half century shows what different times we have seen. When Edward Banfield wrote *Big City Politics*, published in early 1965, he was writing from the perspective of the 1950s and could argue reasonably that urban political systems were functional, orderly, and resilient. Banfield and his generation of urban scholars still believed that cities knew how to function with great ethnic and socioeconomic pluralism.[40] A new generation of urban scholars emerged in the 1970s to challenge Banfield's assertions, writing of "street-fighting pluralism" and continuous urban combat over resources and power. The 1980s fostered more alienation and the regrettable separation of ethnic groups into sometimes hostile enclaves. Historian Kevin Starr has called Los Angeles the Yugoslavia of American cities.

The sad and predictable result of "white flight" to the suburbs has been a polarization of the races, both physical and psychological. As the attitudes go, so follow actions, into overt racial conflict. The Miami riots of 1980 were rooted in a sense of racial injustice. The following decade witnessed an effort in Boston to establish Mandela City, a separate black enclave. An ominous and chilling separation was occurring at the same time, but not by choice, in the phenomenal rate of young black men being sent to prison. By 1992, fully 23 percent of all black men between the ages of eighteen and twenty-six were in prison or on parole. This was not the dream that Martin Luther King, Jr., saw, or that millions have worked to provide the opportunity to achieve. This is a nightmare.

The abandoning of our cities, the murder of the very idea of the civil society, has been accomplished by an accumulation of selfish, short-sighted decisions to pursue individual desires and wrongheaded government policies. One additional price we are paying is an ironic one: the drift to the suburbs has seen people trying to re-create what they feel they have lost. Thus, the edge cities of suburbia go on, naturally, to develop many of the same problems as the original cities now abandoned. It is as predictable as night following day.

This is surely not progress. This is the culmination of a monstrous strategy that assumes an "acceptable level" of casualties in this terrible evolution. Career politicians are oblivious to the meaning of the glowing embers, allowing young men to face a death rate on the streets of America higher than in most wars. With the outbreak of fires in Los Angeles, we witnessed brief glimmerings of concern. Certain ideas and people were momentarily returned from limbo, tossed out on pundits' talk shows: Jack Kemp, enterprise zones, empowerment. Los Angeles drafted Ueberroth as rebuilding czar. Sound and fury signify nothing, for the warnings were clear to the powers that be for decades, since the Kerner Commission. Our leaders in Washington let us cling to the medieval strategy of "drawbridge defense": raise the bridge and remain safe in Fortress Suburbia. Tepid and confusing comments from Washington and governors like California's Pete Wilson reflect their calculated dismissal of votes from the inner cities, seeking electoral victory in the satellite cities of middle America. This morally repugnant course of abandoning America's cities is merely cynical politics. The politicians may be confident. They may be reelected. Yet we will not be safe, nor will they. No wall is high enough, no highway long enough. Any family can be touched tragically. There is no election slogan clever enough to stop a bullet.

Forget It, Jake

"Only death and destruction bring us to South Central Los Angeles," John Gregory Dunne wrote long before those riots. Any thinking human who witnessed the carnage of 1992 Los Angeles, or the physical deterioration of the Bronx or Detroit, is tempted by the question: Why not just give up on cities? Aren't they past salvation? Cities have mixed reputations just as every dream has a dark side. Cities can be centers of innovation and learning, where science, administration, commerce, and arts work together for the enlightenment of the lucky citizens who live there. People of all races and backgrounds can meet and make progress toward agreed-upon goals. Cities also, at the same time, are breeding grounds of crime, poverty, and iniquity.

The tempting question comes as frustration levels are at their highest. From above in society come the pleas of an anxious political and social elite. Glib commentators call for drastic action, to "send in the 82nd Airborne." On a recent visit to Belfast, Northern Ireland, I saw firsthand the results of twenty-five years of military occupation of a civilian populace. The extremists who suggest something similar here should learn the lesson of Belfast: such a move robs the government of any claim to legitimacy and undermines the crucial principle of rule by consent. By the time you have to send in the marines or the National Guard, you have lost that battle. The only solution lies in dealing with problems before it becomes necessary to send in the army.

Frustration also rises from below in the city, the steam venting from those our society penalizes or simply leaves behind. Many in America can understand why that anger occurs and occasionally explodes in outrage. What is inexplicable to most of us is the mindless nihilism of the explosion, the lack of calibration, the failure to avoid destroying what is good in the community in the violent outbreaks. More unfathomable still is the outburst of violence at *good* news. Why would enthusiastic crowds in Chicago, celebrating the Bulls' 1992 NBA championship, express their joy by rampaging through the streets, overturning police cars, and looting innocent shopkeepers? The parade to honor the Super Bowl champion Dallas Cowboys in 1993 degenerated into a violent small-scale riot. When "frustration," a wildly inexact term, boils over into violence no matter what the instigation, we know that alienation from the system is complete.

Bad as all this is, there are worse signs to see than the frustration of a society member at the top of or a gang member at the bottom of the city spectrum. The worst expression of frustration is on the part of the so-called average citizens, black, brown, yellow, or white, expressing dismay by not voting, not participating, not caring. Leaving, first mentally and spiritually, and then packing up and moving to the suburbs if they can. Urban America's answer to its own problems has been a refusal to answer, an abandonment instead.

If I had fallen under the sway of such a mood—and the temptation was there—I never would have run for office. Others might not have joined me in our fight, and our city might never have come back. What I know best of America's cities I know from my own. San Jose's downtown didn't die. Its death was homicide, premeditated and violent, missing only malice aforethought. Some of our shortsighted city fathers and developers of the 1940s and 1950s made growth a superficial and dominant mantra, to the exclusion of all else. They ripped the city's heart out and tossed it far outside, with a callous indifference to the future and to those left behind.

I empathize wholeheartedly with other mayors. When troubles arise, when the problems at hand make residents sit up and take notice, all eyes turn to city hall, and rightly to the mayor's door. City councils cannot or will not provide the effective leadership necessary. As we will see in a later chapter, councils either are structurally too weak or when strong are rent by division and special-interest influence. The comparisons of these legislative bodies to Congress are well made.

So the choice before me in my city was clear. Those faint of heart might throw up their hands and head for an edge city. I could follow, taking the advice given to Jake in *Chinatown*: forget it! I believed instead that we had a chance. A mayor must act. I proposed a heart transplant for the ailing patient.

First, we had to revive the body.

3
HEART OF THE CITY

Oh, a day in the city-square, there is no such pleasure in life!
—Robert Browning

Neal Coonerty was the mayor of Santa Cruz, a seaside resort just thirty miles from San Jose on the Monterey Bay. More than just a mayor, he owned a bookstore, one of the vibrant shops that made up Santa Cruz's unique and homey downtown, a community that had withstood the trends of suburbanization and shopping malls. "Santa Cruz was really different," Coonerty told the *San Jose Mercury News*. "We had a functioning 'Main Street,' the Pacific Garden Mall that had been there for 100 years and kept transforming itself. It was where the Rainbow Lady danced in front of the Cooper House, where the people who lived modestly on trust funds could spend time in coffeehouses."

Then came the 1989 Loma Prieta earthquake. Its epicenter was roughly halfway between our two city halls, but the perversity of nature sent the shock waves more directly to little Santa Cruz and the Pacific Garden Mall. With nostalgia for the sweet old days, and a bit of incredulity, Coonerty told the reporter, "We lost that in fifteen seconds."

Rarely is the heart of a city lost in the blink of an eye. Most Americans have had to suffer the slow-motion degradation of urban life, not a massive coronary. We live with inexorable deterioration of the heart, its muscle and fiber, a slow decline in its ability to pump arterial life through the lives of its citizens. We look back and are unable to point to a specific moment at which a city lost its heart, but we are able

55

collectively to feel the loss. Our eyes wince at this aching sight of an elderly loved one wasting away, year by year, day by day. No one could enjoy that.

John Lindsay, onetime mayor of the nation's largest city, wrote after his experiences in New York: "We can trace all the problems of the American city back to a single starting point: We Americans don't like our cities very much."[41] The appeal of the suburbs, of open spaces and greener hills and bluer skies, pulls us away from the dirty past, out of the city. Individuals pack their bags for cheaper homes and for the sense of safety. Companies follow, lured by lower taxes, the lower cost of land, fewer zoning restrictions. "Less hassle" is the refrain of people and businesses alike.

Many urbanologists (a word as ugly as the pictures they draw of the contemporary city) argue that cities today are the victims of external influences, from the global economy to federal and state governments to the suburbs. I disagree. Too many academics have attempted to explain restructuring and resettlement patterns in purely economic terms, but this misses the mark. Urban transformation involves many forces: diverse changes at all sorts of levels, economic, political, and social. If we are to understand what we have lost, and its psychological toll, we need to understand the psychological aspects that got us here. We need to recall the human dimension.

As a politician, I will accept blame on behalf of predecessors and admit the tremendous level of political ineptitude and stupidity that local leadership across the United States showed during the 1950s and 1960s. Life was sucked out of downtowns across the country. Politicians were responsible in large part, and many paid a price as familiar political machines disintegrated as well.

But not only politicians suffered the consequences. People did. The urban riots of the 1960s were an entirely predictable response of individuals left without hope in abandoned inner cities. Those riots and their associated political and social upheavals were, in fact, a massive *internal* influence, not external, perpetuating the continuing assault on the heart of the city. The violence of the Sixties was both effect and cause, as it set the image of American cities for a generation to come. Cities like Detroit still wear the chains of those events. In 1992, a newspaper reporter could still write plaintively, "Oh, Detroit, Detroit, Detroit. As it tries to overcome its portrayal as an urban nightmare . . . , a string of recent events have repeatedly punctured this proud city's soul and bruised its pride. No other city, residents here lament, has to work so hard to overcome an image." The heading on the story reads, inevitably, "Trying to Live Down What Happened in 1967."[42]

The clichés of pop history label Detroit a postindustrial city, suffering a predetermined decline that befalls all American metropolises. It is difficult to avoid a comparison of cities now and cities then, a look backward. In the comparison lies the sense of what we have lost in the past half century. Quite simply, we have lost our heart. "Megalopolis" was first coined by Jean Gottmann to describe the seaboard stretching from Boston southward to Norfolk, Virginia.[43] This whole area might be called the Eastern City, and I defy anyone—politician or simple city dweller—to define its heart. Center City is developing in the Great Lakes region, including Milwaukee, Chicago, Detroit, and Pittsburgh. What we might even call Western City sprawls between San Diego and Los Angeles, including Orange County, and sometimes seems poised to include San Jose and the Bay Area as well.

Can humans live in a megalopolis and be happy? John Kenneth Galbraith sees in our vacation choices the kernel of what we have lost in a social, aesthetic, and spiritual sense:

> The traveler from the United States or the industrial cities of Europe or Japan goes each summer to visit the remnants of preindustrial civilizations. That is because Athens, Florence, Venice, Seville, Agra, Kyoto and Samarkand, though they were infinitely poorer . . . included, as part of life, a much wider aesthetic perspective. No city of the postindustrial era is, in consequence, of remotely comparable artistic interest. Indeed, no traveler of predominantly artistic interest ever visits an industrial city and he visits very few of any kind which owe their distinction to architecture and urban design postdating the publication of Adam Smith's *Wealth of Nations* in 1776.[44]

A City and Its Stories

If you have seen one city, sneers the cynic, you've seen them all. In 1991, a Miami newspaper reporter uncovered an embarrassing case of Migrating Manhattan. Postcards on sale in Florida stores were captioned "The Beautiful Lights of Miami" but featured a photograph of the New York City skyline at sunset! Yes, lovely Miami, complete with an Empire State Building and United Nations headquarters. The Dade County distributor of the cards explained, "We just assumed it was Miami. You know, I don't know Miami all that well."

Too many today share this low level of civic awareness. Let me describe the constituent pieces that make up one American city today. San Jose has 1,400 miles of roads. (New York City has almost 5,000 more.) We can also count 250,000 street trees, 1,800 miles of sewer lines and over 1 million books in our libraries. Our city has 600 traffic lights, three regional shopping centers, 5,400 city employees, 150 parks and one international airport. There are also a brand-new sports arena, three interstate highways, 250,000 households, and a downtown with 5 million square feet of office space.

But you cannot measure the quality of a city by its parts or its pieces. You will not find the heart of a city in some set of statistics, or in the gleaming glass of an office high-rise, or in the size of its shopping malls or population, and certainly not in the rhetoric of a mayor. If you want to find the quality of your city, you need to look hard, but not far. You need to look to a million places: to one another. And you need to look one place: within. The city's heart is a story that is told by people, by each one of us, a million people, a million differences, a million dreams. Telling that story and reasserting that dream, every day in all our interactions, is the lifeblood of a city.

The very notion of civilization means cities, large populations living together. William Whyte, author of *City: Rediscovering Its Center* and probably the country's best authority on urban environments, has argued that humans gravitate toward crowded living situations. They thrive on density. "Despite what people say," he argues, "the thing that attracts them most is people."[45] Historians can trace the tendency toward self-congestion as far back as one wishes to define the first city, and they point to dense population clusters from the prehistoric Fertile Crescent up through Native American tribes during the agricultural revolution. When they gathered, they settled together. And when they moved on to a beckoning frontier, they searched until they found a new central spot, a welcoming home to nourish the reassembled clan. Our nomadic ancestors were in the business of reinventing their communities, and in California two centuries ago, on the banks of a river, they heard the first heartbeats of what would become San Jose.

Focus on the Heart

History is such a remarkable guide to a city's real strength: its center. The Guadalupe River, before it had that name, was for centuries critical to the first inhabitants of the Santa Clara Valley. In their settlements along its banks, they lived and fished and hunted, knowing they were on the rim of the world in a special place. It was a dream.

The earliest colonists and explorers, Franciscans and conquistadors carrying the cross and sword northward in the late eighteenth century, were impressed by the river they called "Rio Nuestra Senora de Guadalupe." An adventurous band of men, women, and children decided to make a home by its banks. They prospered, mostly. Their bucolic descriptions propelled a mighty torrent of immigrants that descended on the little pueblo as it radiated out from the Guadalupe. They came, wave after wave of newcomers, adapting and building, always building. San Jose was even the first state capital of California in 1850, home to legislators who celebrated so heartily it went down in history as the "Legislature of a Thousand Drinks." Thank goodness the capital moved on after a year.

There was always one constant for the Native Americans, Spanish Californios, Mexicans, and legions of people who arrived in the valley: the dream, reaching for the better life, the better world. Three thousand miles away, Henry Ward Beecher wrote of the marvels he was hearing about San Jose.

> The fame of your valley has come over the plains and mountains and assailed our ears, until, with the description of scenery, of mountains, of mines, of trees, of shrubs, of farms, gardens and harvests, of people and prospects, I will not say that we are wearied, but will say that we were somewhat stunned, and it gave the belief that if nothing else excelled in California, the art of exaggeration was rife. . . . This goodly land which, furtherest from the East, seems to have been the last work that God had in hand, and He furnished it to suit the home of man the best.[46]

Beecher was writing in the early 1880s, just as the good people of San Jose were concentrating on building their first cathedral. The population of the bustling community numbered 15,000. The economy was predominantly agricultural, a cornucopia of orchards. Small businesses dotted what was not really a downtown so much as *the* town, concentrated on Market and Santa Clara streets.

Treat Your Past as Prologue

I grew up in central San Jose, on the same street where I now live. I went to St. Joseph's grammar school, taught by the Sisters of Notre

Dame de Namur, an order that arrived in San Jose in 1851. The nuns teaching me seemed old enough to have arrived on the first wagon train. Our old brick building sat right by the Guadalupe, and when the river flooded in 1956, the students had to help sandbag the school. It was still a small stream, but we learned that the Guadalupe had been the center of civilization in this valley for thousands of years. As a boy, I imagined that era. Today, my mind drifts back to those days, in a bustling downtown that shaped my notions of community forevermore.

There was "the city" itself, with a smattering of "skyscrapers," none more than fifteen stories tall: the Garden City Bank Building, the San Jose National Bank, and the most recent additions of the art-deco era, the DeAnza Hotel,* the Medico-Dental Building, and a stately Bank of America. Rippling out from the core were residential districts with attractive streets, comfortable homes, and well-tended gardens, only a short ride away on "the interurban." At First and Santa Clara streets, you could get off the trolley, weighing your options in the variety of smart shops and stores. Fine dining and dancing were at the St. Claire Hotel, and for a treat there was my grandfather's San Jose Creamery.

To every child, their immediate neighborhood is the whole world. Downtown San Jose had gigantic buildings to a child's eye, like the original Bank of America building, still standing today, with a green bulb on top that I could see from my house. That was the center of the financial world, every bit a West Coast Wall Street. The Bank of America had been founded as the Bank of Italy by the legendary A. P. Giannini, born in a downtown San Jose boarding house. The 1906 earthquake and massive rebuilding projects in San Francisco had given Giannini his empire, but his start had been right here in the immigrant community of Italian-Americans. People in San Jose knew A. P. Giannini, their banker, personally.

A few square blocks of downtown represented the financial center, the cultural center, the transportation hub. All the buses stopped in downtown, all roads seemed to lead there. The train depot was on Santa Clara Street. The town square would have been First Street, with all the department stores and movie houses. I spent much of my time in the Fox Theater, with its elegant lobby and frescoed walls, and the Studio, and the UA. We also had a theater with an interesting nomenclature: more re-

---

*In 1991, a powerful group of corporate executives representing IBM, Apple, and Motorola met in the renovated DeAnza Hotel. There they planned a momentous joint venture that is now shaking the electronics world: the power PC.

cently it served as a porno theater, but it was innocuously known in the old days as the Gay. The only other theaters in San Jose seemed to be out in the country, like the Towne Theater at the bend of Alameda, a twenty-five-minute walk from downtown. Pretty far out there, we thought, though today the restored Towne is easily considered part of downtown. Theaters were a social center on weekends, because you would see everybody you knew in your world.

I had a place in that world. I couldn't serve as an altar boy at early-morning mass or walk down the street without seeing familiar faces. Everyone knew everyone else's family history. San Jose in the 1950s provided me the quintessential small-town environment that Hollywood strives so hard to portray, part Capra and part Beaver Cleaver. Everyone tries in life, through their work or simply in daydreams, to re-create the pleasant things from their childhood. Graham Greene wrote of a traveler who always reconstructs a row of books in any new place when he arrives. At the beginning of my first term as mayor, I saw the opportunity to do precisely that, by refocusing on our downtown heart. I see the past in the present.

Having that sense of place in history is important for any city. As California's first city and state capital, San Jose is now re-creating itself as California's newest city. We have consciously looked back to the pleasures that attracted those first travelers, as we set about supporting the energy and intellect of new immigrants and native-born alike. The heart of any city should represent that dream to its residents, to its welcome new citizens, and to others who may simply be passing through.

Beware the Growth Machine

Every big city, my own included, used the postwar years to ditch the very values and special resources that made our downtowns such remarkable communities. Growth, that two-headed monster, became our watchword. There is a positive side to urban growth, which I will describe quite enthusiastically in a discussion of public entrepreneurship. First must come some truth-telling about the evil side of growth—the dark side of the force.

Sociologist Harvey Molotch is credited with making the seminal argument about "the city as a growth machine," and to understand it is to know much about the extraordinary expansion of urban life in American history.[47] The driving force of the growth machine built modern cities just as it built their great eighteenth- and nineteenth-century predecessors. There is little historical evidence of resistance to the dynamics of "value-free" city building, but let us not be overly harsh with our ancestors. (Others will follow and judge us as well.) They were generally ignorant of problems like overcrowding, intense migration, transportation gridlock, societal anarchy, and so on. Their own values were quite simply those of expansion, development, building, and resettlement. There was money to be made, and the growth-machine elite made it.

A prototypical member of that elite was William Ogden. He arrived in Chicago in 1835, when its population was under 4,000, and it was far from being the nation's "second city." Chicago was virgin territory for a growth-oriented active businessman, and Ogden became its mayor, its dominant railway developer, and owner of much of its best real estate.[48] Like George Washington Plunkitt of Tammany Hall, "he seen his opportunities and he took 'em." Ogden was not unique, not even unusual, in the entire sweep of urbanization from the middle of the nineteenth century on. Social critic Lewis Mumford explained, "That a city had any other purpose than to attract trade, to increase land values, and to grow is something that, if it uneasily entered the mind of an occasional [Walt] Whitman, never exercised any hold on the minds of our countrymen."[49]

The few moments of reflection and questioning were brief and relatively unheralded. Frederick Law Olmsted designed public parks in order to bring qualities of the countryside into the lives of the poor, and the settlement house movement led by Jane Addams tried to ease the squalor of slum life. But their examples were not copied, certainly not as eagerly as the examples of men like Ogden. Money was in the driver's seat. Molotch summed up that century of growth with words that ring true to any mayor in the land today: "The United States became an industrial nation with relatively little constraint placed upon the wheeling and dealing that distributed populations and business activities across the land."[50]

Benign Roots of a Growth Machine

Heeding the words of Horace Greeley, my great-grandfather went west and arrived in San Jose in 1869. A wise pioneer, he waited to leave Iowa until the completion of the transcontinental railroad, arriving in style by train and hoping to participate in the California boom.

The groundwork was set, and the 1880s were a remarkable decade of growth and innovation in the Santa Clara Valley. We had a new cathedral and other investments in our future. San Jose State University, then called the

State Normal School, was already accepting students throughout California and in 1881 opened a second building to accommodate an overflow. The Jesuit fathers at Santa Clara were meting out their particular brand of moral and humanistic training at the oldest center of higher education in the state, now Santa Clara University. San Jose connected its telephone exchange with San Francisco in 1882, and by 1884 (only fifteen years after the Golden Spike) orchards were shipping fresh fruit to East Coast markets in refrigerated railroad cars. In 1886 the Board of Trade, an early chamber of commerce, was formed to bring new pioneers to San Jose and to expand the local economy.

Some bursts in the valley's early boom were lightning bolts of good fortune. In 1885, Governor and Mrs. Leland Stanford suffered the loss of their only son

San Jose in the 1890s.

and in their grief announced a $20 million endowment for a new Leland Stanford Junior University. Today, twenty miles from San Jose, Stanford University is one of the preeminent institutions in the world, nestled on land near Palo Alto once used by Leland Stanford, the famous robber baron, as a summer ranch. The same year witnessed another example of profit being turned to the future, when construction began on the Lick Observatory on 4,200-foot Mount Hamilton just twenty miles to our east, visible from our downtown streets. James Lick, an early businessman and landholder, left his entire fortune *(worth $5 million at the time) to philanthropic causes and specified that $750,000 be used to erect the world's most powerful telescope. In a forerunner of San Jose's cooperative partnerships with Silicon Valley firms a century later, the county spent $100,000 to construct a first-class road to the peak, enabling the observatory to be built and to become a major scientific institution for decades.*

The superintendent of that road work was an immigrant who arrived by train a decade and a half earlier, my great-grandfather Patrick Condron.

After an early explosion of growth, San Jose rested quietly, and its valley from the turn of the century, was devoted to agriculture for four full decades. World War II changed all that. The first taste of the employment possibilities in the new defense-connected technology industry, exemplified by the young Hewlett-Packard and Varian companies, encouraged our city fathers to pursue an explicit goal: make San Jose the Los Angeles of the north through growth and housing for all the workers. In 1950, A. P. "Dutch" Hamann became city manager, and he embarked on an ambitious plan to remake the entire valley. The annexation wars had been declared; the growth machine became a blitzkrieg.

If you wonder how a city like Los Angeles or Phoenix or any other extended Sun Belt city became so large, examine the record of postwar San Jose, for it is of the same archetype. In the absence of a strong mayor or any other counterbalancing voice, Dutch Hamann's administration rezoned large tracts of land, provided easy access to credit for builders, and aggressively annexed nearby territory. San Jose was the Russian Empire of old. By the time Hamann retired almost twenty years later, San Jose had compiled a stunning list of 1,419 annexations. Neighboring communities like Campbell, Saratoga, and Milpitas incorporated themselves during the 1950s as an explicit defense against San Jose's grasp. So did Cupertino—unwittingly preserving millions in tax dollars for its future (it became the headquarters site of Apple Computer and Tandem Computer). These communities on our periphery thus avoided the fate of towns like Alviso and Willow Glen, which now exist on the map only as extended neighborhoods in San Jose.[51]

It was in some ways a well-executed conquest. Hamann's city government extended sewers, storm drains, and roads and capitalized on liberal federal highway grants to build a skeletal (and damned expensive) infrastructure *around*, but not *to*, our downtown. As Silicon Valley's fame grew with the electronics industry, so did the population. Between 1940 and 1980, Santa Clara County's population increased tenfold, from 175,000 to 1.7 million. Countywide employment was doubling in each successive decade, and a large majority of the new workers were immigrants from out of state.

One critical element for the city was cynically ignored: none of those new San Jose residents, were living downtown or in central, established neighborhoods. All were pushed to the far horizon. Rather than living in a vibrant center city, in medium-density housing, the stream of immigrants settled into socially and economically segregated residential communities. This was understandable. The ranch house with the big yard was the American dream.

Hundreds of thousands were now living in San Jose. The absence of a logical plan, a strategy to shape that growth, is a sadly familiar tale in contemporary America. There was no shared vision of common purpose. Laissez-faire held the day, refusing to focus.

The problem was not growth per se. Growth was unchanneled, exploding beyond any constraints that local government might have thought wise—had it thought at all. The downtown atrophied in the pell-mell rush to outlying subdivisions and shopping centers. The growth machine was the engine, greed was the accelerator, and behind the wheel sat the men who murdered the downtown, spiritual inheritors of Ogden of Chicago. Although many were honorable and well-meaning businessmen, others nurtured incestuous relationships, and local government fell under the sway of certain developers, reaping millions from new tracts carved on hillsides miles from our heart.

City hall itself abandoned an interesting Gothic hulk built in 1887 on Plaza Park, sneaking off like a midnight doorbell ringer to a faceless corner on North First Street, two miles away. For years after, city government was adrift, cut off from the once-vibrant heart of the city it purportedly represented but actively undercut. Even the *Mercury News*, putative conscience of the city, moved its offices in 1966 from the very center of downtown on Santa Clara Street to miles outside the city on cheap land further north. Publisher and growth apologist Joe Ridder was once asked about protecting the environment around the downtown's core. He replied bluntly: "Trees don't buy papers." Such was the state of the green coalition in San Jose.

Neal Peirce, observer of urban decline around the country, visited in the 1980s and recognized our downtown hemorrhage. "Blocks were razed for grandiose projects neither the city nor investors seemed able to complete. . . . Whatever new buildings went up tended to be banal. And anti-urban.

Consider Lloyds Bank's glassy high-rise in central San Jose—it was built without a front door to the street! The only entry is through the parking garage."[52]

By 1975, just before I got involved in government, Silicon Valley sprawl had created "commuter hell" on horribly congested freeways, which caused dangerous levels of air pollution and spurred a no-growth movement calling for a halt to further industrial expansion. Housing prices were skyrocketing to nearly the highest in the nation, while builders and their political minions carried on with cavalier abandon, carving residential single-family homes into hillsides and meadows farther and farther from the center. The situation was bleak.

I was not the first to say enough. I would, however, become the most vocal.

Bricks in a New Cathedral

Every city across the country, no matter how blighted, has good people fighting the symptoms of urban decline. Community projects and neighborhood groups pick up the sword every day to fight against decay and poverty and against politics as usual. Many of these efforts are doing the right things but without an overall strategy. You might say that cities—sometimes with the help of city hall, sometimes without its knowledge—are haphazardly laying bricks that might someday make a new cathedral, a focus of pride. I prefer to see a plan before I build, and too many public and private efforts seem almost casual, with hit-or-miss results. But there are initiatives around the country making good, solid first steps. The trendy phenomenon of gentrification, with which inner cities are so familiar, is an example. So is the attempt to stop the faceless, ugly "Sprawlsburg" mentality that characterizes "mall architecture" in every state in the union. The University of Miami now offers an M.A. degree in architecture, assigning suburbs as the key design problem, and students must focus on innovative solutions. A professor describes her philosophy in terms that most suburban dwellers would understand: "Asphalt is a social problem . . . the more there is, the greater the distances between destinations and the grimmer the landscape. Gradually, people stop walking. Neighbors even stop talking."

The professor's ingenious charge to her students: "Take a mall and make it into downtown."[53]

Others know the right things to be doing, but seldom enjoy the support of local government. William Whyte, the scholar of the downtown soul, describes how a new human microarchitecture of inner cities can help enormously. Parking lots, blank walls, sunken plazas and hidden malls are bad in his book. They draw people away from any social interaction and deaden the downtown. The little things that provide warmth, friendliness, and excitement to a city can be critical: chairs, trees, urban parks with waterfalls, benches, and ledges that provide seating.[54]

A small number of activist mayors around the country began to awaken in the 1980s to the loss of heart. Neal Peirce explained the phenomenon as "urban comparison shopping. . . . This new generation of leaders has visited the Bostons, Philadelphias and Savannahs of America, not to mention European cities. It has seen how glorious cities can be and has decided, at last, not to settle for mediocrity."[55] Mediocrity is in the truest sense un-American. It is the antithesis of San Jose and of the city-state ideal.

Now, at the dawn of the twenty-first century, I marvel at how much we have achieved toward that ideal in our community. The next chapter describes our attempt to spark a downtown renaissance. A key element, San Jose's Guadalupe River Park plan, reflects the fact that the river was the first destination and our first identity as a community. The world is being remade every day in Silicon Valley, and it is fitting that we re-create an early axis of civilization, laying new bricks along this green thread of life. We have planned a 500-acre park at our center, radiating through our neighborhoods to the Santa Cruz mountains and to the broad expanse of South San Jose.

The daily fare at the park will be art, ballet, theater, concerts, a new world at the Children's Discovery Museum and the awakening of a young mind in the Tech Museum of Innovation. There is already a place for Sharks to swim—our new sports arena known to hockey fans. Nature lovers will meet joggers, conventioneers encounter lovers strolling hand in hand. The "new" Guadalupe River Park will provide today what it has provided for hundreds of years—a destination, a respite, a home. Once again, San Joseans can walk past the Spanish Plaza Park, now named for Cesar Chavez. Strolling past the two new museums, they will approach the river on Woz Way, named for Steve Wozniak, cofounder of Apple Computer and benefactor of both museums. It is a trip to the past and a look at the future.

The present is a place very close to the past. Today, all cities reflect tremendous change and evolution, good and bad, but their people share the same spirit, the same pride and aspirations as earlier generations. Like those before, we all seek to make a better life for ourselves and our children. We do so only by giving more than a passive allegiance, by making an active commitment to the heart of a new city. When combined with new leadership, willing and eager to look at the city anew, residents can and will face the future with a renewed sense of purpose.

My election as mayor in 1982 was the beginning of a new time for our city, a time when we began to look from city hall on North First Street back to the downtown and to the past. Our team knew it could not perform miracles. But I knew as well what we had lost when we abandoned our city for the siren songs of expansion. I wanted to reclaim it, and as I gazed at once into the past and the future, I had one particular building in sight. It was a cathedral.

4

THE CATHEDRAL STRATEGY: CAPITAL OF SILICON VALLEY

> Everything proud was once only imagined.
> —William Blake

The character of an ancient civilization is often judged by the physical landmarks it left behind. Quite often, that is all a city bequeathed for history's backward glance. Some Egyptian or Mayan cities are remembered only for their pyramids, like Byron's "Ozymandias," monuments to a single ruler's egotism. In Europe, the visitor to Berlin or Paris or Rome stands in awe of the Brandenburg Gate, the Eiffel Tower or the Colosseum. When I visited the imperial city of Kyoto in Japan, I felt drawn to the ancient temples spared by World War II's infernos. And even after decades of Communist rule, cities like Moscow and Kiev retain landmarks of their Christian founders in the mazes of religious structures at their core.

Historians searching for San Jose's character, for a communal heartbeat, would find themselves at the doors of St. Joseph's Cathedral, the centerpiece of our downtown. This magnificent church was built in 1877, the fifth Catholic church on that site. The first was a small adobe frame put up in 1803 by the Spanish settlers as the hub of the Pueblo de

69

St. Joseph's Cathedral shortly after completion.

San José, an oblong group of adobe structures that defined the northern-most reach of the empire of Spain in the Americas. The current cathedral is built in the shape of a Maltese cross, modeled on Paris's Sacre Coeur by architect Bryan Clinch. It is a splendid structure, now well over a century old and restored. Yet the historian, the urban archaeologist, would look not just at the building itself but at the context in which it was born. Today, the massive domes are framed by office towers and hotels, which sometimes shadow the cathedral's imposing presence on old Market Street. That was hardly the case when it was built.

This monument was built by a town of only 15,000 people. The feat was surely technically feasible, but it surprises a modern observer for what it says about those who began such a daunting task. What we see today as a noteworthy edifice in the midst of skyscrapers must have been palatial, almost miraculous, in the midst of a small village of dusty one- and two-story wood structures. Just as the great baroque cathedrals of

Europe are most astonishing for having been built in the Middle Ages, my city's namesake cathedral speaks volumes about the spirit of San Jose. Clarence Darrow said that an idea is a much greater monument than a cathedral, but in this cathedral, a great idea is embodied. Our forefathers left us this hallmark of a soaring faith, built and rebuilt on the same spot, testimony to St. Joseph the builder, the patron saint of the city, and to the valley's obsession with the future.

The people of a city, in any era, can either pursue individually a thousand definitions of self-interest or focus on communal definitions of the public good. The first approach, common in history and so common in American cities today, leads inevitably to confusion, chaos, and failure. Populations wind up leaving, heading for any frontier that looks more attractive.

I suggest the second approach, what I like to call the "cathedral strategy." It requires that a city's leaders agree with residents to act upon a shared mandate, a mission statement for where the city stands, who they are together, and what is most important in their self-identification. Remember Machiavelli's admonition that only "the common welfare" makes cities great.

Most important, the cathedral strategy demands a tilt to the future, a vision of where the city is headed, and a plan to reach the distant horizon. You could define it as a perpetual restating of the big picture. It may be frustrating, for a focus on generally accepted goals and common dreams is difficult to define and requires patience and political skill among citizens and leaders alike. But the cathedral strategy binds the city as it builds itself, leaving for future generations and the outside world a clear picture of what their community attempted and maybe even achieved.

Overcoming an Identity Crisis

When Gertrude Stein said of Oakland, "There's no *there* there," she ironically immortalized the city in an offbeat way. Oakland may be envied by some smaller towns: at least Stein had been there. It probably never entered her head to insult San Jose, a Bay Area neighbor. Now, that is quite a slap in the face.

A city must be reasonable in its expectations. Peoria will not assume Chicago's mantle; recently renovated Newark will not rival New York City. When I first ran for mayor in 1982, on a platform of civic renewal, it would have been unrealistic to expect that San Jose could be transformed through wishful thinking into something that it was not. It was not genuinely a Pacific Rim capital, as Los Angeles could reasonably claim to be, despite its size (bigger than Seattle) and trading links. It wasn't a state capital, not since the old days. It was not (then, certainly) a cultural mecca or a household name for any of the myriad reasons American cities can be immortalized. Furthermore, although there is majesty in this spectacularly beautiful valley, with the Santa Cruz mountain range on the west and the Diablos on the east, San Jose would never have the physical beauty of San Francisco.

I resisted the temptation most mayors succumb to: skyscraper envy. Cities often attempt to set themselves apart with a signature skyline. Since America's first ten-story skyscraper of 1885, only a few cities, like Washington, D.C., have kept the wisdom of a lower scale of structure. More often than not, city planners botch their Tinkertoy efforts. The 1980s were a building boom of high-rise horrors only now being recognized for the indulgences they really were. I read the national figures on downtown office vacancy space now and chuckle. Good planning and a nearby airport (both of which imposed height restrictions) kept our city in scale. Like Jonathan Swift, we worked from a more modest proposal.

I realized the challenge San Jose was up against. We had no soul, no central organizing principle. Gertrude Stein may have said it decades ago, but by the 1980s, we truly embodied her dictum: "no *there* there." The only blip that registered on radar screens was our infamous reputation in the Bay Area as the northernmost suburb of Los Angeles. A *San Francisco Examiner* reporter suggested that, as "a mind-numbing sprawl of shopping malls and drive-through hamburger stands," we might consider our civic slogan to be: "San Jose, Next 11 Exits."[56]

I never really minded such twaddle. I began to realize we had something no other city in the Bay Area, even in the world, had. Right in our Valley, all around us, we had a veritable hologram of the shining city on a hill.

Expand Your Horizons to Fit a City-State: "The Virtual City"

The historian Gibbon, chronicling the rise of the imperial capital Rome, stressed the importance of its surrounding area. "The first and most natural root of a great city is the labor and populousness of the adjacent county, which supplies the materials of subsistence, of manufactures, and of foreign trade."[57]

Few people around the country could have told you in the early 1980s just exactly what San Jose's "adjacent counties" were. Since they barely knew the city belonged on a United States map, they certainly would have had trouble naming its environs. Just after I became mayor, a February 1983 issue of *Newsweek* had an article on the tremendous storms assaulting Northern California. Accompanying the story was a photograph of the devastation along the coast, with a caption reading, "Waves batter a beach house in San Jose." Much to our regret, of course, we are not on the coast. When the local media tried to create a local brouhaha over the big media boys' ignorance, I made light of the incident. "Once again," I told the *Mercury News*, "people are trying to fuel that rumor that I want to annex Santa Cruz."

My plan was much more ambitious. I intended to annex the virtual city of Silicon Valley, to make San Jose known as the "capital" of that ethereal realm.

San Jose had a historical pedigree sufficient to make the claim. It had made an early technological leap with the arc-lamp Electric Light Tower, defining the city to the Bay Area for the four decades wrapped around the turn of the century. In the late 1880s, Santa Clara science professor John Montgomery had used hot-air balloons to launch heavier-than-air gliders, making him a predecessor to the Wright brothers and a pioneer in the history of manned flight.

A City Builds a Beacon

Silicon Valley waited ninety years in the future. Yet, thanks to a dreamer and visionary, San Jose stood at the forefront of a new technology. It takes vision and great persistence to build a beautiful cathedral, but here was something more unusual. On December 31, 1881, James Jerome Owen, publisher of the old San Jose Mercury, saw his dream flash into reality. That day marked the inception of the Electric Light Tower, San Jose's Beacon of the West.

At 6:30 that evening, the gas lights in the city extinguished momentarily. In their stead, six arc lamps on the twenty-story tower, two years in the making, suddenly blazed. Light radiated for two miles from the corner of Santa Clara and Market. It shone with an intensity much greater than the brightest harvest moon. One citizen claimed to have read his newspaper by tower light at a point thirteen blocks away. A farmer in Morgan Hill blamed decreased egg production on the nocturnal light of the tower. To some critics, it was Owen's Folly, a hazard to wild ducks in foggy weather, a meeting place for moths throughout the county.

Nevertheless, for the next thirty-four years until it came down, that light tower served as the symbol of San Jose. Its light shone far beyond this valley, all the way to France. Paris, the City of Light, was chided for not being as pro-gressive as this small hamlet; its own Eiffel Tower was not finished until 1889.

San Jose had even been the home of the world's first broadcasting sta-tion. In 1909, on a downtown corner at First and San Fernando, Charles Herrold flipped a toggle switch to power up a voice radio station, opening the door to modern electronic mass communication. Herrold launched his "Station FN" three years before Congress passed the Radio Act of 1912, establishing the modern licensing system. Having already founded San Jose's College of Engineering and Wireless, Herrold was a pioneer in "wireless telephony" and with his new station began to transmit news and music. His wife, Sybil, was the world's first woman disc jockey. Together, in order to keep the station afloat, they also invented commercial radio advertising. Herrold was a tireless experimenter and developed more than fifty radio-related inventions. Station FN evolved into our modern KCBS, one of the Bay Area's largest commercial stations and a continu-ing tribute to his foresight.

All in all, our city's roots in technology grew deep, in soil that later would nurture the giants of the computer era as they made a revolution. Around here, their names and accomplishments are truly legend and are listed whenever pundits discuss the true birthplace of Silicon Valley. There are many claimants.

One important spot is the Cupertino garage of Steve Jobs's parents' house, where the two Steves, Wozniak and Jobs, built the Apple I and began developing the revolutionary Apple II, precursor to today's Macintosh computers. Earlier, there was the IBM research center in San Jose, where the floppy disk and other computer technologies were invented. Another, more vital inaugural spot for Silicon Valley was graduate student Dave Packard's small garage at 367 Addison Street in Palo Alto, where in 1937 Bill Hewlett and Packard began manufacturing and selling their electronic equipment. An even earlier birthplace could have been around the corner at 913 Emerson in Palo Alto, where in 1912 Lee de Forest pioneered the use of vacuum tubes for electronic amplification, certainly high technology for the time and the cornerstone of computing decades before the silicon chip.

Silicon Valley as a term was popularized only in the 1970s by Don Hoefler, a reporter for the trade newspaper *Electronic News*.[58] The area had, of course, been known as "the Valley" around the Bay Area for quite a while, but the radical economic and industrial changes since World War II deserved the new christening.

Another name change reflecting the same transformation has come subtly to one of San Jose's oldest and largest employers: FMC Corporation. Back in 1910, one of the major suppliers at my family's Farmers Union hardware store was the local Food Machinery and Chemical Company, known as FMC. By the time World War II rolled around, FMC had tanks, not tractors, rolling off its production lines. The company today looks nothing like the orchard supplier it once was; it specializes in high-tech defense contracts. It has, as one wit suggested, "beaten its ploughshares into swords." Their most famous product is the Bradley Fighting Vehicle, which worked well for the U.S. Army in the Persian Gulf War. What didn't? In San Jose's Tech Museum of Innovation, FMC has provided a mock-up of its Mars Rover, which the company has developed with the NASA Ames Research Center up the road in Mountain View and hopes to land on the red planet in a future mission. Today, the official company line is that the letters "FMC" are no longer an abbreviation. They stand for nothing, but in a way they stand for the remarkable story of San Jose's past and future.

The two Steves—Wozniak and Jobs—who helped anchor what has come to be known as Silcon Valley.

One short FMC anecdote that leads to a point: One morning in 1983, I was eating breakfast with Bob Malott, then CEO of the company. Almost immediately he reproached me, verbally attacking me for my seeming agreement with an article calling the Bradley a "billion dollar lemon." He became heated, and Don Tietgens, my driver and security officer, later joked he might have to slap a chokehold on him. Malott went on to retire from the company and become chairman of the board of the Hoover Institution on War, Revolution and Peace at Stanford University, where, coincidentally, I was offered a position as "distinguished visiting scholar." (The post came with no bodyguard, so I turned it down.)

Malott's move reflects the central part played in the virtual city by what might be termed the "new intelligentsia," including not only Hoover and SRI (originally Stanford Research Institute) but also the high-tech R & D departments of the Valley like Xerox PARC in Palo Alto, Apple's state-of-the-art research campus in Cupertino, and San Jose's Dataquest, a high-tech research organization. I have watched us go from food machinery to think tanks in a generation, a generation spurred on by the forward thinking of people like Hewlett, Packard, and Stanford's Fred Terman, the influential engineering dean who encouraged graduates year after year to develop their products and grow their companies. Terman consciously wanted to build "a community of technical scholars," and he and others realized that the combined advantages of the Santa Clara Valley would make this area a mecca for the electronic age.

Today, with an energetic engineering department built by Dean Jay Pinson, San Jose State University prepares more engineers for Valley corporations than Stanford, Berkeley, and MIT combined. Our nationwide reputation should be assured; we lead the nation with the highest per capita level of high-tech exports. Before the cathedral strategy, though, we still had an identity crisis. Michael Malone, who through his books and television work has a reputation as the chronicler of the Valley, wrote very perceptively about the distinctive personality of this city and its region.

> Consider what it's like to be the president of a major San Jose electronics company. In your world, the world of millions of people who work in high tech around the globe, San Jose has no identity problem. On the contrary, it is the largest city in the very heartland of Technology. Japanese computer engineers and French solid-state physicists and Russian space scientists dream of one day setting foot in San Jose, of driving the same streets used by the likes of Packard, Noyce and Jobs. An identity problem? A shortage of visibility? Are you kidding? In electronics, San Jose is the very center of the universe. If anything, it's got too much reputation.[59]

Our Silicon Cathedral

Someone once compared the incredibly complex and detailed designs of integrated circuitry on silicon chips to the intricate maze of a big-city map. Often seen as artwork, these huge chip layouts are produced with computer-aided design software, but they bear in their multicolored, interwoven lines a fascinating beauty. There was even an exhibition of some of the best layouts at Santa Clara's Triton Art Museum.

The sheer intellectual power of the area can be overwhelming. One author, perhaps a little light-headed in the brilliance of a wafer-fabrication clean room, called Silicon Valley "the 20th Century's counterpart of the Fertile Crescent, the cradle of modern civilization in the Near East," where man first began to read and write.[60] For a local boy, that kind of comparison is daunting. It would be my task as mayor of San Jose to dare to make the claim for "capital" status of this revolutionary place.

The daring nature of the claim was entirely within the spirit of the dreamers who founded the Valley. We, like those dreamers, would know moments of frustration along the way. We could take slights like *Good Morning America* labeling San Francisco the center of Silicon Valley. (I am certain that San Franciscans were as surprised about that as I was.) We do not have, as a journalist in that village to our north once alleged, "a silicon chip on our shoulder" because the region is still called the San Francisco Bay Area despite our population surge. The cartographers of Rand McNally were not our chosen audience. I had more confidence in our ability to mentally make the transition from small-town thinking to an entrepreneurial spirit, one that would enable us to accomplish all the economic and quality-of-life goals we had for our citizens and simultaneously nurture a symbiotic relationship with the new industrial revolution occurring around us. Silicon Valley, that entrepreneurial risk center, is an amazing and fragile creation. It exists as much in the mind and imagination as in a physical location. We knew we had to understand this to preserve, support, and eventually annex it.

Not every move we made was from some master plan or high-tech checklist. Looking back, it is in fact quite gratifying that the overall tenor of our approach fits so squarely with prevailing tenets of business success. One expert on entrepreneurship, John D'Aprix, concentrates on pragmatically assessing a region's ability to thrive in an era of change and opportunity. D'Aprix outlines three important factors for "any region hoping to position itself as a thriving entrepreneurial economy," and in retrospect, they describe the components of our effort to rebuild the modern city. First, D'Aprix underlines the fundamental necessity of developing *intellectual capital*. Second, authorities in partnership with the private sector must ensure the development of a substantial *venture capital base*. Third, the city needs the development and sustenance of a healthy *entrepreneurial environment*. The three factors combine for "a rich mix of private sector development enterprise, [which] also strengthens and rebuilds the regional economic base."[61]

Silicon Valley business as a whole has developed largely because of those three factors. But how well can a city do by the same test? Let us chart how San Jose scored on those factors in its own entrepreneurial attempt to re-create itself in the 1980s.

Intellectual Capital. We had a remarkably talented team of winners in and around city hall. No whiff of scandal touched them, and they have all gone on to other significant roles. The team included Frank Taylor at Redevelopment, Dean Munro, Greg Larson, Mary Ellen Ittner, and David Pandori among many others in the mayor's office, Pat Dando in and out of city hall, and a raft of young and dynamic staff members like Bob Trinchero on the city staff and in associated enterprises. In planning we had Gary Schoennauer, an intuitive and experienced director (who is still there), and our key creative lawyer was Gary Reiners. For special projects, we called on an unorthodox deputy city manager I brought in, Dan McFadden. Two council members, Susan Hammer and Shirley Lewis, were kindred spirits and key implementers. They were joined by Judy Stabile and later Joe Head as the inner core of an entrepreneurial council. Senior advisers like Frank Fiscalini, Ted Biagini, Don Lucas, Dan Hancock, and Jerry Estruth and public relations maven Barbara Krause offered our team an outsider's perspective from the business and professional community. For attorneys, the redoubtable Sam Cohen and Roberta Hayashi gave me sage advice, while Ed Storm and Don Imwalle gave me the developer perspective with a clear and unbiased eye. These individuals sparked energetic advances beyond the typical inner-city crisis management—we looked to the next generation, not the next election.

Venture Capital Base. That is exactly what our redevelopment funds provided, and the next chapter outlines how we utilized them. It took hard-earned capital to build a different kind of city.

Entrepreneurial Environment. We were fortunate on two counts. San Jose has a history of forward-looking optimism, related to its frontier past and its optimistic immigration boom. And Silicon Valley itself provided San Jose's entrepreneurial environment within which we were able to operate. Dave Gould, a vice president at the corporate headquarters of Fujitsu America here in town, remarks that "San Jose has a vision of how to do things right. . . . Entrepreneurial fever has spilled over into the public sector here."[62]

A future-oriented entrepreneurial spirit didn't mean that we had our heads in the clouds. Jerry Brown, governor of California just before my tenure as mayor, was rightly criticized for his reluctance to deal with real-world problems in the here and now. People in San Jose begged for the state highways so long promised, highways on which our rapid residential expansion had been predicated, allowing people to get from one side of the city to another. Governor Brown talked of space exploration instead, and magic trains to whisk us from San Francisco to San Diego in a smaller, more beautiful world. His cabal of futurists and purported experts arrived in Sacramento and left eight years later with all our problems intact. That would not be our approach. We represented the future, but a productive future, a future realized today.

San Jose is a new kind of capital city. We are not a governmental capital, with state and federal buildings and high-rise towers housing legions of lobbyists; that's fine for fifty other cities whose names schoolchildren have to memorize.

We are the virtual capital, the metropolis of an imaginary but very real place, Silicon Valley. Our monuments and halls are not made of granite or gilt but of ideas and concepts. Ideas that work in the fight against crime and urban decay, developed in grassroots communities empowered to find their own answers. Concepts here are dreamed up on a Sun Microsystems workstation one day and developed into a top-line product shipped within months, not years. Imitation is the sincerest form of flattery, and those companies I wanted to imitate. We attempted to become a city of new capital, intellectual capital, moral and spiritual capital, a city whose citizens dared to believe they controlled their own destiny and the future of their hometown.

That is all we wanted.

How to Market a Dream

San Jose has no moat around it, nor can any town that wants to succeed. We realized early in the 1980s that a crucial component of revivifying the central city would be plain old marketing—the American way of selling. A modern city has to market itself as it concentrates on building a comparative advantage in the larger economy. The nation has always been a collection of some cities and regions doing well, and some doing not so well. Increasingly in this century, and acutely in the past couple of decades, industry has been flexible enough (for all kinds of reasons) to be able to move and relocate almost at will. Despite our attractive position in the long term, the recent recession definitely hit Northern California disproportionately hard. We lost approximately 50,000 high-tech jobs in the Valley between 1988 and 1993. Many were shifted to other cities or states or offshore. So we compete, and we advertise our strengths beyond the city limits.

Just as power can sometimes be nothing more than a state of mind, economic vitality has a hefty ingredient of positive promotion. We have learned to position our city as a good place to do business, using our chosen high-tech cathedral to attract attention and investment.

With the proper choice of cathedrals to promote, other cities can do this just as well.

Any strategy has to be backed up by the facts, and our promotion of San Jose as the "Capital of Silicon Valley" was underlined by the features we were able to cite to prospective investors, residents, even tourists. We still have the world's most attractive concentration of high-tech industries, with a broad and balanced spectrum of industry segments. The great universities that spawned magical industries are still located here, at San Jose State, Stanford, and Santa Clara. Those schools provide a diverse and skilled workforce, which can support existing and emerging technologies. And our geographic location still serves us well, for West Coast desirability, Pacific Rim access, and a key position in the new North American Free Trade zone.[63]

The Marketer's Nightmare

Selling a new and improved image for a city can be really, really tough, and some cities face much bigger challenges than others. Take the case of Newark, New Jersey, a city about one-third the size of San Jose. Just the name, "Newark," conjures up for many outside its limits the very picture of a dying eastern city. Old. Troubled. Decayed. That reputation dates back to its 1967 riots, which left twenty-seven people dead and set Newark's image for the nation. The image was certainly set for its middle-class residents as well, white and black, who fled city neighborhoods for the suburbs. It takes a long, long time to shake a bad media image.

Sharpe James, the mayor today, has been fighting to reverse not just the trend of decline but the image that can stick even after trend lines reverse. A large-scale downtown renaissance is under way, centering on $6 billion in new office construction since 1986.[64] New downtown residential blocks have been built, a new performing arts center is planned, and Mayor James has supported a remade police force in its crackdown on violent crime.

All this, though, can do little to combat the doubts of outsiders, who have no choice but to contrast James's habitual citation of Newark's "Most Livable City" status (conferred by the U.S. Conference of Mayors in 1991) with the "foot-votes" of residents: 16 percent of its population, 52,000 people, left the city for good during the 1980s. Now, that's a marketer's nightmare. As a mayor, what are you left to say? "More room for the rest of us" won't exactly cut it with corporate investors, or with your own citizens, for that matter.

If a mayor is to be an marketer, he or she must learn from the high-profile flops of assorted charlatans over the years: tell the story, but tell it honestly. Regis McKenna, the marketing guru of many high-tech companies and an oracle of the Valley, notes that without reality behind the hype, without a sense of balance, even the most well-planned marketing will founder on a single shoal: truth.

Boosterism beyond bounds, without the facts to back up a city's claimed stature, tends to fail. In San Jose, we tried to keep our marketing efforts serious and to be led by the overall strategy guiding the city's renewal. We didn't have to be rocket scientists to take advantage of our Silicon Valley home, but we tried to do so in some innovative value-added ways. Our Office of Economic Development published an "Entrepreneur's Guide to San Jose," targeted at potential large- and small-business managers and distributed very widely. The guide provided an excellent manual for business interactions with local government: tips on the planning and permits procedure, the local economic climate and opportunities, and the wide range of city services benefiting business. More than just listing city services, we produced a handbook showing the private sector how to take advantage of everything the public sector had to offer. When I was a small-businessman, back at the Farmers Union in San Pedro Square, local government had been simply a roadblock.

We also made sure that our new downtown renaissance brought in a steady stream of tourists, convention bookings, and business visitors. We had embarked on a mission: becoming a destination city, not just an adjunct to San Francisco–bound travelers or a freeway route for Carmel and the Monterey Bay. By the end of the 1980s, the Convention and Visitors Bureau had retooled all of our marketing materials, tactics, and events to support that goal. We conducted a massive direct-mail campaign to businesses, trade shows, and convention planners on the theme "How to Speak Silicon Valley."

We didn't do everything right. Sometimes people try too hard, and "sophisticated marketing" comes across as desperate begging. Not long after I left office, the city opened itself up to ridicule with one specific piece, featuring a long list of "158 Things to Do in San Jose." I have no idea what bright-eyed genius determined the magic number had to be 158, but to reach it the list compilers in the Convention and Visitors Bureau had to do a little stretching. Actually, they had to do quite a lot of stretching. The list included "breakfast at Denny's," "lunch at Bob's Big Boy," and a raft of other possibly pleasant but hardly dynamic attractions for vacationers. Instead of concentrating on our strengths, the list even went so far afield as to recommend Monterey's Aquarium and the Napa Valley Wine Train. A San Francisco paper called the list "the civic equivalent of hanging a 'kick-me' sign on the city." For once, it was right.

Mayors Must Be Evangelists

Smart city-states know their task: to concentrate their efforts on promoting their special qualities to the outside world. In the massive job of rebuilding San Jose, we knew that the public side of redevelopment called for extensive attempts to scare up financing, in what have been called "search-and-create strategies."[65] Identifying and convincing private lenders calls for strong marketing. As mayor, I considered myself the chief marketer.

Certainly, there are aspects of government that take a little bit of gusto to perform. Executive leadership, as a president, governor, or mayor must exercise, calls on that sole individual to feel passionately about the strength and future of his or her town, state, or country. Being the city's chief salesman might have been a bit uncomfortable at times, but I got used to the "chamber of commerce speech" aspect pretty quickly. More important than being fluent in the message, I fervently believed in the product I sold, and that helped. In fact, I am a subscriber to the new theory of marketing called "evangelism," popularized by Silicon Valley's Guy Kawasaki. His recent book *Selling the Dream* outlines how his marketing team at Apple Computer devised the first marketing campaign for the original Macintosh computer. His experiences taught him that the spirit of evangelism, of passionate belief in the unique value of a product, can carry a marketer beyond rote selling. Kawasaki affirms that the principle works to popularize ideas as well as products, as religious evangelists have proven for centuries.[66]

Local leaders, more than elected officials at higher levels, should believe passionately in the city they represent. Ed Koch was a booster par excellence for the Big Apple. I had little compunction about advertising the virtues and strengths of San Jose. I tried not to be immodest in doing so, but I did try to express the dream our city had of its future, and I was not ashamed to show my passion.

What Goes Up. . .

There he sat, at the right hand of the First Lady, listening to President Clinton's first State of the Union address in 1993. He had earned it, first as

the legendary CEO who brought Apple Computer to the verge of creating a braver new world, and then as the linchpin in a Silicon Valley tilt to candidate Clinton that sent shock waves through the American political scene. No CEO in America had more cachet than this dynamic leader of the most dynamic company in our Valley of the future.

John Sculley was taunted by Steve Jobs to leave Pepsico with the jibe, "Do you want to sell sugared water for the rest of your life, or do you want to change the world?" From the time he arrived in Silicon Valley, Sculley had always helped me. In Redevelopment circles, they still tell of the meeting in which Sculley promised to move Apple's headquarters to downtown San Jose on one condition: receiving the biggest subsidy in the city's history. I liked John's panache. When he thought, it was always of big things. The deal never happened, but it was quite a session.

In June 1993, the guru of the 1980s ended his ten-year reign with a bang. He was forced out, the story goes, but what a great run he had. After all, this is Silicon Valley—two years is a life, ten is an eternity.

The evangelistic mayor is in good company. John Sculley was a top executive at two companies whose bottom lines profited from their image as revolutionary, youthful, and vibrant: Pepsico and Apple Computer. On the subject of marketing, Sculley once wrote: "Advertising allows you to take on the giants and win. Goliath may not need great advertising. But David sure does. . . . it lets you express not only what you are, but what you are trying to become. It's not just a selling tool, it's a leadership tool—a flag on the mountain to rally and inspire your own people."[67]

That's the kind of spirit I like, the kind that motivated me (with John's advice, too) to buy an Apple PowerBook to write the words you're reading now. It is the kind of spirit I feel about San Jose, and it's not a bad role model: Apple Computer, Inc., made the Fortune 500 list faster than any other company in history. While the company now scrambles to maintain profitability, its ascent was dizzying. Things move fast here in the Valley.

Gone with the Windex—OverMarketing

Atlanta skyline. Kevin C. Rose photo.

Hard-charging city marketers inevitably run the risk of selling too hard. Atlanta is attempting to make the most of hosting the 1996 Olympic Games, even hiring a high-powered marketing chief, formerly of Chiat/Day in New York. With a mandate from Mayor Maynard Jackson to act as the city's chief spokesman and marketer, Joel Babbit made plans to raise the city's profile with such gimmicks as naming Visa "the official preferred credit card of Atlanta" to cash in on its Olympic status. More perversely, he embarked on a campaign to raise millions of dollars for the city by renaming streets and parks for corporate sponsors. Aiming at results like a Coca-Cola Boulevard or Pete's Butchers Park, he told the New York Times *in 1993 that "we're sitting, as most cities are, with thousands of non-income-producing assets. . . . We don't get a penny from calling Piedmont Park, the largest in Atlanta, Piedmont Park. I don't think it would hurt anyone or cause any problems if the name was changed to Georgia-Pacific Park, and we got a million dollars a year for it."*[68]

This is an example of when trying too hard to run government like a business palpably degrades the quality of life and the special traditions that bind citizens to their community. What would Scarlett O'Hara say?

More than a Skeleton

When I was in office, reporters used to ask me quite frequently to tell the story of the downtown resurgence. Whenever the *Mercury News* assigned a new cub to the city hall beat, or when an out-of-towner came in to do the "San Jose renaissance" story for the *Chicago Tribune* or the *Washington Post*, I was able to regale them with the tale. I enjoyed it. It was the teacher in me.

That doesn't happen as much anymore. More frequently today, college students, even high school kids, call me and ask a few questions for a term paper. As I tell them how the city government went about remaking San Jose during the now-distant 1980s, I sometimes feel like a Disneyland robot in the Hall of Presidents, recounting a dry history to people who missed it but are curious. The Hall of Former Mayors—now there's an exciting idea. Often, these students will have collected the clippings and newspaper articles citing the numbers: San Jose, the nation's seventeenth-largest city a decade ago, then fourteenth-largest, now the eleventh largest. Yet dry histories fail to capture the struggle, the politics, the heartbreak, the dream propelling it all.

I shared that dream with hundreds and thousands of people in San Jose. We had been a city of sleepwalkers, but once awake, we had a strategy to make the dream come true. That may well be how citizens and their leaders went about building cathedrals and monuments centuries ago. One century ago, only a block from St. Joseph's Cathedral, stood our proud Electric Light Tower. While the tower served as a tourist draw, J. J. Owen's hope that San Jose would become widely known as the Beacon City was never fulfilled. Three sister towers were never built. Eventually, the iron pipe and threaded joints rusted through. On a rainy December day in 1915, in just thirty seconds, the tower collapsed into a fifteen-ton pile of rods and twisted pipe.

Owen's dream, having lived for more than a generation, became its own scrap heap. But the dream of San Jose as a beacon lives on still with every high-tech product conceived, built, and shipped from the Valley. Simply stated, it is the desire to imagine the future and then to build it, over and over again.

Our cathedral strategy for the future was no artificial heart we were intent on transplanting but a synergistic combination of metropolis and industrial magic. Perhaps we had the conceit of Dr. Frankenstein, but we felt we were creating life: a living downtown and livable neighborhoods tied to it.

Part Two

THE TASK

5
KNOW YOUR LIMITS

A man's got to know his limitations.
—Clint Eastwood as Dirty Harry

I was sworn into office in January 1983, with the hoopla that always surrounds a celebration of "local boy makes good." Previous inaugurations had been handled in a manner fit for a small town, which in many ways San Jose still was, with a simple taking of oaths at a regular city council meeting in the council chambers. In keeping with my intention of dragging this city into its rightful spot in the future, I planned a more formal affair. And I wanted it held *away* from city hall.

The new Annual Unity Breakfast was really nothing out of the ordinary for a big American city. The convocation was a public event to swear in the mayor and new city council members and to honor specially selected community activists and volunteers from each of the ten council districts. Most of my contributors during the campaign showed up, along with corporate representatives, local attorneys, and small-business people. So did many ordinary neighborhood residents, almost a thousand, who wanted to be a part of something bigger than themselves, part of the new future I had promised for their city. The *Mercury News* called the affair "flashy," but I think every person who left the breakfast felt good about their community, hopeful for the future, and invigorated to play a role in its rebirth. I do know that the Unity Breakfast tradition has continued—recently it has been an evening affair, to allow wider participation—and my successors will welcome the annual opportunity to make a State of the City address to a wide audience.

The Bay Area media covered the event. The front pages of the nation's newspapers, however, were devoted to chronicling the day-to-day struggle for life of Barney Clark, the world's first artificial heart recipient. Clark became a national hero, surviving nearly four months after Dr. Robert Jarvik's mechanical device was implanted in his chest in December 1982. When he died in March, the country mourned his passing but marveled at the breakthrough for science and health.

I remember thinking, though, that the artificial heart held a negative lesson for our attempt to bring new life to San Jose, with a revived downtown pumping arterial vigor into the city. The Jarvik heart itself was no larger than Barney Clark's original heart, but the device required an awkward external system of tubes and tanks and generators weighing 375 pounds and stored on a cart beside his bed. Some doctors were skeptical about its future usefulness, believing that the artificial heart could serve only as a surrogate, sustaining a patient until a donor human heart for transplant could be found.

In my new desk drawer in the mayor's office, I saved a quote from Dr. Michael DeBakey, Houston's famous transplant specialist. He summed up both the artificial-heart debate and our philosophy in reviving San Jose: "To be a success," DeBakey said, "the heart must restore the individual to normal life. If all it does is keep the patient alive, it has not succeeded."

San Jose was being kept alive by ever-expanding growth, but we wanted much more than just to be big. We wanted normal life, the life of a thriving city and revitalized neighborhoods. We needed a plan for that dream. Luis Valdez has written, in a line I've shamelessly appropriated from him so often San Joseans think it is one of my own, that "the future belongs to those who can imagine it." Without a programmatic vision, we would be no better than Rust Belt cities that were declining with no dream of a better way ahead or even some other Sun Belt cities that were growing haphazardly. Had we wished only to survive, to mark time, we could have relied on the artificial support of Washington, joined other cities' mayors in calling for massive infusions of federal dollars, and limped along with no clear idea of where we were headed.

San Jose deserved better. I had something of a tradition to live up to. The early settlers of San Jose built their adobes and then their grand cathedral. My more immediate predecessors since World War II also held a vision of the city's future, one that relied upon growth and expansion. I may not have chosen that same picture of the future, given the benefit of hindsight. But I certainly admire their drive and proactive style. I wanted to do no less.

Our earlier leaders were thinking in a single dimension when they dreamed of San Jose's future: size. They wished to become the biggest, wrongly equating that with the best in a perversion of the time-honored principle manifest destiny. They did not know their limits.

Other Cities, Other Cathedrals

Most cities could benefit from employing the cathedral strategy. Mayors, other city officials, and bureaucrats, even leading residents, should conduct rigorous and rational assessments of their communities' strengths and natural assets in order to focus on a winning message. Without a strong, consistent, and unified theme, there are no concrete steps to take, no obvious action plans, no rallying cry for all to follow. Less tangibly, but no less important, there is no communal mandate that city government can cite in making the tough decisions to move a city forward.

From the largest to the smallest, America's cities are framing their municipal identities. Gilroy, a once dusty town southeast of San Jose, has worked hard to develop its deserved sobriquet "Garlic Capital of the World." That choice may be humorous on its face, but the annual Garlic Festival brings tens of millions of dollars into the city coffers, and year-round visitors spend even more. Much larger cities need more varied approaches with balanced appeals, but even the largest pay attention to a common city theme. In Los Angeles or Chicago, subcities within these world-class metropolises need to take up the challenge and develop separate but complementary identities that would allow them to benefit economically from local distinctiveness, while reaping the benefits of proximity to greatness.

Through a patient billion-dollar redevelopment, Brooklyn has recently begun to distinguish itself successfully from the behemoth of New York City, after decades of watching its identity as "America's fifth-largest city" disintegrate into the larger Gotham sprawl. The MetroTech commercial and academic complex anchors the new Brooklyn downtown, touted as "Wall Street East," and offers a brand-new infrastructure to support financial and information services seeking to escape Manhattan's high rents. So far, the strategy is proving successful: since 1989, Brooklyn has attracted Morgan Stanley & Company, the New York City Transit Authority, and Chase Manhattan Bank to new headquarters in the downtown, along with a new Hilton Hotel. There are more than

7,000 new workers and countless new retail stores, and from 1989 to 1991, felony crimes in the area fell by 23 percent, attributed by police to the increased number of people thronging the area.[69] Good money drives out bad; in a close corollary, normal citizens discourage crooks and criminals.

Mayors, in particular, are increasingly aware that the United States is really a regionalized economy and that their cities need to specialize to survive. There are many successful approaches worthy of emulation. A mayor or council member could spend an enjoyable junket traveling around the country studying them and might actually learn something. San Antonio, the nation's ninth-largest city, has done a remarkable job in studying and building upon its own cathedral strengths. Drawing back on the Alamo heritage and the tourist attraction the fort represents, the city now presents itself as the "Southern-Facing Anchor of the United States." The brilliant River Walk project, which winds through downtown for two and a half miles along the San Antonio River, has a scintillating Mexican flavor, with a profusion of restaurants, shops and boutiques, cultural attractions, and entertainment spots. In the midst of all the hotels and glitzy shopping, a few blocks from the River Walk, the Alamo of Davey Crockett and Jim Bowie still stands, a tourist magnet. But just as I knew Silicon Valley represented more to San Jose than birthplace plaques, San Antonio's bright young mayor during the 1980s, Henry Cisneros, realized that San Antonio's geographical location promised a wealth of economic development opportunities, presaging the NAFTA era. The city's cultural and historic ties with Mexico make the city a natural gateway to commerce, at the dawn of a century in which a new free trade zone and Mexico's own population growth ensure that U.S. trade with Mexico will explode. Cisneros knew how to build on proximity and imagination.

In 1992 the city was able to persuade Southwestern Bell, the nation's twenty-ninth-largest company, to abandon St. Louis and bring its corporate headquarters to San Antonio. The company's move made sense, since the booming state now accounts for 60 percent of its business, and Southwestern Bell has also taken a major stake in the central telephone company of Mexico. Cisneros's successor, Mayor Nelson Wolff, noted that the relocation "sends a strong signal to other companies doing business or interested in doing business with Mexico, that San Antonio is the place to be."[70] (Wolff sometimes points out that the only picture of a president on his office wall is of Mexico's President Salinas.) Following through on the integrated nature of a good cathedral strategy, the city has helped Southwestern Bell make its new quarters in a building smack on the banks of the River Walk, and 500 new workers are now spending dollars in stores and restaurants all along the old downtown artery. All in all, it is a great play upon history for the future.

The main lesson of the past in urban economic development is that a city has to focus its attention and focus it in a way that makes sense for that community, its history, resources, and potential for growth. Realism is not a very common commodity among city planners, but that's why God created mayors. At their best, mayors exist to cut through the wishful thinking and concentrate on a realistic approach to a city's economic possibilities and plan accordingly. A *New York Times* article in late 1992 sympathetically profiled a small start-up electronics company located in the South Bronx, of all places.[71] The company's young founders had selected the site for one reason only—cheap rent—and were bewailing the fact that "the expertise, the conferences and the engineering community in our field are elsewhere. . . . Ideally, we would be located in Silicon Valley." The author of the piece, like a lot of pie-in-the-sky local officials around the country, seemed to misunderstand the economics of New York City and excoriated the city for "missing the boat" during the 1980s in failing to "establish environments that would nurture high-tech start-ups."

New York City, for all its flaws, is smart enough to realize that its strengths will never lie in high-tech start-ups. Ed Koch was working his butt off in the 1980s trying to ride the boom-years tiger of the Reagan era and ensuring that New York would remain the financial capital of the world. The Big Apple's competitive advantages are, of course, in financial services and real estate, and any attempt to skew municipal priorities in radically different directions would be doomed to failure. As an engineer in the *Times* piece noted, "It's shocking to me how many talented people in the [high-tech] field flood out of New York City." Any resident of Gracie Mansion knows that that particular brain drain is matched, perhaps dwarfed, by the inflow of brilliant young financial managers. We'll take the engineering M.A.s and Ph.D.s. New York City will always get the lion's share of the M.B.A.s.

A city can also build its cathedral quite literally, and many cities use architecture and urban design to define their strengths to the world. Examples abound, but I have always particularly enjoyed western and southwestern cities' attempts at visual self-definition. The best among them are able to combine tradition and modernism in a way that is not cloyingly old-fashioned yet not ugly in a mad nod to modernism. Architecture critic Paul Goldberger has written admiringly of Antoine Predock's "stylistic signature," his buildings in Albuquerque and Southern California that "have become a kind of contemporary expression of the traditional architectural language of the desert and the mountains." One recent accomplishment is Predock's Fine Arts Center at Arizona State University in Tempe, combining a theater, museum, and rehearsal halls for dance and music. Goldberger writes that the building "tells us, as eloquently as any building of the last few years, how it is possible for a piece of architecture to be deeply ingrained in the architectural traditions of a place, yet unlike anything we have seen before."

Memphis has taken a truly inspired step to ensure that its cultural and historical identity is reflected in its design. In honor of its Egyptian namesake, the new Memphis/Shelby County sports arena is called "the Pyramid," because it is just that—an honest-to-God modern pyramid, modeled on the Great Pyramid of Cheops. Now that is thinking on a grand scale. The arena seats 23,000 for Memphis State basketball games, but the building was designed with a multipurpose orientation for music and other community uses. In the base of the building are a music museum, in a bow to Memphis's other great local tradition, and a restaurant. The sloping sides (51.5 degrees, just like the original in Egypt) lead to a skylight and observation deck with views of downtown and the Mississippi River. The stainless-steel building, constructed with the advantages of modern techniques not available to the ancients, is a remarkable structure for the city's future and simultaneously a testament to its heritage as a river city like Memphis-on-the-Nile.

The Memphis Pyramid. Courtesy of the Memphis Convention and Visitor's Bureau.

Centre Pompidou in Paris. Courtesy French National Tourist Office.

Many urban critics argue against spending public funds on sports arenas and facilities, no matter how inspired, when cities of the future will be "knowledge" rather than manufacturing centers or sports meccas. Educational infrastructure, some rightly contend, will be the significant feature of the new global city. Two prominent urban futurologists, G. Gappert and R. V Knight, have written: "One must question the wisdom of constructing gigantic domed stadiums when other cities are building state-of-the-art libraries such as a new British Museum library in London, and the Centre Pompidou and the new Bibliotek Nationale in Paris."[72] Perhaps a new, improved Karl Marx can conceive theories in the former or Émile Zola can write in the latter.

This argument may be persuasive for most large cities; it may be conclusive for some. But it is mostly applicable for megalopolises, for capital cities. It may only be fully true for world capitals or for truly global cities like New York or Berlin. Not every regional city can do the same thing and rely upon a level of national attraction to support "global knowledge workers" in some cybernetic future economy. In any case, even granting the importance of educational infrastructure (and we certainly have not ignored it in San Jose), there will always be the need to reflect the continuing interests of city residents in entertainment, cultural attractions, and, yes, so-called lowbrow events like sports. A cathedral approach, flexibly planned and applied, should enable any city to pursue broad and balanced goals and growth.

Most cities still limp along, struggling to maintain city services in a period of fiscal difficulty but with no long-term strategy to lift their spirits and point the way ahead. Sadly, our neighbor San Francisco is a deeply troubled city, and I see little evidence that its civic leaders have answers to the huge, looming crisis. I am not entirely sure that they even know the questions they should be answering. It is sad that such a great city, world-class in so many ways and so remarkably beautiful, can be reduced to such a pitiful state. The City That Knows How has become the City That Nose-dived. More than sad, though, it is maddening. San Francisco's city hall denizens could solicit some good, commonsense advice in one quick walk around the neighborhoods to canvass the long-suffering citizenry. In such a great city, where residents surely know intuitively what is wrong, it is indefensible for leaders to fail to get it right. The current "citizen-mayor," Frank Jordan, labors mightily to do the right thing, but events (and supervisors) conspire against him.

What can resurrect a city? Beyond leadership from the politicians, sometimes a bolt from the blue can unexpectedly spark a city's first steps on the road to redefinition and renewal. An example: although the biggest cities routinely court the quadrennial political conventions for their delegate/tourist dollars, rarely is the temporary infusion of cash matched by any long-term benefit. One economist minimized the effect, saying, "It's like trying to quantify the effect of one ride at Disneyland." The 1988 Republican convention may have been more significant for New Orleans, though. The city was in the middle of a severe oil recession, and yet it reacted energetically to the prospect of celebrating the passing of the popular Reagan torch.

There was the requisite street sweeping, coats of paint, and refurbishing of hotels and meeting facilities. Beyond that, the event was a tremendous eruption of good feelings, honoring George Bush's nomination and his campaign theme: "Don't Worry, Be Happy." A New Orleans official told a journalist four years later, "It boosted the city's morale at a time we were suffering. The city really cleaned up its act and looked good."[73] Remember, New Orleans was the site of Bush's "kinder and gentler nation" speech, and the convention lent to New Orleans the same tide of goodwill. Never minimize the salutary effect of the grand, symbolic gesture.

A bolt from the blue can also bring ruinous damage to a city, with shocking speed and horrendous, lasting impact. Waco, Texas, certainly had not bargained for the bizarre and deadly Branch Davidian cult siege in early 1993. Moreover, no city leader could have anticipated the instantaneous, worldwide identification of this small, unassuming city as a magnet for crazies. Wacko Waco, we called it, as we checked CNN's hourly "updates from the Waco cult compound." I empathize with Waco's people, who lived through the public relations nightmare. The mayor complained, "The media is making us a focal point of something we had nothing to do with." Life is not fair, Mr. Mayor.

Such a nightmare can destroy a town's attempts to define itself in its own chosen terms, in a swift robbery of communal pride in any shared values, hopes, and dreams. Other cities have seen their imagined cathedrals daubed with controversy or crisis: Dallas and the Kennedy assassination in 1963; New York's fiscal meltdown in 1976; the 1984 MOVE siege and bombing in Philadelphia, the "City of Brotherly Love." In that last case, Mayor Wilson Goode became one of the few leaders in history to bomb his own city. (Boris Yeltsin did it after a coup attempt, with somewhat more reason.)

Sometimes, the best a mayor can hope for is that none of his or her actions directly cause such a catastrophe. In the best of American traditions, after every scandal there's always another day, as plans and dreams are revived and thoughts again turn to the future.

Attempts to Clone Silicon Valley

In 1989, I paid a visit to various Asian countries to broaden West Coast economic ties with the rest of the Pacific Rim. At a stop in Beijing, my hosts introduced me to a young computer engineer who seemed to command great respect among his peers. In a crowded reception room, the translator announced with pride, "This is the Steve Wozniak of China."

The Chinese desire for technological development was so strong that not only were they studying Apple Computer products, they were learning the folklore surrounding its cofounder as well. I don't remember reading any stories lately about multimillionaire high-tech geniuses from China revolutionizing the world, so I guess their Woz was not the wiz they thought, but the reference spoke volumes about the magic of the Valley. Their effort points up the difficulties anyone else has in trying to clone the original Silicon Valley, and Intel Corporation chairman Gordon Moore has explained why: "The talent is here, the infrastructure is here. This area still has the richest broth from which to create a company."[74] I tend to believe Gordon. He was one of the pioneers at Shockley and Fairchild Semiconductor and has led Intel back to international prominence.

Nothing seems to stop others from trying. The London *Economist* once described Silicon Valley as "an engine of growth that is the envy and obsession of the rest of the world." Just as other states have tried to copy California's Hollywood and attract filmmakers, the magic of Silicon Valley and the gleam of its financial power have spurred other cities, states, even countries to attempt the duplication of the phenomenon. After all, if Silicon Valley were a country, it would rank tenth in the world in gross domestic product. That is a rather appealing role model.

Even here in the Bay Area, we have our wanna-bes. San Francisco is halfheartedly attempting to construct what they call "Multimedia Gulch," in its South of Market area, hoping to merge its long-standing artistic community with new software firms, taking advantage of the marriage of computer graphics and art. The East Bay, stretching down from Oakland to Milpitas on San Jose's northeastern border, has made great efforts. Mostly, though, its success has been in fielding new software firms, which are typically small operations employing very few workers. An executive with a software company that was born recently in Berkeley argued that "the biggest advantage of the East Bay is the quality of life. You can have Cupertino and Sunnyvale—it's a cultural wasteland down there. But Berkeley is alive and crazy and it's just a good fit for me and my company."[75] It's a stretch to think of the East Bay as a business climate over Silicon Valley proper. The "business climate of Berkeley" is an absurdity and conjures up more disturbing images. In any case, the East Bay should properly be considered an adjunct of Greater Silicon Valley. By the standards of the rest of the country, much of the East Bay would be counted as a part of the metropolitan San Jose area.

We can't really blame other cities for trying. When San Jose was zooming up the population charts in the 1970s, it was passing cities like Cleveland, St. Louis, and Pittsburgh. Those dinosaurs of the Rust Belt, and other cities around the country, would inevitably like to replace an outmoded industrial base of autos and steel with a productive foundation of clean, light industry.

Massachusetts probably has one of the oldest rivals to Silicon Valley's claim as the center of the high-tech universe in its Route 128 companies. Fortunately for us, they seem to have priced themselves out of the competition, with little foresight to the death knells audible during Michael Dukakis's vaunted Massachusetts Miracle. "Massachusetts will never be a low-cost state," noted Stephen Coit, a prominent venture capitalist. "It will prosper as a high-value-added state. . . . The technology community is growing faster today in Silicon Valley than in Massachusetts," he remarked, but "under a heavier tax burden in California." Governor William Weld has embarked on a campaign to revive the business climate in the state, but I doubt the state's fundamental willingness to go all the way in reconstructing an entrepreneurial environment. It has layers upon layers of an ossified governmental and regulatory culture. San Jose is Nirvana in comparison.

Other states are trying to protect and invigorate their electronics industry. In Minnesota, high-tech firms like Control Data, Sperry, and Honeywell took the initiative to develop research relationships with state universities, and the state government is trying to oblige. Texas, our old rival from the heydays of Texas Instruments and EDS in the 1960s, conducted a huge campaign in 1983 to lure Microelectronics and Computer Technology Corporation (MCC) to Austin. Austin then repeated its competitive drive and beat out California and New York in the 1988 national competition to land Sematech, the federally funded effort to restore competitiveness to the chip industry. This program is a 1990s model of private and federal government partnership, in which the companies (in this case the semiconductor colossals–Intel, Hewlett-Packard, IBM, National, AMD) selected the priorities and matched the government, dollar for dollar. The results have been very positive, and this industry has again taken leadership from the Japanese. Texas also won the political battle to site the Superconducting Supercollider, a massive particle accelerator and public-works program that eventually lost its congressional funding. Winning political battles to build government projects, though, is not true public entrepreneurship.

In the 1980s, North Carolina made perhaps the most sustained and serious attempt to encourage and maintain a Silicon Valley–style environment. In 1981, Governor Jim Hunt established an independent nonprofit corporation, the Microelectronics Center of North Carolina (MCNC), funded by an initial $24.4 million state appropriation "to develop an educational and research activity in microelectronics [and] establish North Carolina as a national center in this significant technology."[76] The MCNC was the state's platform built upon the infrastructure of Research Triangle Park, the area bounded by Duke University in Durham, the University of North Carolina at Chapel Hill, and Raleigh's North Carolina State University. Many of the factors that allowed North Carolina's Research Triangle to attract high-tech firms parallel our own in Silicon Valley. Strong area universities provide human capital and a decent quality of life. North Carolina has a pleasant climate. And the state extends help on taxes, land costs, and facilitating ties among bankers, industrialists, and politicians.

While North Carolina has had a degree of success with Research Triangle Park, largely due to cooperation between the public and private sectors, most of this success story is still a future tale. In most respects, North Carolina's initiative of the 1980s amounted to the cultivation of the *impression* that the state might become the next major computer center, simply because it had the *potential*. Now that the chips have fallen where they may, so to speak, industrial reality has not matched the intensity of the public relations campaign.

Too many PR geniuses have told a mayor or city economic development chief, "Let's call ourselves Silicon City," and waited for the entre-preneurs to come calling. One can only laugh, noting the examples from around the United States. The Austin–Fort Worth–Dallas area calls itself Silicon Plain, Portland claims a Silicon Forest, and there's an appealingly modest Silicon Foothills around Sacramento. Culver City, in Southern California, boasts of Byte Hill, while on the other coast, Long Island pro-moters have used the term Tech Island. Salt Lake City commands the Bionic Valley, while Princeton girds itself with the Telecom Belt. The computer-nerd tourist could scale Silicon Mountain (Denver–Colorado Springs), trek across Silicon Desert (Phoenix-Tempe), whoop it up at Silicon Ranch (San Antonio), and frolic on Silicon Beach (with a choice of Santa Barbara on the West Coast or Dade County in Florida). Read of Atlanta's Silicon Pines or Louisiana's Silicon Bayou, and you find yourself echoing Ross Perot's drawl: "Now, that's just sad."

Most of these are just a name on a PR brochure mailed out uselessly to CEOs at local taxpayers' expense. The CEOs here in the real world recount their junk mail to me with laughter or disdain. And Americans are not alone in this peculiar brand of imitation. Scotland has a Silicon Glen, and similar efforts have been tried in Canada, France, Poland, Brazil, and Russia's Ekaterinburg, among others. Ireland—home to Intel's main manufacturing center—has had notable success.

Cities Can't Be Socially Engineered

As one might expect, our Japanese allies have made the most concerted ef-fort to duplicate our success in Silicon Valley. Sheridan Tatsuno of San Jose's Dataquest research firm has analyzed their "Technopolis Strategy," an attempt to transform Japan into a high-tech archipelago of linked regional cities in a co-ordinated new industrial policy. The word "technopolis" was coined by Toshiyuki Chikami, mayor of Kurume, who wanted the national government to fund his small city's renaissance into a high-technology industrial center.

Tatsuno writes, "Ironically, while we have tried copying Japan, the Japanese have asked themselves a different set of questions: What makes Silicon Valley tick? How can we clone it?" The result has been the identification of nineteen Technopolis Zones across the islands, each with a Mother City, intended to nurture start-up companies, venture capital, and technological innovation. Japan's Ministry of International Trade and Industry (MITI) hopes this blend of American enterprise-zone industrial park and Japanese feudal "company town" will foster new Silicon Valleys, and officials pitch the project as "a nationwide experiment in long-term business planning."[77]

It has not succeeded. I see their glass as half empty, not half full. Japan's previous attempt at federal management of a technological initiative, the famous "fifth-generation computer" project so feared in some U.S. circles, is now admitted to be a total washout. That project attempted to create the computer model for the twenty-first century and instead has been quietly abandoned in failure long before that century has even begun.

Top-down entrepreneurism is a contradiction in terms. In the midst of the Silicon Valley boom of the 1980s, Gene Bylinski wrote, "The Silicon Valley brand of participative capitalism often fools visitors from both socialist and capitalist countries. Socialist visitors think they can create successful Silicon Valleys with government money. But Silicon Valley is a convincing demonstration of the virtues of avoiding government involvement. . . . The industrial powerhouse was built without government planning or help."[78] In San Jose, we have learned the more important corollary: government can do the most good by staying out of the way of economic progress, concentrating its planning on removing barriers to success and having land available where the city wants it to be developed. Make that decision early or rue the day. San Jose's most successful projects were public-private partnerships, with real involvement from the private sector. The city knows its limits, and when it forgets them in a moment of eager giddiness over economic development, the market is not slow in issuing a reminder. Recently, Massachusetts state officials have been wiping egg off their faces with the failure of the Massachusetts Microelectronic Center, now referred to in the press as "a $50 million-plus monument to high-priced good intentions gone bad."[79] The vaunted project was a state-owned chip-making facility designed to educate electrical engineering students as well as attract high-tech industry. It became instead an embarrassing boondoggle, failing to attract jobs, draining $6 million a year in state operating funds and testifying to government's inability to pick economic winners and losers with any certainty. The yellow-brick road to Silicon Valley is paved with good intentions and lost dollars.

Some of these failed cloning procedures can be explained simply by inadequate effort or by overly ambitious officials not taking the time to do their homework on what is really required for a "technopolis" to succeed. Many regions can be disqualified right off the bat. They lack strong research universities, close government/industry ties, talented engineers and professional people, venture capital, and an attractive environment featuring good city services and innovative schools. Most important, according to the Japanese MITI officials who planned their technopolises, is innovative local leadership committed to dynamic public policies and forceful leadership through new ideas and foresight. That is where many American cities fall down.

It is foolish to announce that your city or state will henceforth become a high-tech mecca. It is not accomplished by fiat. There are entire rafts of legal, social, and political obstacles that must be cleared away, refined, or finessed before industry will flow in. Even in San Jose, we continue to walk the fine line between encouraging our entrepreneurial favorite-son industries and recognizing other interests and needs. "Bad-Boy" T. J. Rodgers, CEO of Cypress Semiconductor and an outspoken critic of most governmental attempts at regulating or encouraging industry, has been at times caustic in his remarks about our city's efforts to nurture local business. He has charged my successor's administration with driving electronics manufacturers straight out of town through overregulation. Yet T. J.'s mind is keen and essentially constructive. His favorite anecdote tells of the eighteen months it took Cypress to build a new awning on one local facility. He blames the myriad building codes and other city regulatory mazes. By contrast, according to Rodgers, the mayor of Round Rock, Texas, personally handed over to him a signed, blank building permit giving the company carte blanche to build and alter a new Cypress facility.

Perhaps T. J. will be spending more time in the grand restaurants and museums of Round Rock and recruiting from its major universities from now on, rather than favoring downtown San Jose, with all its amenities, and his alma mater Stanford as he has traditionally done. Although dealing with any bureaucracy is frustrating, the city governments of Round Rock and San Jose cannot be judged by the same terms. San Jose possesses a very complex set of dynamics that are very difficult to replicate. Dave Clements, head of the local Arthur Andersen office and a high-tech specialist for the firm, has said, "Everybody thinks he should be able to copy this. No one has done it with complete success. No one has gotten the whole package, the essence."

No city should slap on a label and cry, "Here stands our cathedral: the new Silicon Valley." That subverts the necessary natural underpinnings of the cathedral strategy. There is a basic human aspect to the notion of "place" that urban scholars describe as vital. "Place" has been described as a sociological phenomenon, a fixed commodity like food. People cannot do without it. They will pay not only for space itself, in buying a home or renting an apartment, but also for the access it affords to other resources like friends, schools, and jobs. That explains why people fight so vehemently to keep geographical relationships intact in their neighborhoods and cities.[80] It is their little spot on the earth.

We know that urban residents are sentimentally, psychologically attached to space. Certain types of businesses depend on community relations for profitability: the neighborhood coffee shop, the corner dry cleaner, the kosher deli, even the local bar, where habituals like Norm or Cliff from *Cheers* might really visit. Those small businesses are attached to one location. Big corporations can move to new locations more readily and can adapt to change more easily, but they are also reliant on their relationships to a community: their peers, their suppliers, their sources of capital. In the case of many electronics firms, that community is right here in Greater San Jose.

To Austin, with Love

I saw firsthand a critical example of the ineptitude of state government when it tries to focus on a key economic prize in the quest for the Sematech Project, a nationally sponsored attempt to regain preeminence in the semiconductor industry. After assembling a generous package of city and private-sector incentives, I traveled to Sacramento with Bob Noyce (founder of Intel), Charlie Sporck (CEO of National Semiconductor), and four other members of the site selection committee. We had an appointment with Governor George Deukmejian. Expecting to receive the key word, "yes," from the governor, we were stunned at receiving instead a standard campaign speech, culminating with, "Gentlemen, we have now surpassed Great Britain as the world's seventh-largest economy." Every eye in the room rolled. Deukmejian and his people had no deal to offer, only boilerplate better suited for a political convention than a business proposal. He was out of touch, with a blandness and lack of comprehension typical of the Duke and his minions.

Sematech and its jobs went to Austin, Texas.

Companies may find new, cheaper spots for certain manufacturing facilities. That can hurt, because those jobs are high-wage, and we miss them. I feel sorry, however, for cities that mistake their success in attracting such facilities for the real key to duplicating Silicon Valley. Nothing is quite that simple. Often, that plant may be just an assembly point, using cheap local labor to cobble together components brought in from outside the community. As any economist would tell you, the roots of wealth creation are kept elsewhere, and any benefits to that local area are limited and prone to evaporate overnight. We in San Jose notice that, while companies may be taking some well-paying manufacturing jobs elsewhere, they still want to keep their headquarters in the Valley, where the action is and where their ideological and historical roots are.

The continuing business in the Valley is gratefully acknowledged, as we recognize our new strength as the affluent "brain" center, the elite control and research center of the next century's industrial giants.[81] We look back now and figure that we were a winner in the battles of the 1980s and 1990s. We took our knocks early, and it gave us a head start. A *Washington Post* article in December 1982 had sounded one of the first death knells, arguing that "Silicon Valley Is Losing Out to the Sunbelt." The article quoted a Rolm Corporation official: "It's hard to find anybody who wants to live" in the Valley, while other spots like Raleigh and Austin "are very desirable places to live , ... where the cities support the expansion of electronics companies."

We learned that 1982 lesson well, and it showed. A decade later, a status report in the *Mercury News* on attempts to clone the Valley had to dampen the hopes of overeager mayors around the country. By 1991, Silicon Valley had 221,700 employees in the electronics industry, three times the number of the largest competing city or region. It had 733 major electronics companies (annual sales of $5 million or more), more than double the number in any copycat area. The *Mercury* concluded, "It doesn't appear that Silicon Valley's environment can be duplicated. . . . Even the Route 128 area near Boston, which some say was the nation's electronics center in the 1960s and '70s, has fallen far behind."

Despite the recession during the Bush administration, the semiconductor industry as a whole retook the global lead in chip production from upstart Japan in 1993. The media were amazed, terming that success "an astounding feat, the first time that a key U.S. industry has regained a dominant market position after being knocked out of first place by Japanese competitors."[82] The chip resurgence was mostly due to massive investment in the future. Just as San Jose was pouring concrete for new educational institutions and a new infrastructure designed to support the city of 2020, companies poured funds into research and development. (Intel Corporation alone has been spending $1 billion a year in R & D.) These companies know how to invest for the future; we have tried to follow these good examples.

I have also spent the last few years watching with some interest as Ray AbuZayyad, IBM's former chief in San Jose and a good friend, aggressively fought to reestablish the computer giant's position in the marketplace and in the forefront of technological advance. In return, Ray has ensured that his employees and corporate coffers will play a role in all the municipal efforts to imagine the future for San Jose. His pivotal leadership on the board of directors for the new Tech Museum ensured that the museum would be born healthy. I remember his sharp rejoinder at one difficult board meeting; in the face of starry-eyed plans, he realistically barked out over and over, to the point of impoliteness: "Implement! Implement!" Ray always kept the board focused on the limited task at hand, with the pragmatism that works in the private sector and should be better known in city halls. Ray and his successor Ed Zschau have kept IBM's local division successful; the parent company could use some of their good judgment.

Our new cathedral's domes are the engineers and risk takers, the brightest minds of a generation. They reflect the spark of opportunity San Jose wants to provide in all city programs. I hope we always have in San Jose the winning entrepreneurial spirit that drives our high-tech pioneers and propels them toward first place. With their examples, I feel San Jose has a competitive edge like no other city. One of the brightest CEOs, LSI Logic founder Wilf Corrigan, says, "Everybody is terrified of the Japanese, but the Japanese are terrified of this place."[83]

6

PLAN BACKWARDS

The physican can bury his mistakes, but the architect
can only advise his client to plant vines.
—Frank Lloyd Wright

The critical first decision in any endeavor is to determine your priorities. When you select one set of building blocks, implicit in that act is the conscious judgment that others will not be used. One of the key developers of San José's downtown, Lew Wolff, has told me often that the old San José of the 1960s and 1970s got an A in planning, and a D– in implementation. Other cities can avoid the pitfalls of implementation by using even better planning.

In a very true sense San José was a start-up company. We had ideas; we had talent; we had accumulated the necessary venture capital to do the first products. The very important decision was to make the right choice on the product line and ensure that we had the expertise to pull it off. As in many companies, it was necessary to clear out the debris and make absolutely certain that the antiquated and obsolete product line was permanently retired. In San José, the old product to be removed was called unprogrammed, rampant growth. When Rodin was asked how best to make an elephant, the sculptor said, "Get a large block of marble and then remove all that is not an elephant."

Our new plan envisioned a different result: a focus on the center. To accomplish that, we had to plan backward, starting from the outside. We were going to draw a line around the city. No housing would be built outside the line, and we concentrated instead on providing jobs. This decision was a covenant that endures to this day and saves us from re-peating the mistakes that nearly ruined San Jose for our children.

Plan with the End Result in Mind

Energetic and successful men and women in local government around the country followed a new vision throughout the 1980s and into the 1990s, doing the same thing at about the same time. Naturally, they were responding to the same national trends. Terry Goddard in Phoenix and Henry Cisneros in San Antonio were two of them. Dianne Fein-stein, brought to office after the tragic assassination of Mayor George Moscone, was holding together a difficult city in San Francisco, with powerful centrifugal forces ever pulling it apart. George Latimer of St. Paul, Minnesota, who served as mayor from 1976 to 1990, was a living embodiment of take-charge government on the local level. Young Richard Daley of Chicago has been innovative since the late 1980s, in-troducing his privatization initiative. He told me recently of his inten-tion "to mold a government that is smaller in size but greater in perfor-mance" through massive spin-offs of services to the private sector. And Ed Koch of New York City—well, New York is still New York, and Koch is Koch.

Those were some of the good ones, the thoughtful mayors willing to challenge the old way of thinking. Most urban leaders around the coun-try today would call it an indulgence to stress vision over the more im-mediate financial woes facing American cities. I heard their refrain in national mayors' conferences for years. They failed to persuade me. They will tell you (they certainly tell their constituents, and they damn sure tell Washington) that their problems can be solved only with an imme-diate focus on money. Big money, money in the billions, poured into city coffers from above.

They are missing the point. Money never drives vision. More to the point, money without vision can be as bad as no money at all.

A detailed vision of where an American city wants to go, and a road map of how to get there, must be laid out to its residents first, with their active participation. Absent that, all the money in the world will not solve a city's problems. We should know that lesson from decades of lis-tening to that giant sucking sound, federal cash being dumped into urban sinkholes. Jane Jacobs, the preeminent city scholar, wrote three decades ago:

There is a wistful myth that if only we had enough money to spend—the figure is usually put at a hundred billion dollars—we could wipe out all our slums in ten years, reverse decay in the great, dull gray belts that were yesterday's and day-before-yesterday's suburbs, anchor the wandering middle class and its wandering tax money, and perhaps even solve the traffic problem. . . . But look what we have built with the first several billions. This is not the rebuilding of cities. This is the sacking of cities.[84]

When I look at the sacking "vision" provided by federal dollars, I find a textbook example of the law of unintended consequences.

Ignore Conventional Wisdom: Washington's "Plan" for Cities

Some big-city mayors deserve honorary citizenship in the District of Columbia for the amount of time they spend on Capitol Hill or in HUD corridors, trawling for dollars. That was never my style. I spent little time in Washington, as little as possible and only for a specific purpose. Robin Williams once said he felt as comfortable in Los Angeles as a hemophiliac in a razor factory, and that summed up my feelings about the seat of federal government.

The U.S. Conference of Mayors was dominated by members of the Eastern old-boy network, most of them without the panache of a Kevin White or Richard Daley. As that noted urban critic James Joyce once said, "They sailed in puddles of the past." At one of the few Conference of Mayors meetings I did attend, I took a seat beside Marion Barry. At least, that's what the placard at his empty chair said. The mayor of Washington was very late to the meeting. Some pressing city business, I assumed. At home, I was often called out of meetings for police emergencies and the like, so I certainly understood—or thought I did. As yet another speaker droned on about the pressing need for increased federal assistance to cities, I was surprised to see Barry enter the room, dressed in a red warm-up suit he must have slept in. He slumped into the chair beside me and closed his eyes. Pressures of office, I thought sympathetically. Look at what the strain can do to a mayor, the strain of meeting increased human needs with decreasing resources.

Suddenly Marion Barry came alive, interrupting the speaker and blurting out a few non sequiturs. The man seemed disoriented to me. Everyone stared for an instant, jaws dropped, and I heard a chuckle of nervous laughter from a staff member. After a moment's rambling, Barry slumped back quietly into his chair beside me again, apparently satisfied that he had made some point, though it was certainly lost on his fellow mayors. Politely, we all acted as if nothing had happened. I recall that someone said soothing words along the lines of, "Excellent point, Marion. Now, back on the subject of block grants. . . ." To paraphrase Ross Perot, we all ignored the crazy aunt in the basement. I have never shuffled my papers as intently as I did the rest of that meeting.

It was only later, when his arrest by the FBI made public his drug addiction, that I understood Barry's behavior that day. But Marion Barry, in his personification to me of the confused paternalism of Washington, D.C., symbolized the inherent dangers of cities becoming wards of the federal government. In office, I always looked at the city of Washington as a warning of what could happen to a city when big-G government took too big a role. Federal involvement, in the domineering manner the feds prefer, always represented to me a loss of accountability, a dangerous diffusion of power, and an abdication of local responsibility. They had been part of the conspiracy that killed San Jose from the 1950s through the 1970s. Mayor Barry, as he disregarded personal responsibility, seemed to anthropomorphize that principle. He fiddled while his city, cradled in the arms of Congress, burned.*

I sometimes annoyed my staff with my repetitious denunciations of Washington, Congress, and their efforts at aiding cities, but as mayor I had to achieve results, not reward good intentions. Sitting on a conference panel in Seattle in 1985 with pollster Pat Caddell, Mayors Bill Hudnut of Indianapolis and Charlie Royer of Seattle, I said that Congress was "brain-dead" and someone ought to pull the plug. Our California congressional delegation did not appreciate the comment; truth is a noxious tonic, especially in Washington. I based my opinions on the historical record.

Like everything else in American governmental life, urban policy still bears the marks of the New Deal. Only in the 1930s did federal policy take on the task of promoting the economic health of cities. In the following decades, local leaders were gradually trained, even encouraged, to look to Washington for solutions to local problems. Mayors became hardened welfare queens.

---

*Astonishingly, in the mayoral election of fall 1994, Barry recaptured the primary win, crushing Mayor Sharon Pratt Kelly's bid for reelection. This election reinforced what Tim Clancy said was the difference between fact and fiction: fiction has to make sense. Barry's election doesn't.

When talking about "urban renewal" from the 1930s on, I am referring to federal programs that took different names under different administrations but followed essentially the same type of heavy interventionist, cookie-cutter grand-plan policies. It was the Robert Moses school of thought without his brains or leadership. Franklin Roosevelt's Housing Act of 1937 set the path of "slum clearance and redevelopment," and the formula was expanded by Harry Truman's urban renewal and housing program passed through Congress in 1949. The objective was large-scale clearance of the "obsolete" features of cities. The terminology was modernized to "blight" in the later lexicon. When you use that old phrase, "a face only a mother could love," I think of all the irreplaceable parts of too many American cities that were obliterated by the total-clearance philosophy. I know that a very important and valuable part of San Jose, critical links with the past and blocks for the future, were destroyed without a sideways glance. It was criminally callous.

In the 1950s urban highway projects were launched, and mayors were eager both to please their federal patrons and to get high-paying construction jobs. All were committed to seeing projects through despite the growing problem of relocating displaced residents, one of the intractable dilemmas cities have always faced in redevelopment.[85] (I was to face it firsthand.) Some residential projects were built, many of them Stalinesque block towers slapped down on razed neighborhoods. The federal urban renewal program is now widely criticized for its destruction of neighborhoods and notable buildings and its botched relocation efforts.[86] The victims of urban renewal and highway developments were the relocated families, most of whom were not well-treated or adequately compensated. The employees and owners of small businesses were never compensated fairly either.[87] It was not a record of honor.

In 1962, at the dawn of what we now remember as the troubled sixties, *Time* magazine ran a glowing five-page cover story on urban renewal, claiming that "the big cities are riding the crest of a renaissance." It made no mention of relocation problems or shattered neighborhoods. Looking back, knowing that the inner cities were about to explode literally, I fail to see how the reporter could have been so sanguine. Arrogance and stupidity can afflict reporters as well as politicians.

The Price of Blindness

The real victim of urban renewal was the American downtown. The inability of local governments to direct the development process was a major limitation on the effectiveness of any cogent planning. Experts made no attempt to consider what the average person needs from a downtown: good jobs, friendly homes and neighborhoods, safe recreational outlets. The redesigned downtown of the 1950s was more like Fritz Lang's Metropolis, with concrete overpasses and blank walls crowding out the human element. Families, individuals, small businesses, all were left out of the federal equation, and the vibrant city they could have combined to create lost its heart in the process.

Without a sense of community, Americans no longer thought of a "downtown," with that word's positive connotations. We began to think and speak of the "inner city" and invested in that term all our negative, prejudiced, even nightmarish images of urban hell. It was the lexicon of an impoverished, intellectually stunted bureaucracy. In the sixties, the images came true.

The response of city leaders around the country to the riots of the mid-sixties should have been to reassert local control and provide singular plans for their communities, better ideas, more participation. No, by that time too many mayors and community leaders were addicted to the federal pipeline, and the solution seemed to be more federal money. Those appeals dovetailed with Lyndon Johnson's goals for the Great Society, which he stressed at home even more as he escalated American involvement in Vietnam. The War on Poverty and Model Cities programs contributed to the transitory relief cities found in federal assistance. Over $14 billion flowed from Washington to cities between 1960 and 1969. Ten times that amount could not have substituted for a handful of good ideas.

The failures of federal policy evident in the urban maelstrom seemed, paradoxically, to spur Washington on. In 1967, the secretary of Housing and Urban Development announced a major expansion of national goals in urban renewal, extending federal involvement to social needs as well as housing and infrastructure. Federal dollars would now expand the housing supply for low- and moderate-income families. Federal dollars would now also be targeted at creating job centers for the jobless. Federal dollars would now support projects addressing "physical decay, high tensions, and great social need."[88] And, as Congress passed the package, it tacked on legislative amendments detailing federal control after federal control. Local governments received funds for narrow programs with strict requirements but were given no more authority. Dully, like a dazed fighter, the city accepted its supplicant status. Rules were now set. Both sponsor and dependent would become inured to the incestuous covenant.

To plan became impossible. The American mayor took on, in many respects, the functions and the status of a pass-through account manager.

Alternating Republican and Democratic administrations kept the spigots open but held the reins of control tighter. Congress played its pernicious role as "ward heeler on the Potomac." The first limited experimentation with federal block grants had begun in 1965, designed to allow more local flexibility in spending federal dollars. But Richard Nixon's 1972 attempt to tilt the balance away from Washington with General Revenue Sharing was never fully implemented and was allowed to wither away. General Revenue Sharing gave cities the dollars and removed many guidelines and conditions on program spending, but members of Congress rebelled.

They fought back to regain their stripped pork-barreling powers and found a respite during Jimmy Carter's single term. Among other expansions of aid and federal control, Carter offered new training programs for the unemployed and Urban Development Action Grants (UDAGs) to stimulate local economies. As Boston's Kevin White said about New York's John Lindsay, "He gives good intentions a bad name." Such intentions walked lockstep with fuzzy thinking.

Just as I entered city hall as a first-term council member, America's cities got a quick dash of cold water in the face. Ronald Reagan's election in 1980 ended the sugar-daddy era. His New Federalism bore out his intention to "get government off the back of the people," and his policies succeeded in getting cities off Washington's dole, cutting federal urban aid by half in ten years.[89]

On my election in 1982, I was entering a brave new world for mayors, where the established rules of dependency no longer applied. Some mayors never noticed and continued to act as wards of the state, bellowing ever louder and wailing their denunciations. Their cities have declined. I was determined to succeed under the new conditions of independence. I did not longingly wait for an unrequited love to be met by the Reagan administration. Californians had known his "commitments" before. A good part of San Jose's growth, from 250,000 to 580,000 people in Reagan's 1967–1975 governorship, had been based on the promised state highways that never materialized.

Silicon Valley's Tom Peters would later write of business's need to "thrive in chaos." Just as Apple Computer, Tandem, Intel, Silicon Graphics and a hundred other high-tech start-ups were doing for corporate America, we were about to rewrite the rules of entrepreneurship for government. I was not about to let my city be sacked again. This time, with a forward-looking plan, we would outflank the Visigoths.

It Helps to Have Dirty Hands

My first effort to plan and rebuild came in my own family business, in San Jose's historic district. A group of vintage buildings make up the Farmers Union, our property that is surrounded by old landmarks. It adjoins the historic Peralta Adobe, the oldest private home still standing in California. The entire district is an interesting area, but in my youth, it was a dying one. The more modern buildings looked in worse shape than the century-old structures. The downtown was deserted, and the Farmers Union had become a conversation piece, shells with an interesting past but apparently no future.

By 1971, our family had two options. We could try to make something again of the old properties and restore a spark of vitality to the central part of San Jose (and to the family name). Our other choice was to sell out, take the money, and cut our ties with the past. Many American families face that decision. Some quite necessarily opt to sell a dwindling heritage for immediate needs. That choice can be practical, make no mistake, but it wasn't for us. My generation felt the chance to preserve a flickering flame. I was newly married and now in charge of the family business, along with my brother John. We made the right decision, taking on the task of rebuilding the Farmers Union into something new. We planned to revitalize the entire area into a "historic entertainment center" rechristened San Pedro Square.

I learned many lessons from that venture, not least the value of hard work and the business end of a shovel. I began to see government the way most people do, from the vantage point of a small business. Local government was more of a roadblock than an avenue of opportunity in our effort to rebuild. When we needed the help of a city bureaucrat, or simple information on some city hall regulation, my level of frustration rose in direct proportion to the amount of time it took us to find what we needed. City hall was an obstacle, and we had to go right through it to accomplish anything. We brushed aside the conventions and the deadwood of the city establishment.

By 1977, the first series of battles was over. We had created a privately financed restaurant row in the center of debilitated commercial areas. The dedication of Oliver Hurtley's huge wrought-iron arch over San Pedro Square was a symbolic curtain drawn over one phase of my life. Our determined attempts to overcome all obstacles gave me the zeal of the convert. I had seen how to re-create one block. I was eager to try more.

Create Alternative Wisdom: the Style of the City

When American and other international visitors arrived in Barcelona, Spain, for the 1992 Summer Olympics, they were roundly surprised at how new and beautifully designed the city was. *New York Times* critic Herbert Muschamp wrote, "Barcelona has broken all records for inspired urbanism in our time." The city achieved success by taking it seriously, up to and including the political leadership. In the past decade in Barcelona, public architecture has become the spectator sport it ought to be everywhere, and in the 1991 mayoral election there, each candidate prominently boasted of his "architectural adviser." The local press covered the architectural aspect of the candidates' platforms so extensively that the vote became by some accounts a referendum on the future look of the city.[90]

We all know what some bad city developments and styles look like. We see them all the time. William Whyte has made a career of pointing them out, particularly with his "photographic record of outstandingly bad [public] spaces." He has said of New York City that it may be the king of bad urban planning decisions: "They are not peculiar to New York, save in scale—New York's worst examples are so bad that one is almost proud of them."[91]

San Jose's history had shown us as much. The leadership from World War II on had simply wanted a big city, the bigger the better, and had used "growth" as the answer to all ills. A San Jose city clerk from that era,

Frank Greiner, said in retrospect, "With that policy, there wasn't much they had to study. They just had to let the developers build."[92] That is exactly what happened, with no oversight, investigation, or questions on what effect such growth would have on the city.[93] Architect Daniel Soloman, a thoughtful young designer who wonders why we build such bad cities, has written that the "sanitized anti-urban world" we created in California (and exported elsewhere) is "a place of diminished experience and diminished insight for its inhabitants."[94]

Some mayors never learned the lesson of the bad old days. Tom Bradley was always associated with strong growth policies in Los Angeles, exhibited through his hyperactive Community Redevelopment Agency and its build-first, ask-questions-later approach. At the 1990 groundbreaking for a seventy-three-story Library Square building, he said that every great city that has tried to stop growing has died.[95] That begs the question. The point is not whether to grow; our families and our families' families give us no choice. The issue is *how*. Urban critic R. V. Knight has called the guided development of a city "a social learning process whereby cities learn from their past experience, from the experience of other cities," but he also notes that few cities have institutionalized the learning process.[96] San Jose was determined to learn as it innovated.

The late Spiro Kostof, a professor at UC-Berkeley and one of the nation's preeminent architectural historians, outlined in his masterpiece *The City Shaped* five major prototypes of urban form through history.[97] San Jose has either lived or flirted with each of the five since its earliest days. Most early American cities preferred one, developing on a grid, or "orthogonal plan." On a visit to Philadelphia in 1842, Charles Dickens wrote: "After walking about for an hour or two, I would have given the world for a crooked street." He knew that such an authoritarian planning method was no way to capture the heart of a community—much less to provide an interesting walk.

Three of the other styles noted by Kostof are pursued today by city planners with more chutzpah than imagination. The "grand manner" features a heroic scale, ceremonial boulevards and vistas, all sorts of baroque grandeur of the kind seen in Paris. The "city as diagram," favored by utopians like Jeremy Bentham and Thomas Jefferson, used strict geometric circles and polygons to achieve some sort of cosmic significance. Of this style, Kostof remarked, "In real life, we know better." And the "urban skyline signature" is still a popular style among mayors, planners, and developers who want to put a vertical signature on their city. Kostof was skeptical, as am I. San Jose has developed a gentle skyline all its own without needing to pierce the sky with immense, heroic towers.

San Jose was not partial to any of the trendier and more conventional approaches. We preferred the oldest of Kostof's five categories: when our earliest settlers found the Guadalupe River and nestled on its banks, they organized along "organic lines," like most other early communities that grew up along rivers or trade routes. Our heart, our downtown, was still alongside the river and it was still viable. There was no need to raze what had gone before. We knew the style we wanted—a combination of the grace of our past and tradition with the energy of the future—but we had to have all the specifics, the building blocks required in a cosmopolitan central business district. Those were the pieces that we had lost in the previous decades and that we would find again.

We began to plan in earnest. We had the economic infrastructure of the city to keep in mind and the social infrastructure as well. For the former, land is the most important asset; we hold most of the improved industrial land still available in Silicon Valley. We needed buildings, millions of square feet of available industrial and office space at competitive rents. We had to attend to the transportation network and find ways of more efficiently connecting prime industrial districts with residential areas. The social segment was no less important, though. The social character is what makes our cities and towns more vital, exciting, livable and beautiful at the same time. We would pay attention to public space design, creating a sense of place and community in our architecture (and with art in public places). Our redevelopment process placed a priority on community participation as we looked for successful strategies to involve our citizens in this revitalization. I looked forward to a new downtown that fostered and protected urban traditions, like festivals celebrating diverse communities. We were interested in identifying all the elements that could nourish a town and bind it together. Sometimes it was painful; always the process was positive. These ideas came from city planners, certainly, and from architects. But they came from city dwellers as well, whether expressed in the hundreds of public forums I had attended over the years, in the barbed questions tossed at city council meetings, or in sharp letters to the editor—which I read every day, whether I had to or not.

Hire Alter Egos

The San Jose Redevelopment Agency, in its original incarnation began in 1956 but as a creator was dormant for over twenty years. The agency created a desert and called it progress. In 1979, as I sat on the city council, we decided to take seriously our official role as the ex officio board of directors of the agency. The council directed a new activist path for redevelopment, grounded in the most basic desires of our citizens. The new course began in 1979. That year, we selected Frank Taylor as the new executive director of the Redevelopment Agency. In 1980, the city stole a march and won state approval to pool our property tax increments from multiple redevelopment areas into a single fund. One small step; one giant financial base. Since 1982, San Jose's Redevelopment Agency has become one of the nation's most active, with an annual capital improvement budget of more than $130 million. In a decade it contributed nearly $1.5 billion to downtown San Jose.[98]

Frank Taylor was a native Bostonian whom we recruited from Cincinnati, where he had gone to school and participated in a large redevelopment program. It has been said that by the age of fifty, you get the face you deserve: Frank had an Irishman's red beard and laughing face. He also had an innate love of cities. I soon discovered, to my satisfaction, that he epitomized what has been called the "new type of public entrepreneur," characterized in the words of scholars Bernard Frieden and

Frank Taylor, San Jose Redevelopment Czar.

Lynne Sagalyn: "Operating with a strong sense of personal mission, they brought a free-wheeling style to city government. Comfortable taking risks, cutting deals, and pressuring reluctant colleagues to keep projects moving, they were ready to change course abruptly in a crisis. . . . They valued results on the ground more than the traditions of public administration."[99] At its height of activity in 1990, my last year as mayor, the agency had two-thirds fewer employees than Leonidas had Spartans at Thermopylae, but our band held the pass.

Frank had an educated yet intuitive understanding of what we needed in San Jose. "We can always get budget hotels, discount department stores, and second-class office buildings," he said, "but we will never achieve a downtown worthy of a great city if we do so." The agency's annual reports often featured soaring rhetoric unusual to government documents, but he actually did express our dream: "We are capturing in the briefest of times the elegance and romance that great cities build over centuries."[100] Frank liked to say that he wanted San Jose to be a place where lovers could stroll hand in hand. I used to add: "and children with their parents." It was a very nontraditional view of planning, but the only one for San Jose.

One thing we knew we had to continue: our refusal to allow further fringe development on our hillsides, on the farthest reaches of our sprawling empire, and even by the airport—especially by the airport, a potential competitor three miles from the downtown. We kept fighting proposals for airport hotels through Gary Schoennauer in the planning department. Gary worked in concert with Frank Taylor, as the planning department reviewed all planning proposals outside the downtown. A man of Napoleonic temperament, Schoennauer was a local product, a San Jose State graduate, and was evangelical about controlling the development community. He held the line. We were directing our energies to the inner-city neighborhoods and the downtown, and all our cylinders were firing in sync.

Not every city has such a good planning team, often because too many mayors are afraid of appointing strong, independently minded team members. In our case, these egos were in fact *alter egos*, reflecting the same vision emanating from the mayor's office. Los Angeles, the nightmare model we try to avoid, has a planning department that over the years has become so inept that the entire office should be subjected to a little "bureaucratic cleansing." A 1991 city-commissioned audit charged that "planning in Los Angeles is at a crisis level," and found "an over-politicized department. . . . [that feels that] the mission of our division is to do pet projects for the city council and keep them hap-py."[101] It is a recipe for calamity.

San Jose has had no such problems. If anything, our decision to pro-vide professional, self-assured leadership for redevelopment has led some to conclude, wrongly, that city hall and elected representatives are not in control. In 1992, the city auditor conducted an internal audit of the Redevelopment Agency's public accountability and charged the agency with supposedly leaving the city council in the dark about some minor spending decisions. After I left office, one lonely gadfly on the council charged that the agency needed major attention, that it had been too high-flying and independent, and that the council, as the agency's board, should crack down. He was apparently trying to make the agency a whipping boy for political purposes. "[McEnery] didn't want us to mess with Frank Taylor. He'd go crazy," this council member said. "Now we have another chance. . . . Those guys work for us, too. It's about time they learned who's boss."[102] With such politicians, only disdain and dis-tance can be ample palliatives. Taylor and Schoennauer were able to deal with the few "wackos" in easy style.

Back when I *was* boss, I worked closely with Redevelopment officials. I had been elected to act as a hands-on mayor, and not a drawing or design escaped my scrutiny. I remember the time a particularly annoying set of plans was laid before me by a developer and his minions in my conference room at city hall. The plans were the same woolly-headed, suburban "Century City"–style proposals that I had specifically warned them not to submit. In a fit of drama more calculated than impulsive, I scooped up the entire set and angrily heaved them out the window. Once the chastised team had left, I had a good laugh and looked out the window to see where the papers had landed. We did not see those plans again.

I always enjoyed the Tinkertoy nature of studying the designs and plans, although I think we avoided fairly successfully the dangers of de-signing the city in a vacuum. Daniel Soloman has written that one of the major evils introduced into modern public architecture was "the large-scale introduction of the magic marker. . . . Since 1965, the urban structure of the American city has been reduced to a rudimentary orga-nization of land-use blobs, freeways, and arterials."[103] I tried to avoid that level of abstraction. One of my favorite ways of handling the stress of the mayor's office was to sneak away for a midday walk, and I often took along Frank Taylor or David Pandori. (When I just wanted to listen to a nonstop monologue, I would take police chief and accomplished crime novelist Joe McNamara.) We would walk the neighborhoods, the downtown, the Guadalupe River area, and ideas would germinate and percolate into concrete plans—only some of which involved concrete.

Major Redevelopment Projects, 1983–1990

Convention center
San Jose Arena
Guadalupe Parkway/Highway 87
Highway 85 improvements
Downtown Transit Mall
Children's Discovery Museum
Tech Museum of Innovation
Retail Pavilion complex
San Jose Museum of Art expansion
Silicon Valley Financial Center
Fairmont Hotel
DeAnza Hotel
St. Claire Hotel
San Jose Hilton Hotel and Towers
Plaza Park renovation
Three-mile Guadalupe River Park
Housing
Preservation of historic buildings
Neighborhood Business District revitalization

We identified quickly the most important building blocks we needed for the new downtown core. I had spoken of most of them in my inaugural speech: hotels, including one five-star among them, and an urban to-scale skyline of premium office buildings intermingled with shops, restaurants, public arts, parks, and museums. Also needed was a first-class convention center and a sports and entertainment arena. Perhaps even a baseball stadium might be added to the mix.

Highways: Unclogging the Open Road

The Bay Area's four major freeways—Interstates 280, 680, 880, and State Highway 101—all converge in San Jose. We are the unique nexus of the Bay Area. In 1984, we finally addressed head-on the fact that our industrial growth was creating intolerable rush-hour traffic. I worked on the issue with a county supervisor and Peter Giles, then president of the Santa Clara County Manufacturers Group (founded by David Packard), the premier industry association of the high-tech world. We masterminded a campaign for Measure A, which asked for a half-cent sales tax increase. Peter was clearly the lead, whereas I added my name and fundraising ability to the campaign. County voters passed the measure, approving over $1 billion for road improvements and creating the Santa Clara County Traffic Authority, a model for self-help in California. The eventual results were significant: Highway 85, the eighteen-mile West Valley Freeway with a mass transit median quickly linking Palo Alto, Mountain View, and points north with Silicon Valley South, looping around the west side of the city to link up again with 101 in the south. Measure A also paid to widen existing freeways 280 and 101 to eight lanes and to upgrade State Highway 237 in North San Jose's Golden Triangle to full freeway standards. We had waited for the promises of previous governors: Brown, Reagan, and Brown again. Deukmejian was proving a disaster of closed mind and meager thought. We finally did it the old-fashioned start-up way: by ourselves, with our own money.

That menu of construction was not enough. When we realized that state funding for freeway access was lagging far behind our own building program, we decided to do something else almost unheard of: we spent $40 million of our own redevelopment money to build our north-south artery freeway. Highway 87, the Guadalupe Expressway, provided a new corridor for commuters coming up from our southern residential areas to new jobs in the industrial parks. The "Guadalupe Parkway" section, opened in 1988, links the downtown directly to the international airport three short miles to the north.

Overall, we spent over $84 million in redevelopment funds for highway construction from 1977 to 1990, representing about 15 percent of the total redevelopment funds, and we committed another $45.3 million in the first five years of the 1990s.

Mass Transit

Daniel Soloman is designing an urban-village-style development, on San Jose land still owned by the pioneering Bettancourt family, known as Communications Hill. As an architect of a new kind of city, he believes that the resurrection of a pedestrian townscape "demands that town builders understand cars the way lion tamers understand lions."[104] That sums up our whole approach to mass transit, light-rail, and particularly the Downtown Transit Mall through which the new trolleys glide.

Mass transit has been a nightmare issue for city planners for decades and probably will continue to cause headaches for quite a long time to come. No system is perfect or satisfies all the important criteria, from ease of use and attractiveness to riders to cost per rider or beneficial impact on the traffic situation. Even Washington's Metro, so popular among commuters and tourists, has been criticized by a *New York Times* columnist for being so expensive that it "scarfs subsidies like an armada of stealth bombers."[105] Each ride costs the taxpayer nearly $9. Nothing, however, should stop cities from pursuing the goal of efficient mass transit. Los Angeles is now opening links in its new Metro rail system. Kevin Starr, USC professor of urban planning, is optimistic: "The Metro system will encourage some three to four decades of retro-fitting and reurbanization, as Los Angeles doubles back on its center and reurbanizes properties made valuable by the public transit system. The Cold War is over, but transportation has replaced defense; and connected to transportation is a construction boom that will see Los Angeles County well into the 21st century."[106]

Back in the 1970s, because of the shortsightedness of our Peninsula neighbors in San Mateo and our own narrow thinking, we refused to allow the BART (Bay Area Rapid Transit) heavy-rail line to reach San Jose. Ironically, San Jose merchants were afraid it would take shoppers away from the downtown. We gave up on that system for the time being, but we are not about to give up on mass transportation. We have simply looked to our past, to the old "Peninsular trolleys" of a bygone era—a line of over 100 miles that carried one from Palo Alto to Los Gatos or San Jose and to the eastern foothills. It had been dismantled in our "orgy of progress," bought by new energy and highway cartels. At the dawn of the 1980s, city and county officials determined that we would best be served by a high-tech light-rail system. Portland's activist Mayor Neil Goldschmidt a decade before had planned a similar system, for which he was rewarded with an appointment as President Carter's secretary of transportation. I spoke to him in San Jose in 1980. He was a good promoter. We emulated Portland's successful network with a $421 million state-of-the-art light-rail. The first nine miles opened in 1990 centered on the Transit Mall, and the line expanded to twenty miles in 1991, reaching deep into residential South San Jose.

We took advantage of the fact that only a short stroll from stops along that new mall sits the old Cahill Street Train Station. The CalTrain commuter rail service now run by Amtrak links downtown San Jose with San Francisco. From the train you can see plants belonging to GTE, Apple, and Hewlett-Packard up and down the valley between San Jose and Palo Alto, where once only orchards grew. In 1992, Amtrak opened a new thirty-mile extension providing access all the way to Gilroy, passing through South San Jose with a link to light-rail at Tamien station.[107] Thus was our downtown linked with steel bands to all of Silicon Valley's major industrial and residential areas.* Today, public transit for tens of millions of riders annually is located within five minutes walking distance for most of the San Jose metro population.

Don't Neglect Pieces of the Puzzle

Not all our transportation links are earthbound. The San Jose International Airport has actually received no redevelopment funding, but it is a key piece of our economic growth engine. Located only three miles from downtown, it is now among the world's thirty busiest airports, used by over 7 million passengers a year. We achieved a major goal in 1988 when San Jose International was made a West Coast center for American Airlines. That partnership gave us vital trade linkages, including a direct flight to Tokyo. To support American's major presence, we began a $516 million expansion project, including a new sixteen-gate terminal that opened in 1990. Like another growth turbine, the water pollution control plant, the airport is an enterprise activity that funds itself on user fees.

*In 1992, voters approved the dramatic expansion of light-rail at the cost of $1 billion by taxing themselves. The measure passed at the same election that sank the hopes of our borrowing the "San Jose" Giants from San Francisco.

Beginning at the airport and running south is the new three-mile Guadalupe River Park, which when finished will feature lakes, floral gardens, and public access points. Once the biker, jogger, or casual stroller reaches the new downtown, he or she will find many activities that predate the redevelopment era. The San Jose Symphony, the oldest symphony west of the Mississippi, was founded in that exceptional decade before 1885. It shares the Frank Lloyd Wright–inspired Center for the Performing Arts with the renowned San Jose–Cleveland Ballet and the Civic Light Opera. The San Jose Repertory Theatre will actually move within a few years to a new 575-seat home, built with redevelopment funds in the San Antonio Project area.

Redevelopment also funded a beautiful new wing for the San Jose Museum of Art. Opened in 1990, the wing blends well with the sandstone walls of the 1892 Richardson romanesque main structure and is a wonderful example of how we have managed to set the new with the old. The half of the building that is a century old began its life as San Jose's first post office and in my boyhood was the city library. It has evolved as the community has needed it, a functional metamorphosis that now houses art from a partnership with New York's Whitney Museum.

Revive The Downtown Heartbeat

We designed our public spaces downtown, at least in part, with William Whyte's "Street Life Project" in mind. Whyte used time-lapse photography and other observation tools to see precisely how people used city spaces, particularly streets, plazas, and arcades. His films and photos are fascinating. In New York City, he has spent a career cataloguing so many awful public spaces, sterile and empty; they are good only to walk across on your way elsewhere. He also points out some excellent spaces—street retail where people window-shop, plazas where strollers congregate, lounge, eat, and enjoy city life.[108]

Whyte feels that quite often bad projects come about when the relationship between a city and developers is too cooperative. City officials sometimes aid and abet a developer's desire to do as little as possible for the life of the city, caring only about the bottom line. As a result, some cities have had monstrosities like Detroit's Renaissance Center or New York's Times Square Hotel dropped in their midst, with the impact of a neutron bomb: its presence kills all the people, but the building still stands! So many buildings from the Sixties, Seventies, and, yes, even the Eighties present only huge blank walls to onlookers, with no contribution to street life or city vibrancy whatsoever. Whyte says of such buildings that they dominate a block "like a gigantic mammoth frozen in the tundra." That is not true of our elegant Fairmont Hotel. Owners, the developer, and the city staff worked together with the same vision: a truly first-class hotel that would be accepted by the public as an integral part of their new downtown.

We needed more. We needed to provide a commercial raison d'être for the rest of downtown, for the visitor staying in the comfortable Fairmont, and, more important, for the year-round residents of our own city. Again, we looked to the past for guidance. The thriving American downtown of the late nineteenth century had one obvious heartbeat: retail development. The downtown department store was the nucleus of the vigorous commercial center. By the turn of the century, the heart of downtown in most big cities was a popular retail district replete with department stores, specialty shops, restaurants, and the like. The lifeblood was foot traffic throughout the day and night.

After World War II, everyone wanted and could afford to buy a home and a car. Department stores followed people out to the suburbs. San Jose was a willing model. By the time mayors woke up to the desperate reality of a dying downtown, the retail had fled. They had forgotten the human heart of the city. In the frantic 1950s, leading experts in urban redevelopment made a strategic error: they redesigned downtowns to create more space: space for highways, parking garages, parks, massive cultural centers, and huge concrete plazas. America had forgotten what average people wanted in a bustling downtown. Frieden and Sagalyn write that "the new downtown was profoundly out of touch with popular taste," built by developers who normally built for a mass market. "The key decisions on new downtown projects . . . [were made] by a professional staff who hoped to attract a trendsetting elite."[109] The elite stopped coming, whoever they were.

Only after the pain and destruction of the 1960s did some big-city mayors and their allies find a better path. Hoping to rebuild and revitalize their downtown, some began to believe, as Philip Langdon writes in *Urban Excellence*, that city design needed less emphasis "on the individual building and more on how the building contributes to a broader sense of place and a sense of community."

Slowly, through retail centers, a few cities ventured to change the character of downtown. The new centers competed with the suburban malls and were designed to draw large numbers of ordinary people back downtown. My firm intention was to place San Jose among the leaders in what has been called a "golden age of downtown retail development."[110]

We studied closely other examples of big-city downtown retail developments: Quincy Market in Boston, Pike Place Market in Seattle, Town Square Mall in St. Paul, Horton Plaza in San Diego, all built in the 1970s and early 1980s. Not all of them were completely successful. Horton Plaza was built around the historic heart of San Diego's downtown but did little to save neighboring Horton Plaza Park, an urban disaster. The *San Diego Union* in 1990 was still able to cite the park as "an attractive gathering place for our city's underclass."[111] Even the presence of a new convention center and thousands of visitors doesn't deter the panhandlers, who have created a scene straight from Dickens. San Diego has not yet been able to clean up the park. On the other hand, Quincy Market, a key component of Boston's Faneuil Hall complex, has been phenomenally successful, and many cities are trying to emulate its special vitality as a festival marketplace. The complex benefits from a close combination of office buildings, retail, entertainment, and housing.

We planned a similar mix in San Jose. First, we set aside a dozen parcels for office development, including four potentially one-million-square-foot office sites suitable for corporate headquarters. By the end of the 1980s, we had about 5 million square feet of office space downtown. Second, we planned and built downtown retail space in the Pavilion Shops complex and the neighboring San Antonio historic district, including a large number of 30,000- to 200,000-square-foot sites for department stores, supermarkets, and destination retailers. Third, we included a focus on downtown housing: twenty development sites targeted for 8,000 new housing units, plus a related 15,000 housing units planned along the city's major transportation corridors within the existing urban-service line around the city—to quote Colonel Qaddafi, "a line of death" beyond which no new housing could go. Overall, our plan calls for 45,000 new housing units citywide during the 1990s. We were not "no growth"; we favored thoughtful growth.

We had to make sure that we were the ones making the decisions, not the developers, since that is what created our problems in the 1950s and 1960s. We had watched our predecessors and our peers in other cities cave in to the demands of developers quick to cry outrage at any imposition of city control over their projects. Facing the threat that a developer might pull out, mayors and councils and planners usually give in. "Civic officials rarely call such bluffs," says William Whyte, "especially when the city finances are in straits, as they so often are. A city in that stance is a developer's city, and a great many in the United States are exactly that."[112]

Winning the Battles

No single assessment can detail who wields power in cities. What an observer can do is thoughtfully assess the strength of the forces arrayed on either side of a particular issue, at a particular time. In the 1980s and early 1990s in San Jose, redevelopment was the single most predictably contentious political issue in town. As mayor, I was battling against the status quo, at least as it has traditionally been defined in cities. In 1987, Stephen Elkin wrote of American cities in general that "the battlefield of city politics is not flat but is tilted toward an alliance of public officials and land interests. Those who want it any other way must push uphill, whereas such an alliance only has to sit still and wait until the task of pushing the rock up the incline grows too burdensome. This alliance is the status quo."[113]

I was pushing uphill, attempting to recast the way the growth machine had been defined for our city. Certainly there were strong opponents, development and real estate interests primarily, and the debate still rages in a fight I took up a dozen years ago. Housing or industrial development—which to choose? Instant gratification or long-term investment; the choice is ages old. Our general plan allowed another 11,000 homes to be built inside the line we drew in 1983, and the city should not plan one more anywhere else until most of those are constructed and occupied by taxpayers. In our southern reserve, the Coyote Valley, San Jose should allow no housing to be built until industry continues its inevitable expansion there, providing industrial taxes to the city's coffers to pay for the police and libraries those new homeowners will demand. The line still holds.

Other cities are trying to hold a line against rapacious development. Sacramento lost the battle in a massive rezoning of land for development interests in the mid-Eighties, when the lure of an NBA franchise and an arena was put on the ballot against the mayor's wishes. In San Diego, a heated political debate is being waged over the "North City Future Urbanizing Area," a 12,000-acre preserve representing the largest privately held undeveloped area in the city. Developers have pressured the city council to rezone the area from "future urbanizing" to "planned urbanizing," which would remove a requirement for voter approval of any building project. The area had been set aside in 1979 at the height of San Diego's building boom, but not everyone has the gift of vision. A developer who owns one-third of the acreage told a journalist, "We find zoning means nothing, and it is all up for grabs politically." In a *New*

York Times piece on the story, the reporter opened with a great pun: "Next month, the City Council will consider a measure that could pave the way to construction. . . ."[114]

San Jose's downtown focus would probably not have succeeded had we focused only on building shiny projects, a criticism that was lobbed frequently by self-appointed "neighborhood activists," but without the virtue of being correct. The activists charged that neighborhoods were being shortchanged, but they never would acknowledge the previous "underground subsidies" of old San Jose in highways, sewers, and services. We made sure on our watch to support all the various pieces of a strong community, not just houses. Redevelopment funds paid the bulk of construction costs for a new fire station in 1992, which also became the home of our Hazardous Materials Incident Team, designed for any emergencies in the new industries we beckoned to San Jose. Early in the 1990s, the CityTeam organization opened its new facilities for the homeless, built with $11.6 million in city redevelopment funds. The money allowed CityTeam to double the number of beds available each night for the homeless and recovering addicts and to plan another new facility specifically for female addicts and their children. Still in the design phase is the Mexican Heritage Gardens, a project supported by redevelopment funds featuring a heritage library, classrooms, senior housing, and a large plaza and performance center for cultural events. Although controversial and mired in fights with the local school district over turf, it could be a fine project.

No mayor can rebuild anything larger than a shed single-handedly. The three allies the mayor's office relied upon the most in our decade of renaissance were the mandate of the citizens, Frank Taylor's Redevelopment Agency, and Rob Elder's editorial page at the *Mercury News*, backed up by the gray eminence of publisher Tony Ridder. Frank constantly weathered criticism from outside second-guessers about his leadership style. Facing a charge by the city auditor that the agency lacked accountability and was too headstrong, Frank replied in the press: "I have to improvise every deal with a developer. People have said 'slow down' for eight and a half years. I haven't and don't intend to."[115]

Rob Elder, just as forthright in his support for the path San Jose had chosen, played a critical role in all our success as editorial page editor. In any city, the local media tend to play a role as active growth proponents. In our city, they did so thoughtfully. The *Mercury News* once ranked Elder among the ten most powerful people in San Jose, in a 1990 review of power in the city. His own paper reported that "year after year, the editorial page has cheered Tom McEnery, endorsing virtually every project that the San Jose Mayor has advocated and every candidate whom he has backed. Other city officials say the support has greatly enhanced McEnery's influence." It did indeed. Elder particularly touted the Guadalupe River Park, the Tech Museum, and regional government, the last an idea whose time may never come. He explains his role: "Joan Didion says the *L.A. Times* more or less created the idea of Southern California as a region. I think what we're trying to do here is something very parallel to that. We want to shape the way people think about this area."[116] He did, and it has helped tremendously to make San Jose a better place for the next generation.

The loudest complaints over our rebuilding projects were those I had least patience for: arguments that the tax revenue flowing into redevelopment coffers could have been better used to fund traditional general-fund operations or should have been funneled to counties instead. My response was always the same: I had made my priorities known to the voters, set them in stone for all to study and judge in the most open process known on earth—the democratic election. When I won, I carried a mandate. Not a personal one, but a mandate for my ideas. When I won reelection by an even larger margin after four activist years of carrying out my agenda, I sealed that bond.

The battles will continue, of course. The redevelopment agenda is far from over. The 5-Year Capital Program from 1993 to 1997 anticipates spending another $572 million overall. By law, $85 million will go to the 20 percent of housing subsidies that are set aside for low- and middle-income housing, and $86 million will go for operating costs for ongoing projects and the work of the Redevelopment Agency itself. That leaves a pool in the neighborhood of $400 million that the city of San Jose has to invest in its own future. The money is theoretically already budgeted, of course, but then, the agency's board of directors is actually the city council. Politics will inevitably rear its head, and my hope is it will not be Quasimodo.

The Big Score

Our successes did not go unnoticed. My staff always put on top of my "in" pile the clips from the national media. In the fall of 1990, in the waning days of my second term, the kind of coverage you never can buy appeared in *USA Today*. An article entitled "Best-kept Secret in U.S.A. Is Out" featured our city as an exemplar of a new wave of cities of choice, "offering a future, and a safe and pleasant place to live."[117] A year later (exactly 365 days later, oddly enough), when I was out of office and back to the exalted masses, my eye caught a very gratifying *San Francisco Chronicle* column. Under the heading, "A Downtown That Came Back to Life," it proceeded to sum up exactly what we had been hoping to achieve. Praising "a project that took tons of money and a great deal of political energy and shows it," the columnist pointedly compared us to his own San Francisco, reminding our neighbors to the north that we had created "a handsome, sparkling clean centerpiece for a city that thinks of itself as the focal point of the Bay Area."

I enjoyed that kind of approbation, particularly after fighting media battles and municipal anonymity for a decade. But more gratifying was when other cities seemed to sit up and take notice. Cupertino, our Silicon Valley neighbor and the headquarters of Apple Computer, began to stir in the 1990s and notice that it had no heart, no center, no soul. Local critics have condemned the city for "drifting its way into the future," in comparison to San Jose's rigorous attempt to plan creatively. Cupertino is finally coming around and is now considering an interesting proposal to convert the suburban drag of Stevens Creek Boulevard into a European-style grand boulevard, lined with trees and linking shops with housing clusters and pedestrian preserves. Across the bay, Concord has begun to face the same dilemma San Jose did in the 1970s. The city is a sprawling suburb that has grown to become the largest city in Contra Costa County, with 115,000 people. In one of the fastest-growing counties in the United States, Concord is only now beginning to face the difficulty of creating a traditional downtown for itself, though one never existed there before. A new long-term development plan that will last the rest of the decade features plans for a downtown events center for the performing arts, office complexes and retail space, a ten-screen movie theater, and high-density downtown housing linked to the BART station. The project hopes to mix tens of millions of dollars in public redevelopment funds with millions more in private investment.[118] People want to invest in what so many have cast to the wind: a living downtown.

We can only guess at the ultimate look of other new cities as the millennium approaches. The second half of the 1990s will not feature the building boom of the 1980s. Los Angeles built itself a huge skyline with tens of millions of square feet in office space in the 1980s, but entire floors sit vacant in those gleaming towers as the city suffers one of the highest vacancy rates in the country. (Compare L.A.'s 28.4 percent in early 1993 to San Jose's 16.3 percent and San Francisco's 12.8 percent.) In Chicago, which underwent the same imbalanced boom in office construction, work was stalled in 1993 on some twenty large towers that already had their approvals but no tenants in sight. One of the buildings planned—but with no construction starting date—is a 125-story skyscraper claiming the title as the world's tallest building.[119] If you believe that, as Art Buchwald says, I have a savings and loan to sell you.

San Jose does not believe in that particular ambition. That is not our city, and our backward planning should keep us from such pitfalls. There are still many other things to do in rebuilding the heart, enough to keep San Joseans occupied productively into the next century. Our new Downtown 2010 Plan was conceived at the dawn of the 1990s by a 34-member citizens' group. The Downtown Working Review Committee was led by Susan Hammer, now mayor, and Frank Fiscalini, the closest thing this city has to an elder statesman. In 1992, at nearly seventy, Frank was elected to the city council, his first political office, after a career that had taken him from star baseball player at Santa Clara University to superintendent of the East Side Union High School District, one of the largest in the country. The Downtown 2010 report follows in the tradition of the Horizon 2000 plan a decade before, as our city continues to imagine a future and plan for it. We still need more housing, particularly exciting downtown urban housing. We need a project on Communications Hill, a major in-fill site, and we will need development along our major transit corridors. We are still intent on attracting major department stores back downtown, to match the days of Hart's when I was a kid. That goal will take awhile. And our dream remains for more corporate headquarters in the heart of the city, symbolizing our capital status for Silicon Valley. All that will come. And someday soon we will move city hall back downtown, completing the broken circle.

As mayor, I received credit for the vision we began to reclaim.[120] Much of that credit actually belongs elsewhere. If anything, my role was only an extension of the efforts my family made in restoring San Pedro Square years ago. We knew the result we wanted; we planned what needed to be done, and we set about accomplishing it. Art Lund, a good friend, lawyer, and local powerhouse, was once quoted in the *Mercury News* on my role in rebuilding downtown. "McEnery," Art observed, "was able to say, 'Damn it—run the train down the track!' Which is what a business person does." I do enjoy being the engineer.

7

PUBLIC ENTREPRENEURS

> Instead of lamenting the absurdity of the world,
> let us try to transform the corner of it into which we were born.
> —Andre Malraux

If the business of America is business, then government needs its own refresher course in Business 101. The wrong way to assist local economic development is to follow Washington's lead on "urban policy." The right way is for localities to set off independently in search of opportunity, growth, and commerce.

The traditional arm's-length distance between the local public sector and private enterprise is driven by mostly fear or ideology trickling down from a generation of federal planners. Robert Wood, HUD secretary during Lyndon Johnson's Great Society, recently renewed the suspicious attitude in an article, complaining that "at least since the Civil War the private sector has built our cities, determined the location of jobs and households, and either covertly or overtly determined public urban policy."[121] Too many municipal apologists stop there, laying bare their antipathy toward business involvement in shaping public policy.

The new city-state attempts to recast the relationship so that city hall is no longer a junior partner but the leading edge in the process, able to harness the prodigious power and energy of the private sector—this time, to the city's own purposes. The private sector, as the invisible hand of the market, may play a key role in determining a city's future, but leaders can and must identify options, declare a vision for the city's future, define the steps that get us from here to there, and then lead people along that path.

Mayors have counted too long on "the market" alone, lazily waiting for their ship to come in. They need swimming lessons.

Our job at the local level is to take advantage of business, not to serve at its mercy. The market can cause great damage in a vacuum. Growing cities could build housing from here to the horizon, until dragged down by the cost of servicing those new residents. In the real world, we cannot wait on the possibility that the right kind of renewal will occur just because developers and companies wish to do the right thing.

Redefine the Growth Machine

City-states, if bold, can take the traditional concept of the urban growth machine and make it their own. Cities have always had a primary interest in promoting economic growth, but for years urban "experts" tried to tear down this assertion, arguing that the benefits of economic development are only narrowly distributed. They have always been able to make a case that sounds convincing by citing increasing income inequality and the proliferation of social problems.[122]

The city-state is now redefining the growth machine. It includes all the diverse elements of a city, together under the leadership of city hall and therefore within the control of the democratic process. Popular will, expressed through elected representatives, now drives the growth machine. A city can still view growth as beneficial, just as developers and business interests have for decades. Now, though, the discussion will represent a wider spectrum of diverse but interlocking interests, a coalition coordinated by government—a coalition that works for the community's interests.

The 1980s were a boom decade for partnerships in city building between private developers and public officials. The first stirrings of the new growth machine saw entrepreneurial mayors realizing that the driving forces of settlement and development were still in the private sector. The results were developments like Boston's Faneuil Hall, Chicago's Water Tower Place, Baltimore's Inner Harbor, and Atlanta's Underground. None of them would have happened without their city halls soliciting partnerships with private developers in the planning, financing, and building process. But mayors had to be active to make it happen. "Urban renewal" became a more flexible concept, and mayors and city councils began to operate more flexibly. Some have even said, admiringly, that mayors began to act like developers themselves—willing to negotiate special deals to suit each project, spending money before a deal was completed.[123]

As cities began to offer more enticing and elaborate aid packages, they also became more involved in project supervision. More money meant more control. To handle development negotiations successfully, city governments had to create new organizations and hire people with business and technical skills. Local governments weren't satisfied any longer in simply regulating deals; citizens demanded more and deserved more. In San Jose, we relied on our small but focused Redevelopment Agency staff and on a new breed of energetic staffers in city hall. We set up ad hoc groups where needed. The new flexibility we brought to the table allowed for more creative problem solving and greater speed, traits we had to learn from the private sector.

At the same time we removed roadblocks, though, we had to make sure that we were not letting the private sector off the hook too easily. Familiarity with the business sector can help local government know how hard to push. Over two decades, we have developed a sophisticated program of charging impact fees to help finance our planned growth. In 1972, we began imposing property conveyance and construction taxes, which financed all the urban services our new residential population demanded: parks, libraries, fire stations, and other public works. Today, the construction tax is $150 for each single-family dwelling and $75 for each unit in a multiple-family building. By the early 1980s, we knew that we had not encouraged developers to make their full contribution for the housing they were building, and we raised the sewer-connection fee from $23 per single-family dwelling to $780 per house, with similar increases for commercial buildings. No more unconscious, unseen subsidies lacking formal authorization. We now have a full program of development impact fees that we charge any developer, including commercial and residential construction taxes, conveyance taxes, sewage connection and storm-drain connection fees. Individual developers often complain, loud and long, about these charges, but they are designed to finance the 100,000 more residents we will add during the 1990s and to influence a "pay as you grow" mentality among city planners, developers, and the citizenry at large.[124] The bottom line, of course, is that this civic virtue also brings in to the city somewhere between $30 million and $50 million a year (depending on the general state of the economy in a given year). This revenue helps to keep the community at large from shouldering the burden of growth alone.

Not every city has the good fortune, the legal statute, or, more fundamentally, the political will to impose such impact fees. In Florida, for instance, state law severely restricts the ability of local governments to raise revenues this way. Orlando's mayor Bill Frederick responded by promoting the use of "enterprise funds," which are quasi-autonomous agencies that have to generate their own revenues, which are then turned toward public buildings or projects: a new airport, sewage treatment plant, and basketball arena all in the last decade.[125] It is the time-honored method used at San Jose's airport and its sewage plant. The latter began with an 1880s brick sewer line to the outreaches of the bay, ten times the diameter we needed then. Some early mayor had either great vision or a brick contractor for a son-in-law.

Cities using their own devices are able to innovate some interesting arrangements. Los Angeles is planning a $14 million face-lift of downtown's oldest park, Pershing Square, which is now a concrete eyesore. The city is using the same talented Mexican architect who designed San Jose's Children's Discovery Museum, Ricardo Legoretta, but the financing arrangement is unlike one ever attempted here. While the Community Redevelopment Agency (CRA) will be contributing $6 million, the remainder will be picked up by surrounding building owners through an "elective tax district," targeting revenues specifically to the Pershing Square project.[126]

Some cities are coping well in their efforts to harness the growth machine to a unitary purpose. Atlanta is cited by an observer as a town "still held together by interacting government and business elites."[127] But a city can be hostage to its businesses as well. I have already mentioned Seattle as an example of how directly a city's fortunes and quality of life can be tied to the fate of a single company. Seattle enjoyed glowing media attention in the late 1980s and early 1990s—the *San Francisco Chronicle* headlined it "A City That Knows How: It has its problems, and it is solving them." As that article pointed out, "while Boeing [the region's largest employer] continues to do well, so does the city. . . . Boeing's profits were in the billions last year."[128] Unfortunately, in 1992 and 1993, Boeing's bubble burst, with tens of thousands of layoffs sending a shock wave through the city's economy and abruptly altering the long-term projection of municipal health.

Acting in the business environment, city officials learn the harsh lessons of the real world. Ed Koch came to office after New York City's fiscal crisis of 1975, caused in part by the city's overly generous policies on welfare, housing, and social services it couldn't afford. Under Koch, it was a different city. "The main job of government," declared newly elected Mayor Koch in 1978, "is to create a climate in which private business can expand in the city to provide jobs and profit. It's not the function of government to create jobs on the public payroll."[129] Tact was not Ed's strong point. I like that. When Koch visited San Jose in 1991, I asked what impression he had of our city. "Oh, nothing, really . . . hmm . . . no, no impression at all." Quite a flatterer, that Koch. His anti-suburban bias once cost him the governorship, when he blurted out during the 1982 campaign: "Suburban life is a joke." The lesson seems to have been lost, but at least he still speaks his mind.

Focus on the Bottom Line

Some mayors deserve gold stars for adapting to private-sector approaches. When the book Reinventing Government *was just a gleam in a Visalia city manager's eye, long before it became the book every government official quoted but never read, Richie Daley in Chicago was running his government with a passion for innovation. Daley's focus on the bottom line has made him a national leader in the privatization movement.*

He has explained to me his evangelical belief in spinning off government services that the private sector can do better and cheaper. Chicago's drug treatment program has been entirely contracted out to private agencies, and, according to Daley, "the results were spectacular." No city employees lost jobs—they either went to work for the agencies or were transferred to other city work. He aggressively rattles off the list of services now being privatized: "sewer construction, repair, and cleaning; towing of abandoned cars; janitorial services; parking ticket adjudication; maintenance and management of Department of Housing properties; servicing of housing loans; management of the city's central library; vehicle maintenance for new garbage trucks and street sweepers; curbs and gutter construction work; and custodial services at police headquarters."

The only job on the city payroll that may be safe from privatizing is the one in Daley's office. If he succeeds in his mission, with a government smaller in size but greater in performance, then no one would begrudge him his zeal. Other American cities would be better off studying his successes. In fact, I can think of a few towns that might benefit if their mayor's position was contracted out. I will name no names.

Enterprise Zones

Harry Truman once said, "When a man starts telling me how religious he is, I reach for my wallet." There are many devoutly touted "ideas" for reviving the American city, but I am suspicious of trendy terms and the attention they receive until I hear the experienced testimony of a real, live mayor who has tried them out. "Enterprise zones"—the trendy buzzword of the 1990s for urban renewal—are a case in point. I would normally ignore the ethereal realm in which the idea has been debated. One thing, though: we have already established an enterprise zone in San Jose. With a lot more empirical data than Lincoln Steffens had, I can say I have seen the future, and it works.

In some ways, the concept behind enterprise zones is not new at all. Cities have always used variants of creative financing, ad hoc approaches for "incentivizing" business formation. (I do not like words like "prioritize," and "incentivize" is a ghastly word for a simple concept that works.) In the mid-1970s, ailing city governments could not afford to give cash handouts to retailers and developers to encourage new business, nor could they get the feds to do all of it. Instead, they offered other incentives: tax abatements and loans to be paid at below-market rates or on deferred schedules. They were beginning to learn the chief disadvantage of federal funds: the loss of local control.

The first use of the term "enterprise zone" came from Great Britain. It originated in the minds of some academics, Cambridge dons no less. There were eleven such zones established under Margaret Thatcher's iron economics in the late 1970s. Companies operating within specially designated districts got generous perks, including a development land tax abatement, less bureaucratic oversight, and fewer planning restrictions. The programs worked, to turning around deteriorating urban dock and warehouse areas with a burst of laissez-faire capitalism.

By some accounts, San Jose did in fact have the first local enterprise zone in the nation. In 1981, Ronald Reagan was in his first year in the White House, and I was on the city council. Conservative business thought was ascendant. The country was embarking on the longest peacetime economic expansion in national history, sparked in part by supply-side economics. Although the long-term impact of Reaganomics would be far less salutary, I was determined to use any and all tools we could on a local level to advance our economy and begin the downtown revitalization. I didn't care where an idea came from or about its partisan ideological pedigree. I asked if it was good for San Jose.

That is how an enterprise zone was introduced to our city. I proposed to the city council in 1981 a downtown central incentive zone, four square miles that we soon rechristened the San Jose Enterprise Zone. The city offered a number of attractive inducements, focusing on exemptions from business license fees, utility taxes, and large sewer-connection fees. Later, we added a small business loan program and employment and training referral services.

The idea was sound, the benefits were appealing, and I had no trouble persuading pragmatic colleagues to pass the measure. Within three weeks, San Jose had one of the nation's first operating local enterprise zones.

Few cities were as proactive as San Jose. Florida instituted a state incentives program in 1980 responding to Miami's Liberty City riots. The state tried to attract business back to burned-out areas by offering some of the urban-renewal incentives we now associate with enterprise zones. Only later when the term became a buzzword did state officials slap that label on it. Connecticut launched the first officially named "state enterprise zones" in October 1982 when it dedicated six cities—Bridgeport, Hartford, New Britain, New London, New Haven, Norwalk. Their primary inducements: a five-year, 80 percent abatement of local property taxes, a ten-year, 50 percent credit on state corporate business taxes, exemptions from state real estate conveyance taxes and sales taxes on machinery replacements, plus a $1,500 grant for each new job created (as long as 30 percent of all hires were local).[130]

Today, Connecticut has a total of eleven zones, but the state is learning that an enterprise zone is no magic bullet. Bridgeport recently gained national attention not for its zone but for declaring municipal bankruptcy in 1991.

From California, however, often the pioneer state in new ideas, came only silence. Sacramento's reluctance to experiment with enterprise zones—even to test the concept in pilot areas—was regrettable, given the fact that in San Jose we were already finding vigorous success with our local version. In the fall of 1981, two Republican members of the California state assembly attempted to introduce enterprise zones into California. Their efforts went for naught, though, as naysayers defeated their proposal. Liberal Assembly Democrats opposed the experiment, although they were proven wrong. Partisanship would continue to murder good ideas, strangling them in the cradle.

Surprisingly, though, even Republicans were too wedded to the status quo to consider the utility of the idea. Pete Wilson, then mayor of San Diego, joined the lineup of pessimists who testified against the proposal before the Assembly Economic Development Committee. To the committee, Wilson gave a stunningly bureaucratic argument on enterprise zones: "It's certainly true that various forms of over-regulation, if eliminated, will be a significant incentive. Whether that will be sufficient to produce a really significant response, I question."[131] Pete Wilson's wishy-washy, timidly conservative approach helped to doom enterprise zones in the state for years, and his 1981 testimony presaged the lack of vision for the state he has shown in the governor's office the last few years. No wonder economic vitality is unknown in California anywhere above the local level.

By the mid-1980s, new manufacturing companies were being started in Silicon Valley at the rate of three per week, with fifteen other kinds of companies being born each week as well. We intended to make sure we got our fair share—more than our fair share, in fact. In focusing on downtown and industrial zones, I was following the Silicon Valley entrepreneurial code, developed, surprisingly enough, two centuries ago by the French economist J. B. Say. He coined the term "entrepreneur," defining it as follows: "The entrepreneur shifts economic resources out of an area of lower productivity and into an area of higher productivity and greater yield." That is exactly what we were doing on a large scale in the city, trying to halt sprawl and its subsidies and provide a tax base for the kind of city our people wanted and deserved. With our enterprise zone, we were creating the basis for new areas of higher productivity and yield.

By the beginning of 1993, our enterprise zone had netted $9 million in direct benefits to the city of San Jose, not counting the much higher indirect contributions to city coffers and overall synergy of the economic engine of the city. We are using that success to benefit other areas, too. Since eight of ten San Jose jobs are in small businesses, it has always been important to nurture those as well. In 1989, the city created the Enterprise Zone Loan Program to provide critical small loans (which banks normally avoid making) to small businesses located within the enterprise zone. By 1992, the EZLP had worked with sixteen participating banks to arrange $2.4 million in small business loans.[132]

Avoid the Twilight Zones

Sacramento finally got around to forming an enterprise zone program in the late 1980s. Hidden in the California Office of Community and Local Development, the state program was begun in 1987 with ten designated zones, including San Jose—a belated tip of the hat to our early success. In the next five years, the program operated almost unnoticed, although by 1992 officials claimed credit for creating almost 25,000 jobs, according to the state Department of Commerce. When that figure surfaced, questions were raised. By the time San Francisco won one of ten more second-round designations in 1991, the press was skeptical of the effectiveness of the state zone. A *San Francisco Examiner* business reporter wrote that the "costs and benefits of the 4-year-old program remain hazy." The state auditor general has charged that the California Commerce Department had no idea how to monitor the impact, successful or not, of the program. "They had somebody drive around," the auditor general laughed, "and say, 'There's a new building,' 'There's a for-sale sign,' 'There's a help-wanted sign that wasn't there before.'"[133] I am a big fan of keeping in close touch with the community, with life in the streets, but for a state program monitoring the impact of millions of dollars of tax cuts, this was ridiculous.

California has still officially designated only twenty state enterprise zones; for a long time San Jose's was the only one in the Bay Area. Oakland, possibly the Bay Area city most in need of urgent economic life support, had its application turned down for zone status in 1991.

Our state-designated zone in San Jose now covers ten square miles and includes the downtown central business district. Businesses within any state zone, whether established or just moved in, are eligible for state incentives including hiring-tax credits and sales-tax credits for new machinery and equipment; a fifteen-year net operating loss carryover; business expense deductions for certain property purchased for use in the zone; and tax-free returns on investments.

Overall, I would judge that the state enterprise zone designation has been helpful for San Jose. I am happy to see any effort made to support our own drive for economic health. The question now arises of how long American cities must wait for the federal government to take meaningful action in supporting new local enterprise. Federal zones are necessary because most business taxes are paid to the federal government, of course. We waited for years for the federal government to establish federal zones so that we could match our city and state zone borders to the federal ones, thus multiplying the impact and really focusing our energies. That federal help, like the cavalry reserves to Custer, never came.

The federal government was completely inactive on enterprise zones, despite a decade of lip service, during the Reagan and Bush administrations. Jack Kemp proved unable as HUD secretary to back up his vision of using zones to make "America's cities models of entrepreneurial capitalism." Vision without the requisite implementation is not very helpful. Meanwhile, thirty-five states and hundreds of cities were establishing their own. By my count, as of 1993, there were some 4,270 enterprise zones across the country. Estimates of the employment they have created range up to 890,000 jobs, with an estimated $55 billion in private investments spurred by the public incentives.[134]

The federal attempt came only in response to the Los Angeles riots of April 1992. President Bush's first proposal, immediately after the disturbances, envisioned 300 urban enterprise zones featuring capital-gains tax breaks and other incentives. That was too good to last.

Along the way, as spring turned to summer and summer to fall, the bill picked up a variety of tax-cut and tax-hike amendments, tacked on by individual congressional members, until the total weight of the bill dwarfed the amounts of aid envisioned in the enterprise zone provisions. It was classic Potomac mania. Both Republicans and Democrats added on provisions, seemingly indifferent to the original intent of the program: helping the people of inner-city America. The episode seems to contradict the "rolling stone gathers no moss" theory. The stone became an invisible blob of green.

Once the bill emerged from a Senate committee, though, it allowed for only 25 zones. Jack Kemp intervened and pushed senators to raise the number to 125 zones, but on the other side of Congress, the House version designated 50 enterprise zones, only half of which would be urban. The rest were designated to be rural, as a sop to members of Congress not from urban areas. The major attraction of the bill was an employment credit of 15 percent on employees, but only up to a maximum of $3,000 per employee annually, and a 50 percent exclusion for capital gains from new zone investments held for more than five years. One interesting note: the absurd federal criteria for zone creation in the bill would not even have included south-central Los Angeles or any section of the second largest city in the country. Legislative staffers and special-interest lobbyists had set the criteria to favor Eastern city patterns of urban blight, ignoring by definition California cities, which demographically have developed differently but present no less economic need.[135]

By the time the conference committee had finished its patching work, and after the pork-barrel process finished with it, it resembled more a classic public-job-creation scheme rather than a private-enterprise-zone approach. In November, President Bush used the thirty-seventh and next-to-last veto of his administration to kill the $27 billion "urban aid bill." He said at the time, "The original focus of the bill—to help revitalize America's inner cities—has been lost in a blizzard of special interest pleadings." Among the special interests he failed to mention were Republican lobbyists behind an expanded tax break for IRA accounts. Bush

also forgot to mention that he had tried and failed to get even more un-
related items added to the bill in the Senate.[136]

We must not blame only George Bush and his administration, as the
bills were created in Congress. Our bright members of Congress were responsible for the idiotic debates over criteria and political pork barreling
that delayed and denied any help to south-central L.A. Meanwhile, the
debate continues on the national scene over the utility of enterprise
zones. Jack Kemp and his predecessor Robert Wood squared off in the
pages of the *New York Times* in July 1992. Wood asserted that existing
zones in almost forty states had found "disappointing results" and criticized them for springing "from the loosely woven tapestry of ideology
where aspirations lose touch with reality." Kemp countered that decades
of Great Society/New Deal approaches had shown that "we know government doesn't create jobs, entrepreneurs do."[137]

We are finally at the point where something might happen. President
Clinton began his administration with a commitment to enact a federal
zones program, and Henry Cisneros at HUD is a strong proponent. Henry
established two zones himself in San Antonio, creating some 1,200 jobs
in the process. A real mayor always knows. Governors may not have such
firsthand knowledge of the details, though, and some critics have
ridiculed Clinton's own Arkansas enterprise-zone performance as marked
by more quantity than quality. The 800 zones designated by the state of
Arkansas exist mostly in the minds of bureaucrats and on maps in their
offices. The state director acknowledges the patronage tint to the system,
which has zones, lots of zones, in each of the seventy-five counties: "We
got 'em going across bodies of water—everywhere!"[138] As soon as
Clinton began planning his federal zone plan in early 1993, gnomes in
the bureaucracy immediately set about squabbling over definitions, regulatory minutiae, and the ultimate scope of the program.[139] The president's plan has evolved into a broader scheme of "empowerment zones" as
well, and some elements seem more designed for political correctness
than job creation.

We have answered the debate for ourselves, ignoring ideology. I realize that local government's efforts are only an additional fillip to efforts
that the private sector makes with its own investments. In 1992, Silicon
Valley's twenty-five largest venture capital firms invested around $700
million in high-tech companies, fully a third more than was invested
during the year before.[140] The bottom line, though, convinces me that
enterprise zones are an important tool for any city committed to smart
competition in the battle to influence the decisions of industry.

Redevelopment Financing and Bonding

I realize that a detailed discussion of municipal financing can be a dry subject. Most citizens and too many mayors leave the details to others and miss an important point. The money is where the action is. Control and use of a city's money are holy grails for politicians. In boomtowns like San Jose, "redevelopment" is the pot of gold.

The San Jose Redevelopment Agency has quite a simple mission: to combine public entrepreneurship with private investment to create an attractive environment for economic development in the area that the state and city designate as "blighted"—an unfortunate, inaccurate, and frightful term. The agency builds infrastructure: roads, bridges, and the unglamorous but essential pipe-laying side of the city. Redevelopment finances public building projects, and it also works with private developers on selected projects ultimately designed to rehabilitate the city's declining areas.

Our overall redevelopment strategy has been to allow downtown to exploit suburbia after all the years when the advantage was tilted the other way. George Bernard Shaw once said that when you rob Peter to pay Paul, you will always have the support of Paul. Our Paul was an impoverished, dying downtown, and Peter could well afford the contribution. The Redevelopment Agency pays for its projects with "tax increment financing," a method whose only controversy appears to be the jealousy it arouses among those not sharing in the revenue. Tax increment financing freezes the assessed value of property in a designated redevelopment area at a certain point. From that moment on, that baseline amount of property taxes continues to go to the city, county, school districts, and other tax-supported agencies, just as it always has. The *increased* valuation year by year, the "tax increments" above the frozen baseline, funnel into the Redevelopment Agency. As the designated area gets redeveloped and becomes more valuable, the tax increments flowing into redevelopment coffers increase. It may not literally be a magic pot of gold, but the dynamic can be very powerful if the right decisions are made on property redevelopment. We strived to make the right decisions.

The tax increments rely on two industrial areas in San Jose, one booming and one simmering, that have contributed most of the agency's wealth and on eight other much smaller downtown areas that are net beneficiaries at least for a time. Altogether, the redevelopment areas total some 7,500 acres, about 7 percent of the city as a whole. As I noted before, in 1980 we were granted permission by the state to pool those ten areas into one revenue stream, to be used anywhere in the redevelopment areas. The agency also issues bonds, which are later retired with the additional property tax revenues from new developments. The bonds are not a debt of the city or the county, but people are still sometimes wary of the agency's bonded indebtedness. One point to keep in mind is that we sell the bonds publicly to private investors, which ensures an ultimate "reality check" for city officials. They have to be attentive to business concerns, since business investment is the financial cushion keeping the city afloat. I learned that lesson very well in 1984, in the city's bond-loss episode.

The tax increment policy has been vindicated by its success. The combined tax increment collected each year from the two industrial parks, Rincon and Edenvale, has increased 230 percent from $27.3 million in 1984 to $64.3 million in 1992.[141] In the policy's first ten years, 1980 to 1990, the total amount contributed to redevelopment from the two industrial parks has been approximately $390 million, while the downtown area itself contributed about $30 million. With the additional funds from bonding, and with significant public-private partnerships, the machinery was a tool that we used for a textbook case of successful redevelopment.

Today, our two redevelopment industrial parks are humming engines for the capital of Silicon Valley. Rincon de Los Esteros is considered one of the most successful industrial parks in the country and a premier location for high-tech industry. We set aside 4,669 acres of prime industrial land in North San Jose back in 1977 and in the next fifteen years continued to improve the area's transportation, housing, and commercial amenities. By 1993, Rincon was booming with over 1,700 employers and some 77,000 employees. Companies like Hewlett-Packard, Watkins-Johnson, and Rolm led the way, followed by Hitachi Instruments, Toshiba America (relocated from Irvine in Southern California), Canon, and Zuken America. All were attracted to Rincon manufacturing sites, as well as homegrown Valley companies like Mentor Graphics, Conner Peripherals, and Cadence Design Systems. Sony America opened a 500,000-square-foot operations center at Rincon in 1993, and other companies have recently purchased land with plans to build in the future.

The Edenvale/Silicon Valley South industrial park—2,300 acres of prime industrial land in a pastoral campus setting at the foot of the Diablo hills—is truly an investment in our future. It remains one of the only large preserves of available industrial land in the Valley. Since 1977, the Redevelopment Agency has used some $37 million for improvements, including infrastructure enhancements like the new $5 million, six-lane Fontanoso Bridge, connecting the area with Highway 101 and with residential areas. The new light-rail system directly connects Edenvale with the northern industrial areas, including the Rincon park, as well as with residential neighborhoods and connecting transit systems. Edenvale currently supports almost 20,000 employees and some 175 employers, including IBM, Litton Applied Technology, Xerox Engineering Systems, and Cybernex. Because of the foresight we held to a decade ago, it has the space and the infrastructure to attract many more.

Setting aside Edenvale and the nearby Coyote Valley for industrial development required more than a little political will in the early 1980s, since those rolling plains were eyed like raw meat by developers. That crowd had been used to decades of unfettered expansion and saw Coyote and Edenvale as just the next meadow to be carved up into single-family lots for commuters. They believed that political principles would wilt in the San Jose sun—as always.

San Jose would have remained a bedroom community had we not taken a stand in favor of economic development *first*, before the homes were built. The Horizon 2000 task force in 1983 had concluded that we suffered a major deficiency in our planning strategy. While we had thousands of acres of vacant industrial land, very little of it was planned for large-acreage parcels. Yet the task force found that the expansion plans of local Valley companies would require sites of at least twenty-five acres, and preferably fifty acres or more. Following the recommendations of the task force's report, we determined to set aside areas in our southern reaches to provide a solid foundation for bold, diversified development *in the future*, without compromising the existing levels of city services within the "urban service area" where people live now. Planning and zoning controls for Edenvale and Coyote Valley, our areas of future focus, were set to ensure a high-quality, campus-style setting for larger sites. We determined that no residential development would be allowed in Coyote until the jobs had arrived there first, jobs and industrial development that would provide the taxes to pay for services to new homes. We pulled back from the fringe to the center.

Oops! The Bond Loss

Only in pulp fiction, the movies, or on your deathbed do you normally get to see your life flash before your eyes. There is, on rare occasions, one other spot: in politics. I had that dubious distinction on that day in May 1984, when I first became aware of the great bond fiasco.

Looking back, it seems like such an easy affair to head off, so apparent in retrospect. One of my city council members, Jerry Estruth, a stockbroker by profession and a victim of the events, expressed it this way: "I've seen a lot of investors who start speculating, get the taste of very easy money, and they just get sucked in and never get out. My sense is that [the city bureaucrats involved] were very well-intentioned people who got into something very far over their heads." It was a charitable interpretation, to be sure.

They were also victims of the rapid growth in San Jose. One of the guilty parties had started his career at a counter issuing dog licenses, when San Jose was just a small, agricultural city. Exponential growth in the city put him in charge of a $500 million portfolio.

The chronology of events is now clear, and sickening. The city's investment managers, in some crazed attempt to earn larger returns on our money, had taken a monumental risk. They had speculated on the interest rates, borrowing against the city's assets, to obtain positions in the bond market. That move sank the city deep into illiquid investments. Using two instruments, a "repurchase agreement" and a "reverse repurchase agreement," the city basically built a huge investment pyramid that was in danger of collapsing at the slightest additional stress. The single most important factor in financial planning is a cash-flow analysis, and that was absent. Such an analysis would lead, as it always does, to the purchase of short-term securities so that temporarily idle funds are always ready to meet the city's needs, such as payroll, capital projects, and so on. While some municipalities hold their bonds and securities at an average maturity of less than a year, San Jose had allowed its portfolio to reach an astonishing seventeen years. Our money was tied up. And the very speculative reverse repurchase agreements allowed the city to raise cash for investments by selling bonds purchased from other agencies and then agreeing to buy them back at a set price on a future date. The city was also agreeing to pay interest at a higher rate than an investor could get elsewhere.

Reports from our Price Waterhouse audits for the previous three years had indicated no alarm. Only minor tightening in our portfolio was necessary, we were told. No big problem.

The tip of the iceberg appeared in early May 1984, when Deputy City Manager Les White discovered that we had invested and lost $2 million of redevelopment funds in Lion Capital, a government securities firm now bankrupt. Our city manager, Jerry Newfarmer, was diligently dealing with certain weak spots, but oblivious to problems in what was considered one of the superstar departments of San Jose. It fell to White to bring the urgency of the impending disaster to the attention of the city manager and his staff.

I was notified, in that dramatic afternoon rendezvous at St. James Park described in this book's introduction, and I called a few trusted council allies for advice. When the crisis management team was assembled, it included Newfarmer, White, a few of their deputies, Frank Taylor of Redevelopment, several outside experts including a team from Goldman Sachs, Jerry Estruth, Dean Munro of my staff, and me. We met through the weekend.

The toll was alarming. The city had on hand for the month of June about $600,000 to meet a demand for payroll and assorted expenses of nearly $20 million.

The speculative buying had topped off only at about $500 million. A good number of records for this massive portfolio had been kept on a desktop calendar—"the Snoopy calendar," as Estruth called it. It was beyond belief, a disaster choreographed by the Marx Brothers. I knew the feeling expressed some years later by the CEO of Allied Stores, who was so astonished after the hostile takeover of his company by Campeau that he felt he "had been broadsided by a trainload of clowns."

As I left city hall late on Sunday night, I was not thinking about whether I would survive politically. I was wondering whether this city of such massive potential would survive. Nothing in my public or business life had ever depressed me so or made me feel so personally responsible for hurting others. It was easily the worst moment of my career.

With San Jose's neighborhoods still dark early Monday morning, we met in time for the bond markets opening in New York City, three hours ahead of us. As agreed, the city hedged over $300 million, and then sold outright the remainder of its portfolio. On that sale of $108 million, we took a loss estimated at $60 million. A reporter asked me on the phone later for my feelings. I retreated into gallows humor, reaching for the line from the old Timex commercial: "Takes a licking, and keeps on ticking."

Titanic *Lesson (1): Don't Trust the Experts*

I do not believe the captain of the *Titanic* was ever again given a post on the high seas. In government, such a move is a regular occurrence. I chose not to fire the city manager, although our finance director, city treasurer, and investments officer were, of course, "terminated," to use a bureaucratic euphemism. They had wildly and insanely violated the prudent investment policy of the city; they were canned. Although I would never again place my total trust in the "professional" management of the city, I was not on a hunt for scapegoats. Newfarmer later proved to me how little he had learned by leaving on a month-long vacation to Europe within five weeks of the disaster and by resisting to the last the firing of one of his deputies responsible for financial management. Some people just never get it! Newfarmer would stay for a time, but it would be under a different form of government.

I decided then and there to convene a new city charter review committee to drastically change San Jose government into a "strong-mayor" form of government and shift the balance of power away from the appointed city manager. The responsibility, as well as the buck, should stop at the mayor's desk. Few among the public at large even knew who the city manager was. This anachronism dated back to my grandfather's days on the council and the Dutch Hamann era of paternalistic management from above. It had outlived its usefulness.

In 1986, the people agreed, approving several reforms in financial management. The charter revisions put budget power in the mayor's office and allowed the mayor singularly to select the manager, now more of a chief administrative officer, and to present that selection to the council. One of my outside advisers, Dean Marshall Burak of the San Jose State Business School, told me that the bond-loss episode "allowed San Jose to develop a strength it never would have developed." We turned the bond loss into an opportunity, to enshrine the strong-mayor concept that Pete Wilson had tried to implement in San Diego. Pete's attempt had failed; we succeeded, in a bloodless coup.

Titanic *Lesson (2)*: *Tell the Truth*

The second lesson I learned from this dismal episode was the value of the truth. Some politicians and administrators tell it only as a last resort. As I commented once on Sacramento politicians, their general mediocrity was varied only by cases of spectacular mendacity. "Learn or Die: Tell the Truth," should be a reminder on the desk of many an elected and unelected official. When I learned the full extent of the financial imbroglio, I immediately insisted that a reluctant Newfarmer accompany me to the editorial board of the *Mercury News* to explain how bad the situation was. The manager wanted to hunker down in the bunker and say nothing—a frightfully wrongheaded course of action. We went; we explained; we survived. We also granted what interviews we could with the local print and electronic media. The following week, I went on television with a live, prime-time speech on what the crisis meant to the citizens of San Jose. The truth was our best and only ally in those days.

I reflect back on those trying days with anger. I still feel my blood pressure rising when I write of the episode. Sixty million dollars. I felt as responsible back then as if a city truck had killed a child in a crosswalk. I had few restful nights that summer, and walking the beach in Santa Cruz offered little respite or relief. I had an enormous sense of letting down the people who believed in me, who relied on me. This, I promised, would never happen again. Nor would I ever again allow a group of un-elected bureaucrats to hold the type of unfettered power that was enjoyed in San Jose from the Hamann days to the Night of the Bankrupt Bonds. Just like the regal Bourbons of France's ancien régime, the green eyeshades had "learned nothing, and they had forgotten nothing." That was not to happen in San Jose. I would see to that. The meaningful reforms we instituted were made possible only by getting out the truth about the magnitude of the error.

A postscript: In September of 1984, San Jose filed suit against thirteen investment brokers and the accounting firm of Price Waterhouse, for violations of state and federal securities laws. We charged that the brokers had basically hoodwinked gullible money managers by recommending unsuitable securities. We won. In 1990, a federal court awarded San Jose nearly $20 million in damages.

Titanic *Lesson (3): Think Long Term*

The bond-loss episode details our experience with short-term thinking, and I learned a third important lesson. Although we did eventually receive much of it back in the settlement, the original money lost would have been enough to pay more than 100 police officers for ten years or to open twenty new branch libraries. We owed it to our citizens to make new hard choices for the long term and to ensure that the financial arm of the city changed its ways thoroughly. Deborah Larson, whom we hired after the bond loss as San Jose's chief of treasury, wrote later that we plunked her down in "a trembling financial environment, which had lost the confidence of its public, management, media, and elected officials."[142] Her judgment was correct, and she worked hard to reinstitutionalize the virtues of thinking for the long haul. (We later promoted her to director of finance for the city, and she has followed that with spectacular stints in Seattle and now Phoenix/Maricopa County.)

Short-term thinking still abounds in cities, of course, and not just in smaller towns that can't afford professional oversight and planning. New York City in 1993 announced plans to seek a $250 million bank loan using *uncollected* property tax bills as collateral. The idea, which the *New York Times* diplomatically called "an unusual scheme," was one way Mayor David Dinkins hoped to close a $2.1 billion budget gap in his 1994 budget. I am sure that every mayor around the country wishes he or she possessed a municipal credit card on which to draw a cash advance, but if wishes were horses, beggars would ride, right into city hall. (Perhaps they already have.) Other officials did not view the plan so kindly. Allen Proctor, head of the New York State Financial Control Board, which oversees city finances, judged that "all this does is make 1995's problem bigger. It is nothing but pure putting off until tomorrow what you don't want to do today."[143]

Government officials desperate to balance a budget are tempted to look to all kinds of alternate sources of revenue. As in San Jose or New York, city portfolio managers can take a shine to risky investment schemes. State pension fund managers may get wacky and go in for junk bonds. I find it most alarming when government gets gambling fever. Since New Hampshire launched the first state lottery in 1964, 35 other states have followed, and more are attracted to the lure of more money from taxpayers, dressed up as "playing a game." One Southern California psychologist specializing in gambling addictions says that "gambling used to be looked upon strictly as recreation or diversion. Now its major thrust is to raise revenue for governments."[144] California established its own state lottery in 1985, with the gilded promise of supporting schools with the proceeds. Actually, since then, our lottery has put in only 3 percent of the state's public education spending, and the source is so unstable and erratic that educators now know better than to count on lottery revenue as a savior. I sympathize with the anger of teachers who see parents encouraged, in state advertising, to buy more tickets because "Our Schools Win, Too." No one stops to think about the long-term effect on society of our government actively encouraging a gambling mentality. A Colorado minister opposed his state's lottery, bitterly complaining that "you cannot get anybody in the media to even be objective about the lottery, let alone critical. There are only stories about the winners. There are no stories about the people who take bread off their table to buy these damn tickets."[145]

The trend is unfortunately reaching the local level. Chicago has plans to put slot machines in O'Hare Airport terminals to take advantage of captive travelers. Card clubs proliferate in towns throughout California, and San Jose just recently has begun to rely quite dramatically on special tax revenues from two expanded clubs. (The city used "budget crisis" as the hook, but more important to many observers were major contributions to city council members.) The U.S. Conference of Mayors, always a good place to look for a dubious idea, has gone so far as to promote what it called a "precedent-setting national meeting," bringing together mayors from across the country and "leading authorities" in a two-day conference on "Gaming and Gambling: Playing to Win," held in an appropriate place: New Orleans. Among the speakers, predictably enough, are the mayors of Reno, Atlantic City, and Las Vegas.[146] Eager cities are following their examples. Such short-term thinking offends my understanding of governmental leadership, which should strive to reflect and encourage the highest values of society, not pander to and reward the lowest common denominator just for the sake of revenue.

Pride and a Tax Base

Not all California cities have been as successful as San Jose in managing their redevelopment efforts. Let us look at Los Angeles. Former mayor Tom Bradley exercised much of his long hold on power in Los Angeles through his control of the CRA, the immensely powerful Community Redevelopment Agency. While the city council often tries to nose into the CRA's affairs, the mayor has the power to appoint the members of the board of directors, and Tom Bradley's CRA operated largely independently of the city council. Unfortunately, the CRA is often caught up in the special-interest squabbling that afflicts cities like Los Angeles or San Francisco. It remains to be seen how Dick Riordan will free the paralyzed city from a long-running dispute between the mayor and the council over redevelopment control. The council has established a special committee to attempt some oversight.

The only city with a larger redevelopment effort than Los Angeles is New York City, and New York has also had its headaches. In fact, the recent "ICIP boondoggle" may teach only one lesson for other cities: how not to finance redevelopment. The Industrial and Commercial Incentive Program (ICIP) was begun in 1984, when the New York city council tried to stop the granting of subsidies on a case-by-case basis to developers. Reformers argued that such a review process was open to corruption. Instead, the new program became a free-for-all, with incentives and cash subsidies offered hand over fist, for all intents and purposes on a first-come, first-served basis. No one should have been surprised when developers began wholesale exploitation of a program with so little oversight. By 1992, ICIP was the city's largest single economic development program, but the *New York Times* called it in March of that year "a bonanza for developers of all kinds." A state senator judged the program "a total flop."[147] The city council lost control of the entire approval and review process for industrial and commercial incentive projects. The mayor? Well, then-Mayor Dinkins was actually out of the loop. Developers like Donald Trump had been taking massive advantage of the program. In 1992, when the state legislature tried to step in and halt the boondoggle from handing out hundreds of millions more dollars, the New York city council gave ICIP a reprieve, voting to "study" the program and its problems. The bottom line, according to the *Times:* "still business as usual in city politics."

In San Jose, we have tried to keep a level head and a long-term focus. The merged revenue from the ten redevelopment districts was funneled into our sixty-block core redevelopment area. From 1977 until 1990, we spent $554.7 million in redevelopment funds. When leveraged with other partnerships, we were able to invest around $1.5 billion in the new downtown. State law is quite specific on what the city can and cannot do with redevelopment tax increment revenues. By law, a fifth of that money goes right off the top into low- to moderate-income subsidized housing construction. From 1981 to the mid-1990s, redevelopment funds will have contributed some $155 million toward homeless shelters and housing. Most of that money, 85 percent of the "20 percent set-aside housing fund," goes to support low- and very-low-income housing. Also by law, redevelopment funds can be used only on capital improvements such as highways, buildings, and parks in the designated redevelopment areas. This point is often missed by agitators who argue that the "pot of gold" should be used for other city needs. Funds cannot be used for operating expenses, for general fund purposes, or even for maintenance of existing buildings. The synergy of redevelopment, though, brings into the city treasury millions of dollars in increased sales tax and other tax revenues, which the city can devote to its more traditional priorities of libraries, police officers, and city services. In 1979, the city collected only $7,000 in sales tax, utility tax, and downtown hotel taxes. By 1989, the year we opened our new convention center, the downtown was pulling in $4 million. In 1992, as a result of redevelopment, the new downtown provided more than $6 million to the city's general fund, as sales tax revenues and other business transactions escalated. I calculate that by 2002, new taxes collected from the downtown will be adding at least $20 million annually to the city's general fund.

This money goes to one simple cause: to create our glittering new cathedral city. Downtown means two things: it is both a source of pride and a new tax base. Another way of calculating the bottom line is to realize that from 1980 to 1992, the projects supported by redevelopment brought nearly 100,000 jobs to all of San Jose. And while the redevelopment areas make up only 7 percent of San Jose's total land, they now account for a remarkable 40 percent of the city's employment, and the property tax base of redevelopment has grown 50 percent faster than the tax base of nonredevelopment areas.

From city hall, I tried never to lose sight of the small-business impulses that had first led me to government. In partnership with individual city council members, and with some pointed prodding from certain members, we made certain to supplement our downtown focus with support for neighborhoods. Redevelopment funds have been used to support eight Neighborhood Business Districts, strengthening commercial streets with streetscapes, storefront improvements, and even specific retail promotions. In the five-year plan adopted in 1992, more than 15 percent of all capital improvement funds (some $61 million) will be going to neighborhood business support. Perhaps one could see this as San Jose's way of atoning for the annexation wars that brought Willow Glen and other neighborhoods within our orbit.

Back downtown, all the signs of a revived city are present. The new public and private investments have added some 14,000 permanent jobs downtown, making a total today of 25,000 people working in the downtown daily. Another 17,000 are expected by the end of the decade, most as a result of redevelopment.[148] All in all, I feel vindicated whenever I walk on one of our newly bustling streets. I feel the life of a city, a city-state itself, with a true heart.

8

HIGH HOPES
AND HARD HATS

> Make no little plans, they have no magic
> to stir men's blood.
> —Daniel Burnham

Graham Greene's traveler in *The Comedians* visits Duvalierville, a grandiose vision named for the Haitian dictator. The traveler is shocked to discover, instead of shining projects, nothing but empty fields, half-built foundations, and broken-down construction equipment. "And the cathedral?" he asks his guide. "It will be over there, beyond the bulldozer" is the reply.

I paid my own first visit to a Haiti, my first glimpse into an outer garden of hell. I was shocked to discover it here in my own city, in one of my own pet projects.

I had not laid eyes on one of the centerpieces of our new downtown social services, the Julian Street Inn, and in the fall of 1989 I figured it was high time. Churchill once said that we make our buildings, and then they make us. The genesis of this project was grounded in the best possible reflection of that noble thought. It had been conceived to be a state-of-the-art, humanistic, and safe center for the homeless in the central city. There would be 100 beds only, but it was carefully modeled to provide the very best treatment for those with significant mental or psychological problems.

157

The Julian Street Inn.

One early evening, I made the trip with Frank Taylor of Redevelopment and City Manager Les White. (Les was promoted to the top spot after Jerry Newfarmer's departure and was now a right-hand man.) A partnership among the city, the Mental Health Agency, and a well-regarded architect, the center had followed some laudable concepts. Since at least the Middle Ages, religious and other charitable organizations have taken the lead in sheltering the homeless and needy. The architect recalled that honorable tradition in the form and materials he planned for the shelter, which resembled a medieval cloister.[149] The structure would turn monastically inward with a perimeter living area wrapped around central courts and the dining hall. Items like courtyard fountains and a beautiful garden would give the place a special look, along with flying buttresses in the dining hall and real tile in the bathrooms. The pivotal mental health unit would have a human face, treating its patients just as you would want a member of your family treated. Frank, Les, and I had all been pleased to see such caring reflected in the design. I was anxious for my unannounced tour to the much-ballyhooed Julian Street Inn.

I was totally unprepared for the sight that appeared before my eyes. As the three of us entered the building, it was apparent that this was no brave new world, no new approach to the treatment of these unfortunate people. We got a view of the past—a distant and disturbing past. Several people greeted us at the entrance with vacant stares. The check-in hall was unattended. As we proceeded through the first floor, we encountered numerous individuals who seemed to be confused and disoriented. Others babbled incoherently in the corners. Parts of the building had a pungent odor of the foulest kind.

The physical condition of the building was 180 degrees away from the project that I had seen outlined in so many reports. Where plans and updates had indicated "garden area," there were the barest of dirt patches. In the stairwells, large parts of the drywall had already been destroyed. The store-room area for supplies was covered with debris and filled with construction material. Nothing was as it should be. Everything was in chaos.

I was in shock. I stared at my surroundings the same way that the famous Native American Indian Iron Eyes Cody stared at a piece of litter on the open range. I was ready to scream or cut someone's head off. After seven years as mayor, I was used to an occasional screw-up; this was inexcusable. To allow the weakest among us to be subjected to such conditions was criminal. When a staff person finally joined us with a lame offer of assistance, I used all my reserve to stay as calm as possible. As we asked incredulous questions, we three visitors were told a tale: schedules far behind, memos ignored, budgets with incredible elasticity, and a flawed Pollyanna design.

The devil may indeed be in the details, but here we had an example of a more disturbing sin. The disaster happened not because of details; it happened because the guiding concept was too large and too far off the mark to be implemented. From the beginning, inspired concepts created problems. The "design-as-you-go" style of architecture was ineffective and interfered with construction crews. The increased time and cost, in turn, reduced the number of beds from 100 to 69. The project ground to a halt when it was discovered during the site layout that the revised building plan did not fit the lot.

Certain types of material used were downright cheap. The beautiful Spanish motif tile was nice, but cleaning it was impossible. Using a particular type of wall covering is impressive for show and style, but you stop being impressed when you see how easy it is to kick in the drywall of a stairwell. Areas reserved for greenery are great additions, unless they remain bare dirt and blanket all their surroundings with a patina of dust. The best-laid plans of mice and men often go astray, but I had never in my time as mayor seen anything so grand and worthy wind up so betrayed, reduced to a horrible hovel. Having long ago been struck by Graham Greene's descriptions of the horror of Haiti, I felt we had paid a visit to Port-au-Prince.

Eventually, everyone cooperated to make it a workable center. Not all of our projects were as disturbing and botched as the Julian Street Inn. Some were more like open heart surgery, with risks and complications but a healthier patient afterward. In reconstructing a modern city-state, you do not have the leisure of the erstwhile masters; they were building from scratch. You are, after all, operating on a living patient, and you endeavor not to be disruptive. You must decide on those few priorities that will transform your city into the best possible living space for those people who have put their faith and trust in you.

My plan for our city was drawn on a clearly visible blueprint that had been discussed in a hundred community meetings, candidate forums, special TV shows, and campaign debates. It had been endorsed again and again by citizen groups and blue-ribbon panels. Later, if I received criticism for some particular action, I would admonish the critics; while they might disagree with the direction or quibble with the implementation, I expected to receive at least a small gold star for consistency and keeping my word. That quieted some faultfinders but for others marked only a momentary pause in a nonstop monologue. The major failing of San Jose's leadership in past efforts, familiar in many cities, had been the reluctance to keep to the agreed plan on either growth management or downtown rebuilding.

The city-state must be built on one vital assumption, namely that the city's legitimate leaders, not an invisible government, will decide in what direction such a mutable community will grow. In San Jose, politicians and expediency held the field for decades after the war, and their work had been deficient. It was now time to return to the old virtues of our valley, and to utilize fully the area's creativity and independence. As we put on the hard hats and began to build, it was necessary, as Lincoln said, to think and act anew.

Build Your Capstone First: The Fairmont

Each time President Clinton visits San Jose, which he now does regularly, he stays in the same hotel that countless other presidents, potentates, and dignitaries have chosen for eight decades: the Fairmont. It was, however, to the Fairmont in San Francisco that so many other important people had gone. The forty-second president of the United States has the opportunity instead to stay closer to the political action, the swing voters that he needs in the heart of Silicon Valley. Clinton stays in San Jose's spanking-new Fairmont Hotel.

Just a few brief years before, such a visitor could stay only at either the Hyatt Hotel, well outside the downtown and nearer to the city of Santa Clara, or the much smaller 232-room Holiday Inn beside our old Civic Auditorium. One of our top priorities was to procure the finest hotel possible for the entirely new heart of the city. We decided to place the hotel just where California's first state capitol had stood more than 100 years before, now only a parking lot in the middle of the long-promised San Antonio Plaza redevelopment project. We knew that by using only the best talent and experience could we hope to overcome our dubious and unwanted second-city reputation. We turned to our master developer in the downtown: Kimball Small, a man handpicked by Frank Taylor. We were also lucky in having close at hand just what San Jose needed, the highest-quality hotel and the best people to be associated with, the Swig family of San Francisco.

The Swigs were no strangers to me. Ben Swig, the late patriarch, was an old friend of my father's. The family had helped build the Democratic party in Northern California in the late 1940s by electing strong candidates in the Truman mold and had raised to prominence men like Pat Brown, our governor in the Sixties (and father of Kathleen and Jerry Brown). Ben Swig started his career in the early Forties by buying the Fairmont Hotel—and paying in cash. His prominence in San Francisco's real estate world led many local and state officials to his door with offers of public-private cooperation. He once told a gathering, "The Democrats are little people who don't know how to handle their money. Then they come to power and get some money. They don't know what to do with it, so they hand it over to big guys like me."[150]

Ben died in 1980, and by then sons Mel (who died in 1993) and Richard were directing a significant financial empire that stretched from Manhattan high-rises to their signature hotels in San Francisco, New Orleans, and Chicago. When you deal with the best types of people, honorable and resolute, good results occur. This was the case once again in the tale of the San Jose Fairmont.

We knew, of course, that this had to be a public-private partnership, and the city leadership was prepared for a significant subsidy. After all, we had been subsidizing a dangerous and potentially destructive type of growth in the city for many years, where the subsidy went underground, literally. When we had built roads and sewers in a crazy-quilt pattern, we had expanded San Jose into what my predecessor called in a cogent moment a "moth-eaten tablecloth." (It sounded like a well-scripted phrase.)

Now we would use our resources in the most productive and cost-efficient way, as a business does. The cost of the hotel would be in the $100 million range, and a portion of that would have to come from the city. We encountered a significant snag with a condition of the agreement with the Swigs stipulating that we would arrange a federal UDAG grant of nearly $5 million. It was an election year in 1984 and although Democrat Walter Mondale had no chance of winning, many on my team assumed that we might have a shot at a UDAG with the help of U.S. Senator Alan Cranston and San Jose's Don Edwards, the dean of California's congressional delegation. We also could call on the vaunted congressional muscle of Norm Mineta, a former mayor and great friend of San Jose.

I had grave misgivings. There was one big flaw in this deal, and I attempted to explain it to our team: UDAGs are rarely given on merit. They are political plums dispensed to the well connected, and the strange criteria of poverty seem to eliminate the San Joses and San Diegos and San Antonios, steering pork toward the Northern and Eastern cities of the Frost Belt and the Rust Belt. (President Reagan virtually eliminated UDAG programs in his second term, making the right decision for the wrong reason.)

Our attempts to have ourselves included in the UDAG's intricately worded "pockets of poverty" section was an exercise in futility. To deal with that sprawling conglomeration of inefficiency and inertia known as HUD at any time is difficult, in this case impossible. To make matters worse, the application actually made the city lie through its teeth in order to make the request. Our consultant, rather, told the lie, but the nuns taught us in grammar school that a lie once removed is still a lie. We were required to maintain that this project would not go ahead without the UDAG grant. Nonsense. That kind of brinkmanship-as-management style was not something our city has engaged in. Such a lie meant that, even with $440 million of money available, San Jose was coming hat in hand, begging for the kind of aid actually intended to bolster economically anemic cities that truly do need financial CPR.

I had had enough. San Jose decided, as it so often has, to take care of itself. We would make the loan with city money, raising the city's share to $23.5 million and the Swigs' to $80 million. We made the right deci-

sion. The final result was a nineteen-story five-star hotel across from Plaza Park smack in the heart of the city. Helmuth, Obata, and Kassebaum designed it and planned a generous sprinkling of retail uses in the ground floor.

At the ground-breaking celebration, the cake was five feet tall and had an amazing likeness to the hotel's eventual look. Headlines heralded a "finish to urban renewal's failures" as the exciting project was begun. The seventeen-year saga of the San Antonio plaza project was over, capped by the Fairmont. It had been a fallow period for our downtown, beginning the year that Bobby Kennedy was assassinated and Richard Nixon elected president. Now it had finally ended in the fifth year of the presidency of the former head of the Screen Actors Guild. The long road had seen the collapse of the efforts of Taylor Woodrow of London and a San Francisco group led by architect Corwin Booth. While these developers, their attorneys, and assorted politicians and bagmen fiddled, the life had been snuffed out of our downtown.

Many who gave their all and fought the good fight to preserve downtown for posterity did not live to see the rebirth. But the new and improved San Jose took form with the first shovelful of dirt for the Fairmont and the Silicon Valley Financial Center office complex, on a sunny day in September 1985. I said that morning that, while other buildings signify birth and transition, this one speaks volumes about maturity and quality. I am proud of it, for our citizens deserve no less. When the grand opening took place at Christmastime 1987, they got a present they deserved, a gorgeous hotel any city would love: the San Jose Fairmont.

Act One: The Convention Center

Recently, *Architectural World* magazine selected our new convention center as one of 100 most significant structures built in the past century. Until that moment, the building's primary claim to fame was a gigantic portal sporting thousands of porcelain tiles by the Royal Copenhagen firm and an interior causeway 1,100 feet long. I always point out that if stood on its end, the center would be the equivalent of a 100-story building. It is one of those remarks that always brings a smile to the faces of small children and chamber of commerce executives: "Gee, we *are* a big city!" For all the ballyhoo, this building was not conceived in the inner recesses of a planning committee or a blue-chip architectural think tank. The real story had a much more prosaic genesis.

Although the concept of a convention center had been debated and endorsed by Frank Taylor's Downtown Working Review Committee, it was just one good idea among many. Other pieces of the puzzle were of great significance to San Jose. All of them seemed to require either massive federal help or major decisions by bankers and the private sector. There were, in addition to the convention center, an arena, the light-rail Transit Mall, four-star hotels, and the Tech Museum. All were improvements that would measure whether San Jose evolved into a major American city or remained in municipal limbo as a city that would suffer an identity crisis ("if only it had one," remarked the *Boston Globe*.)

Woody Allen once gave a summary of Tolstoy's *War and Peace*: "It's about Russia." There is a beauty to simplicity. The question to our community was quite simple: Which of the crucial building blocks that are necessary for the economic rebirth of San Jose were entirely in the city's control? It was not a long list, consisting of one item, but that one was critical. Only the convention center was within the total control of the city to approve, design, build, and operate. I decided to go all out on this initial project.

The strategy began in the languid interregnum in the summer of 1982, before I was sworn in as mayor. That crucial six months was afforded me by a clear victory in the primary and no need for a runoff in the fall. I put the time to good use by preparing for a crucial debate. The convention center could be placed in the downtown core, as I wished, or out by the airport, three miles away. One rather vociferous band of lunatics lobbied for the airport, led by the old laissez-faire growth crowd. That would, of course, be repeating the mistake of putting city hall outside the downtown and placing regional commercial development on the city's fringe.

My choice was easy, but there was a complication: the downtown site stood among a neighborhood of single-family rentals and a handful of small retail businesses. They might fight redevelopment, or they might welcome relocation. As in most things at city hall, when you have a difficult situation, get some first-hand information. And do it yourself!

Early one Saturday morning, Susan Hammer and I walked the entire area. Susan represented my old downtown council district. Anytime politicians venture into the real world and away from the cloistered halls of government, they are amazed and enlightened by that great misnomer, the average citizen. In that all-too-brief tour, we encountered an aide to the late Senator Bob Kerr of Oklahoma, a former salesclerk at my dad's old Farmers Union store, a family whose children had gone to school with me at St. Joe's, and a man deathly afraid of being bombarded by ultraviolet rays from outer space. A random sampling, to be sure, but a lively one. They did not cleave to the NIMBY ("not in my back yard") philosophy in the slightest and recognized the importance of the convention center to the city, its economic value. I saw in them a real willingness to sacrifice for the good of all. That is a great lesson in civics for a student *or* a mayor. I told each of those we visited that they would receive fair, sensitive treatment from the city and that on this they had my word.

Government shifted into high gear. Support for the convention center was both genuine and carefully orchestrated. At the four public hearings, there were probably fifty speakers in support. It passed the city council unanimously, bolstered by positive editorial comment from the *Mercury News*. Rob Elder's editorial pages were in strong support of the downtown's rebuilding. They say that converts to a religion become the most zealous of practitioners. So it was with Elder, the transplanted Tennessean who, while always thoughtful, became a passionate proponent of the new San Jose and a foe of the "growth-at-any-cost" gang.

The first budget estimate for the convention center was pegged at $75 million. From that point the project and the dollars moved quickly. We began the design in the summer of 1983 and the city swung into action to acquire the property. The city manager was instructed to use the highest amount of sensitivity with the renters and older home owners. With those directions crystal clear, I moved to other issues. I would only later remember the response that the Duke of Wellington gave to the man who inquired about the quality of his troops. "I don't know what effect they have on the enemy," the wily old commander said, "but, sir, they scare the hell out of me!" I understood the comment when our city "experts" had finished with the relocation effort.

To make a long, tragic story short and tragic, let it suffice to say that the handling of the relocation was neither sensitive nor efficient. Despite direct instructions that bilingual relocation assistance would be available at all times, it was not. In the midst of demolition of certain sites and relocation of some businesses, there were still people living in some of the homes. Problems with rodents, fleas, dust, and the general commotion of a multi-million-dollar project made for a dreadful and very hot summer in 1986. Wonderful timing: it coincided with a council election in the same district, and my own mayoral reelection campaign. We first received hot criticism from the news columns of the local paper for not treating the renters fairly, and headlines blared the daily chronicle of incompetence. In the midst of the consternation, I kept faith with my initial commitment to treat the renters fairly—too fairly in the minds of the *Mercury News,* in fact, which later flip-flopped and castigated me for giving the renters too much in city relocation dollars. We were using "eminent domain," a concept I found distasteful and justified only in the most dire of municipal predicaments. I was imposing (with a capital I) our domain on the lives of those neighbors, and the price was a high one. I was willing to pay it. Everyone involved paid a high price, and years later I think of the precept of Nietzsche: "What does not destroy me, makes me stronger."

When the convention center was dedicated in April of 1989, the reviews came in. The *San Francisco Chronicle* architecture critic, Pulitzer Prize winner Allan Temko, called it the best public architecture in the Bay Area in a generation, and the smiling faces far outnumbered the frowns. I was able, after all the tears and turmoil to holler that favorite line of Michael Keaton's in *Beetlejuice,* "It's show time!" as the curtain was dropped on the orange-, blue-, and white-tiled entrance. Off the long concourse were an elegant ballroom and thirty meeting rooms. Indeed, it was time for shows, and for new taxes into the city coffers. High-technology firms, as well as conventions and local entertainment, now have a public home. Apple and IBM showcase new products here, and 10,000 volleyball players in the Junior Olympics could soon play in the 1.2-million-square-foot center.

It is a new look for a site where one prominent civic mover and shaker almost put a Burger King just ten short years before. San Jose has the best. To my way of thinking, it was exactly what the people deserved.

Gigabytes and the Junior League

In the Dashiell Hammett story immortalized by Humphrey Bogart, the Maltese Falcon is the thing that people will lie, cheat, steal, even murder for. Cities seek the same in the landmarks they choose to construct, though most mayors draw the line before that litany. There are certain projects worth taking a great risk to attain. Sports facilities usually prompt civic leaders and politicians to pile all the blue chips in the center of the table and say, "Deal the cards." In San Jose, it was no different.

In 1983, my first year as mayor, there was a much shinier prize to be achieved, a prize that could turn the heads of presidents, corporate titans or a child of twelve. It would solidify our position of regional hegemony and make us a true rival of San Francisco. It was an economic and regional home run, a slam dunk at the buzzer—metaphors do not convey the magnitude of this goal. In the parlance of Silicon Valley, San Jose was to push the outer envelope beyond the edge, showing exactly how serious we were as a community. We were going to reach for the biggest prize of all, the stuff that dreams are made of: Silicon Valley's Tech Museum of Innovation.

It was not ours from the beginning. The Tech was a vision shared by high-technology wizards like Bob Noyce, founder of Intel Corporation; civic boosters like Tony Ridder, newspaper dynasty scion; and most immediately the Junior League of Palo Alto, which actually originated the idea. It was a game lofty enough to attract the attention of near-icons Bill Hewlett and Steve Wozniak. The Tech was an effort to chronicle the second Industrial Revolution, the amazing achievements that have occurred in the wide swath of land from Stanford to South San Jose in the decades that followed World War II. It is a story of inventions, from the klystron, which helped win the Battle of Britain, to the personal computer, which changed the world. Mostly it is a tale of heroes, replete with names that fill the pantheon of an entrepreneurial hall of fame: Terman, the Varians, Hewlett and Packard, Noyce and Moore, Jobs and Wozniak, Treybig, McCracken, on and on. There is sound and fury in the story, and we wanted a way to capture that and tell it to future generations. In my first State of the City address, I listed the Tech's construction as the "highest goal of our city."

The Junior League's initial organizing group planned a huge building, with an early working name of the High Technology Museum, that would be a regional, national, and international mecca for those who sought education and inspiration. The Junior League's plan envisioned a technology center, part museum and part adventure, where the public could experience an array of sophisticated games, exhibits, and industry wonders. Displays ranging from a single byte of information to gigabytes' which would focus on chip manufacturing, communications, computer-aided design, clean rooms, aerospace, defense, genetic engineering, robotics, space exploration—the range of industrial magic covered was dizzying. The museum's first director said, "We think it's all right for people to be confused when they leave."

To many, it would be the West Coast equivalent of the Chicago Museum of Science and Industry, a place where the young could be inspired and take those first steps to their own successes. The *Los Angeles Times* has called it the "Smithsonian of the West." But for the Junior League, the immediate question was location. Every Silicon Valley city wanted the Tech. To see one of the others take it would signify that San Jose was still the same old home of faint spirit and second-raters.

I promised the League that in my first year as mayor, becoming the home of the High Technology Museum was an explicit sine qua non of San Jose's future. The stakes were clear, though. Although Palo Alto had dropped from the race, two other aggressive and wealthy suburban cities, Sunnyvale and Mountain View, were vying for the honor and for the tangible benefits accrued by hosting up to 1 million visitors each year. To the winner would go increases in hotel revenues, entertainment spending, and related tax income. Also, a title was at stake: center city for the Valley. The *Los Angeles Times* referred to the competition as "the type of backbiting and mudslinging usually reserved for the meanest political campaigns."[151] I had spoken to the reporter for the story. "I really think the losers will be the people behind the museum project if we don't get it," I told him. "Some of those other sites are nice places to live, but I would not want to visit there."

The lobbying campaign was very active. Mountain View, home of NASA's Ames Research Center, offered a $38 million package that included a building and twenty acres of land in its 1,500-acre North Bayshore redevelopment area. Rock-and-roll entertainment legend Bill Graham added clout to its presentation; he had built his money-making Shoreline Amphitheater in Mountain View. Sunnyvale offered acreage at its Baylands park and an increase in its transit occupancy tax to service revenue bonds that would cover the capital cost and partial operations. In ad-

Bill Hewlett (right) was an early booster of the Tech Museum of Innovation (left and below).

dition, revenue generated by a future hotel on the site would be added for a grand total of $40 million over twenty years.

I was personally involved in making San Jose's case, speaking and giving riverbank tours on the Guadalupe River to members of the unbuilt museum's board of directors. When the final presentations were given, the major pitch was delivered by me and Frank Taylor in the boardroom of the *San Jose Mercury News*. Our task was eased by two factors: First, I knew I had the support of one of the best friends a city could have, the chairman of the museum's board, *Mercury News* publisher Tony Ridder. His presence buoyed my expectations. Second, I knew we had an upper hand on the numbers alone. We made our offer, and it was commensurate with the prize: $30 million in capital costs, including over 1000 parking spaces, and the real sweetener: $2 million in operating subsidies over the life of the museum. That kicker was valued at $20 million at the least and quadrupled our initial offer. I had negotiated the sweetener directly with Ridder. I hoped it was the type of boldness that business people and entrepreneurs would appreciate.

Within a week, the museum was awarded to the city of San Jose. The *Mercury News* said in a lead editorial that the decision "recognized the ascension of the view that Silicon Valley is maturing from a tilt-up, overnight, suburban phenomenon to a stable, developed region ready to concentrate its energies in a unified, central core."[152] We were that core. Palo Altans were miffed, losing their initial progeny, while Mountain View and Sunnyvale were truly steamed. To quote the witty onetime senator from California, Sleeping Sam Hayakawa, about the Panama Canal: "We stole it fair and square." San Jose pulled a piece of larceny to enshrine itself as the Capital of Silicon Valley with a substantial landmark. Not bad for a city that had not even been on the radar screen of national attention for so long and had played only a partial role in the thirty-year history of the Valley. A little ethical larceny is necessary if a mayor is to build a city.

Steve Ross, the Deal Maker

When Steve Ross died in 1993, the obituaries filled the papers. Here was a man who had taken a modest undertaking business to the heights of an entertainment colossus: Warner Communications and the incredible Time-Warner merger. Magician or charlatan, he was said to have irresistible charm. I saw it once. When Warner in 1984 bought Atari Computer, the game company that revolutionized adolescent habits, Ross came to town with our mutual friend

Lew Wolff to seal an impressive land deal. He strode into my office with a combination of flair and deference, difficult to capture. In the press conference that followed, a reporter asked one key question: "Mr. Ross, why did you come to San Jose?" Without blinking, he gazed back angelically and replied that he was "drawn by the pro-business philosophy of Mayor McEnery." Now, we had known each other for just twenty minutes, but he was so convincing, I almost believed it myself. I realized I was in the presence of a master schmoozer, deal maker, and a world-class flatterer. How could such a shtick possibly be successful? Ask the master egos of Hollywood and Wall Street, none of them impervious to this larger-than-life impresario.

Someone once said that the problem with the future is that it takes so darn long to get here. For us, a big part of the future arrived in 1988 when one of the Tech Museum's educational pieces was launched: Project Mindstorm. I visited tiny Gardner Academy elementary school to see the project, in the shadows of downtown's high-rises. The school is in a small Latino neighborhood, an area that has provided shelter to hosts of newly arrived immigrants, from turn-of-the-century Italians to recent refugees from the turmoil of Nicaragua. IBM had joined with the Tech Museum to tuck into the neighborhood a piece of the future.

I waded through the narrow aisles between the desks of fourth and fifth graders and was inspired by what I observed. Here from the children of my city I received one of the best lessons on what is important in a community. The students were hard at work at their personal computers, using a software program and a special teaching method designed and monitored by noted professor Seymour Papert of MIT. Papert is a man noted for coloring outside the lines. With his methods, and the natural exuberance of youth, something wonderful was happening at Gardner Academy. Only a few weeks previously, students were staring at the alien boxes that had been deposited on their desks. The machines were frightening, as technology can be, and so intimidating. Admiring the tutelage of Papert and his on-site assistant, doctoral fellow Carol Sperry, I watched these young children embrace the concept of "the big pencil": a computer is only a highly sophisticated and maneuverable pencil, with the ability to do so much more. In a seemingly miraculous metamorphosis, the children and their new pencils were transformed. One student was writing a poem, another was designing a fantasy family room, while a third was solving a small-business problem for her parents. Their horizons were far beyond the fourth grade.

Few of us get to plan for the future and to enjoy it also. Visiting Gardner Academy was a great morning for a mayor.

In October of 1990 the penultimate stage in the saga of the Tech Museum gave us an additional bit of instant gratification, Silicon Valley style. The finished first-stage building consisted of many of the same parts originally envisioned by those present at the creation almost eight years before. The Tech came alive at the downtown site of the old Civic Auditorium, a vintage WPA project from 1935. We called this initial facility "the Garage of the Tech Museum." That name distinguished it from the permanent site to be finished later in the 1990s but also paid homage to those pioneers who had built this Valley with electronic wizardry from their garages. One of them, the always generous Bill Hewlett, contributed $1 million to ensure that the site opened. Others in the Valley community donated up to $25 million to the venture in cash or in-kind assistance.

Visitors—heads of state, Nobel laureates, and twelve-year-olds alike—have entered the hall and met a startling array of the past, present, and, most of all, the future. The evolution of the calculator, the fastest bike in the world, FMC's Mars Rover and its exact path on the red planet, the history of robots from Hollywood to factories, all in a whirling amalgam amidst a cacophony of noises like a wild scene from Disney's *Fantasia*. If you could hear the sound of a young mind at work, that indeed is the loudest noise you would notice in the room. We had put our faith in the ability of young minds to adapt and expand, and we were not disappointed. All of it had been done in the tested and true tradition of the Valley. Ed Zschau, former congressman and now CEO of IBM's local division, was the Tech board's new chairman. At the grand opening, Zschau noted eloquently that the museum had been built in the style of a genuine start-up company.

Although the budget would eventually rise to $39 million of city assistance, and the starting date on the final structure would not arrive until the mid-1990s, it is still clear that this is a project like no other. The permanent building is being designed by Ricardo Legoretta of Mexico City, along with our local Steinberg Group, and will boast 80,000 square feet of exhibit space, an OmniMax theatre, and labs and information lounges already prototyped in the Garage. It is going to be one of the premier educational facilities in the world and a tourist and convention draw of grand proportions.

Field of Nightmares

The city-state sometimes goes beyond its borders in search of a little credibility. An early, perhaps most notable example was in the eleventh century. Citizens of Venice, a rapidly growing city at the mouth of the Adriatic Sea, were in the market for something of marquee value to put the emerging commercial center on the map. Abner Doubleday was still several hundred years in the future, so they couldn't steal the San Francisco Giants or Brooklyn Dodgers. As happens in many wanna-be cities, Venice had a brainstorm. In the Egyptian city of Alexandria was a prize even better than a ball team. In fact, it was biblical: the body of St. Mark. In a feat of derring-do worthy of a James Bond saga or a Spielberg movie, Venice set out to steal the corpse.

Once they exercised their peculiar interpretation of habeas corpus and snagged the body by night, Venetians began a world-class campaign of medieval marketing. With statues, songs, and fanfare, Venice became the City of St. Mark. To millions of lovers strolling through that lovely cobblestoned plaza, not to mention to the pigeons, it would never be the same. The acquisition vested immediate prestige for Venice and was certainly the first recorded attempt at municipal larceny. Venice had its cadaver and patron saint and bragging rights in the Mediterranean. It was a wonderful lesson for future mayors and chambers of commerce. Many cities would attempt to follow suit. Most would have a good deal more trouble.

Most people love sports, and mayors are no exception. When St. Petersburg, Florida, finished constructing its shiny new Suncoast Dome in 1991, city leaders were certain that the stadium was their ticket out of the minors and past second-city status. St. Petersburg had been known as "God's waiting room," the butt of national media jokes. *60 Minutes* jocularly noted the billboard ads for cremation. Cops cruised the streets in golf carts, looking for coronary cases. Now elected officials had risked $139 million to build a stadium, seeking respectability with the same zeal as Ponce de Léon's quest nearby for the legendary Fountain of Youth.

Unfortunately, the campaign to woo a tenant team for the dome has been a long ride. No fewer than eight teams showed interest, among them Chicago and Seattle, only to back off. In late 1992, the occasion of a signed contract by the San Francisco Giants set off bonfires throughout the city reminiscent of V-J Day, certainly marking the dawn of a new era. But it was not to be. There was a last-minute West Coast effort to save the team, with a bout of concessions to the team's new owner (replacing the disillusioned and sincere Bob Lurie) offered by Mayor Frank Jordan in San Francisco. St. Petersburg was once again a bridesmaid or, more accurately, a minister with a beautiful cathedral and no congregation. Today, the 240,000 residents of that sleepy Florida town are still paying $1.5 million a year in operating costs and $8 million in debt services. That is nearly $10 million each year for an empty stadium that was built on the promise that it would turn a profit!

The story of the Giants has a couple of regrettable San Jose chapters as well. A mayor, above all, must be adaptable and able to seize opportunities when they present themselves. In the spring of 1985, opportunity came knocking. Owner Bob Lurie was eager to move from windswept, antiquated Candlestick Park. The owner of the Forty-Niners football team had once even referred to the facility as a giant urinal, and the Giants were just plain unhappy there. Lurie was intrigued by the possibility of a relocation to the warmer climes of the Santa Clara Valley in San Jose. Here he would find not only better playing conditions but the geographic center of his fan base, in a middle-class family community. San Francisco residents account for only 25 percent of the Giants' total attendance. A move was ideal, or so it seemed.

I was able to enlist Tony Ridder again, and Phil DiNapoli and Lew Wolff. These two businessmen had played key roles in the initial rebuilding of the downtown. Lew, as part owner of the St. Louis Blues hockey team (and later part owner of basketball's Golden State Warriors), was knowledgeable about the financing of sports facilities. The allies were in place for the quest to capture the Giants. These were excellent tacticians and strategists.

Time was short, because of Lurie's timetable to escape his Candlestick lease. The task was at once both simple and enormous. We were to plan, construct, and build a major sports facility in the amount of time that it normally takes to get a committee together. It was a test of our ability to make our city move in somewhat the same tempo and style as a private-sector company. The goal was a 45,000-seat outdoor stadium. In my first meeting with Lurie, at Mel Swig's Fairmont Hotel office, I convinced the Giants' owner that we were serious about luring his franchise but told him that this project could not jeopardize the rock-solid priorities that we already had on our public-private Tech Museum and the $27 million that I had set aside for the initial stages of a separate indoor sports arena. In addition to that, we had an ambitious program of infrastructure improvements and downtown revitalization of nearly $500 million. Those were the givens; Lurie understood. The major players were now on deck. Then things began to move rapidly.

Almost immediately, we lined up an attractive piece of land, 118 acres in North San Jose near the Milpitas border. The land was an old bus yard publicly owned by the Santa Clara County Transportation District. In possibly the best business terms that I ever managed to arrange for the city, or anyone else, for that matter, the terms were set at a one-dollar option, plus a price to be determined by agreed-upon appraisal in the next few years. Nothing need be paid for twenty years. The main land-acquisition cost was deferred for a generation in one stroke. The County Board of Supervisors, which was never very fond of San Jose and had been a thorn in our side for many years, had finally performed acceptably, if only when a little moral suasion and a baseball bat had been waved in its direction.

The financing for the stadium was assembled using a combination of creative mechanisms. The most significant lay in the novel but not altogether untested method of financing via the sale of luxury boxes. Many corporations had been using the plush and richly accoutered enclosures since they first appeared in the Houston Astrodome twenty years earlier. They had been used only once to finance a stadium, and that was in Miami just a year before. The Dolphins had put together a 72,000-seat, $90 million stadium using the sale of 234 luxury boxes at a price range from $29,000 to $65,000 a year, and they also included 10,000 special reserved seats at prices ranging from $600 to $1,400 a year. The tactic netted over $7.5 million annually and had cinched the deal. We hoped to utilize the corporate might of Silicon Valley to sell 100 boxes, another first for our young Valley. Advertising could bring in millions more, including the sale of the stadium name, though I preferred to save that for San Jose—Atlanta's "Coca Cola Boulevard" was not a welcome approach in our new city.

We anticipated other barriers but were certain that they were only obstacles to be overcome.

A Cold Wind from the North

Plans for the stadium came to a screeching halt in May 1985. I received a phone call from the mayor of San Francisco, Dianne Feinstein (who would later go on to the United States Senate). She spoke in her best deadpan voice, reminiscent of Claude Rains in *Casablanca* stating that he was "shocked, shocked" to find that gambling was going on at Rick's place, and then being handed his winnings. Dianne was "surprised." Weeks after being notified by Lurie of his intention to leave, and presumably after reading the spate of headline stories in all the major dailies in the Bay Area, and after viewing a continuing soap opera of stories on television, Dianne was now calling me in surprise that we were approaching the Giants. She notified me that I must cease and desist from tampering with the Giants—or else. "I intend to make use of every legal remedy available to San Francisco to compel the Giants to honor their lease. Furthermore, I want you to know that any efforts by San Jose to encourage the Giants to breach their Candlestick Park lease will be treated as an inducement to breach a contract," she recited, as if from an aide's script. "Please be advised that if the Giants are induced by San Jose to breach their lease, San Francisco will hold San Jose liable for all resolution damages."

A letter that arrived the same day confirmed that she had been reading her comments. "Tom," she concluded in the letter, "I would hate to have the fine relationship enjoyed by our two cities disrupted by this issue." Feinstein seemed to take it personally, as if our efforts were an attack on her mayorship or political honor. I liked that in a mayor, particularly when the vital interests of a city seemed to be at stake. It was a bit like the U.S. president sending the bombers to Baghdad while expressing the hope that it would not harm relations between the two countries.

Dianne's tough talk was strengthened by the fact that she was on firm legal ground. Our lawyers gave me the bad news that once San Francisco contested the move, the die was cast. Although Lurie was still optimistic, the deal was as good as dead. With so much of the financing plans hinging on private sources, the threat of litigation and suits froze all the private money. Feinstein knew it, and I knew it. Most of all, our investors knew it. There would be no San Jose Giants—at least for now.*

The time had come to turn to other projects that were more directly in our control. And a far more controllable and fascinating project was ready to be implemented. It would ultimately be a more usable major sports facility, a multipurpose arena. This one would not need the agreement of a billionaire owner or the poohbahs of baseball hierarchy, or any rival mayor. It would need the resolve and collective will of San Jose.

Planning Another Cathedral

San Jose has its St. Joseph's, Washington the National Cathedral, and in Southern California television evangelist Robert Schuller has a giant glass "Crystal Cathedral." But in the last quarter of the twentieth century, there has been only one type of building that cities like to construct that can embody such awe-inspiring magnificence: an arena or stadium. Today, the San Jose Sharks spark national attention and local thrills in a cathedral of sports that was opened in 1993. Back when I became mayor, the site was a parking lot. People ask how San Jose managed to build an expensive new facility downtown, when other cities try and fail. The story of ups and downs should be studied.

In early 1984, I commissioned a task force to study the possibility of a sports arena for San Jose. It was not your normal committee, however, the kind of place where good ideas are lured into a cul-de-sac and knifed. The Arena Task Force was a fourteen-member group cochaired by two trusted allies: Ted Biagini, lawyer and banker, and Frank Fiscalini, former protégé of my father. Also on the committee was can-do member of the city council Jerry Estruth, a guy you could rely on. Our initial inclination had been to locate the project across the street from the old Civic Center on Almaden Boulevard, between the planned convention center and the planned Tech Museum. The task force, though, displayed a

---

*In 1992, in the teeth of a national recession and a dramatic local economic dive, my successor, Susan Hammer, and Bob Lurie went to the ballot with a $300 million stadium proposal at the old bus yard in North San Jose. It was crushed at the polls by an angry 60 percent of the electorate.

strong tilt to build an arena out at the publicly owned Santa Clara County fairgrounds, abandoning the thought of a downtown site. The thought of free land three miles away had temporarily distracted us.

Not on my shift! My judgment always said, when in doubt, slam it in downtown. That is exactly what we proceeded to do. The amount of planning and analysis that a project of this magnitude takes is almost enough to put off even the hardiest souls. There was a long and laborious process of analyzing three potential sites. The old bus yard in far-off North San Jose (later considered for the baseball stadium) and an FMC Corporation property in the warehouse district were each considered too remote or redolent with potential toxic problems. We decided that the best was the most central location, on West Santa Clara Street. Everything went quite well—for a while. By 1987, I saw portents of an easy approval process for the arena, just as we received for the convention center, the Tech Museum, and the Fairmont. All the lights were green when I felt a strange foreboding. All mayors who survive have it; it must be akin to the running back who can sense a linebacker on the blind side or a seasoned fighter who knows when to slip an unseen punch.

The problem unfolded with lightning rapidity. One council member began yelling fire in the theater, and, worse than that, began to pour gasoline. The old Rosegarden neighborhood of San Jose, the council member's sleepy home base, was a mile farther down Santa Clara Street, as it changes to the Alameda and winds its way to the old mission on the Santa Clara University campus. That was the route the *pobladores* of San Jose, shaded by three rows of willow trees, used to trudge every Sunday on their way to mass. We envisioned no such traffic from the arena; this neighborhood should have stayed asleep. In the parking plan, we specifically planned to funnel all traffic into the downtown, away from residential neighborhoods. No red-blooded sports fan would walk from this faraway neighborhood area to the arena. Nevertheless, a panic overtook some in the Rosegarden. A neurosis was fanned by arena opponents, using that old NIMBY doctrine to scare residents into believing that their property values would plummet and that their neighborhood quality of life would be changed forever. It was a classic example of scare tactics, and it worked well.

The battle lines were drawn. Every enemy that I had, and a few new ones, accumulated and assembled into a strange host of malcontents, no-growthers, low-income advocates, anti-downtowners, and renegade art patrons, including my predecessor as mayor, the hapless but still popular

Janet Gray Hayes. They failed to stop the approval of the favored Santa Clara Street site, which won on a lopsided vote in the city council, but they had a significant weapon left in their arsenal: a ballot initiative.

Citizen-sponsored initiatives are a time-honored piece of Californiana, one of the revered reforms left to us by the Progressive movement that cut such a wide wake through the state and the nation during the opening decades of the twentiethth century. (My grandfather had been a leader in the Progressive wave that destroyed "bossism" locally.) Sometimes political tools, like people, are a bit more likable in the abstract. The initiative turned the debate over the arena into a fight to the death, and the head on the chopping block was my own.

I knew that it would be easy to get citizens, for or against the arena, to sign a petition taking the issue "to the people," enabling an up or down vote on its approval rather than trusting the city council with the final decision. It is always easy to oppose something as expensive and complicated as $100 million public building. There will be mistakes, errors in analysis, miscalculations, and outright bungling. Politicians will make misstatements and bureaucrats will falter. Having government succeed at a large project is extraordinary, like a dog that plays the piano. It's not that he plays well that is amazing, but that he plays at all! The arena project in the heart of the downtown was massive, leaving much to go wrong. Using the name People for Fiscal Responsibility, the opposition coalition needed 5 percent of the registered voters in the city to qualify the measure for an upcoming ballot. Predictably, the opponents emphasized the lament, How can you build an arena when there is crime in the neighborhoods, too few books in the library, homeless on our streets? Fill in the blank with any discontent.

They got reams of signatures on the initiative, proclaiming in a scant nine days that they had reached their goal to qualify for the ballot. When their leader attended a council meeting to announce their great achievement and to ask for a city count of their qualifying signatures, I thought of the proverb that I always hated and still do: "There go my people, I am their leader and I must follow." I hoped instead to outflank them. When they submitted the reams of petitions, I had a new city ordinance ready, eschewing any count, yet immediately adopting their petition item for the ballot. My new approach held that city money could be spent for a sports facility only after a majority vote of the people. Approval would give the green light and an open road back to the city. Simple. Concise. We had retaken the high ground, placing the measure up for a vote. We denied the opposition even the satisfaction of counting the petitions.

The election was set for June 1988, and everyone believed that it would prove decisive to my two terms as mayor, the prospects for the arena, and the future of the city.

What is This Meeting About?

We all remember the recurring bane of our college years when we awaken from the terrible nightmare of arriving for a final exam and knowing absolutely nothing. Every Mayor has a parallel experience: sitting in a meeting, without a clue of the topic. It happened to me one early evening in City Hall when I met with the man who created the business of rock music, Bill Graham. He escaped the holocaust and as a boy traveled alone to New York and finally, in California, found the future.

We sat together and spoke of mutual friends and the Tech Museum and movies. (I enjoyed his work in Apocalypse Now). The time passed and although he was a born raconteur, the hour was late. Finally, I told him I had a subsequent meeting and asked what could I do for him. He gave me one of the great looks of all time and responded: "I thought you wanted to see me." At that revelation, we laughed and laughed, and stayed for another hour discussing events great and small. With Bill Graham, there were no half measures, and he went on to help the city and me in the Arena Campaign, designing the finished facility, and advising on the mix of shows. He stepped forward after the quake of 1989 to put on benefits and distribute funds through my relief effort; he was a 'detail guy' and called me once to warn of the dangers of a particular rock group appearing at Spartan Stadium at San Jose State. "No control, Tom, they'll be trouble", he predicted. Even with additional security, a small riot occurred. He hated screwups.

Bill knew his business and gave a lot to others. I went to his house, Masada, on a picturesque hilltop overlooking the Golden Gate to plan a benefit for San Jose schools. He always had a new venture: a tour with the Rolling Stones or Amnesty International or a children's affair or anti-

drug campaigns. A few weeks later his helicopter hit a power line and the creator of an entire raucous, fantastic world was dead. Bill Graham was the most interesting person who ever entered my office . . . . even if I didn't know why.

I wanted to win. There would be no armistice, no more cease-fires. "The forces of the night versus the army of tomorrow, for a new and improved San Jose"—that was how I chose to present this moment in the life of the city. And coincidentally, that is exactly the light in which I saw it.

Win Your Battles Before the Concrete Is Poured

The campaign for approval to build the arena was my real political battle royal. Toward the end, the media seemed to equate my chances with those of a tinhorn dictator teetering on the edge of overthrow—news stories took on a tone of, "Your plane is fueled and waiting at the airport, Your Mayorship." A loss on this one would have been a substantial obstacle in my quest to build a new metropolis.

The all-important ballot measure was really a simple question: "Without imposing additional taxes, shall the City of San Jose build an indoor community arena for entertainment and sporting events using public funds to finance its acquisition and construction?" The anti-arena forces knew they would be badly outspent in the campaign, but they were confident of victory, knowing full well that voters are usually eager to slap down any large expenditure of money for a project that could be portrayed as a white elephant or boondoggle.

I called in the redoubtable Frank Fiscalini to serve as chair of the pro-arena campaign, and recruited the energetic and savvy David Pandori, one of my chief advisers since his days with me as a college intern. (He is now a city councilman in his own right.) Richie Ross, a tough Sacramento campaign consultant with a clerical background, acted as our media and strategy consultant. My primary advice came from Dean Munro, Greg Larson, and Pat Dando in city hall; my wife, Jill, and my brother John; and old allies Mike Fox, Harvey Armstrong, Phil DiNapoli, and Lew Wolff in the private sector. Longtime friends Rich Cristina, Mike Rawitser and the utility player, Al Crema, were there to help also. In the community Gayle Jones and Barbara Walsh did it all—and raised money too! My personal lawyer, Ken Machado, was a key and courageous supporter as a candidate for council. This group had been part of every decision I ever made as mayor. Money would not be a problem, but energizing a community that had so often had the brass ring snatched away from it was going to be a task. The *Mercury* and Rob Elder's editorial staff were solid, as usual. Their support was phrased in careful pragmatism.

We had made sure that there would be no large dislocation of homes, as there had been with the convention center; only two residences were on the list. The total number of businesses to be moved was twenty-five. With those sources of potential opposition answered, we could concentrate on our own agenda in a strategic campaign. That strategy centered on me. The campaign was my baby and I would determine the plan, lead the rallies, solicit the money, work the precincts, and even narrate the commercials. The theme: the sports arena will be the entertainment centerpiece of a new city. If I failed to get the arena for the people of San Jose, then I would feel I had also failed all those citizens still to be born or to move here. I would have flunked the future.

Initial opinion poll results asking general questions were quite optimistic. We carried the campaign through the balmy days of spring, but as the weeks to the June election ticked off, something began to ring false. It slowly became clear that, somehow, the campaign was not going well. It is sometimes said that generals are always fighting the last war. This is often the way with politicians and their political consultants. In Richie Ross we had chosen a flamboyant person, cocksure of himself and his judgments. Rapidly, the political circumstances were changing. All our carefully budgeted, sophisticated targeting to get out our message was missing a big point. Questions still abounded about the cost of the final project and about how the traffic might affect nearby neighborhoods. It dawned on me, slowly for a politician of my supposed intuition, that the battle would not go to the swiftest in fund-raising or the strongest in editorial support but to the side that could better draw a picture of our future, a vision with a resonance among the voters.

Other cities might learn something from our mistakes. Our first and least effective campaign strategy stressed the simple theme that in our own arena, San Jose fans could see all of the things that San Francisco or Oakland could see. Basketball, hockey, circuses, ice shows, concerts by everyone from U2 to Neil Diamond, all this and much more lay in our future, if people had confidence in the city. Great idea, but it wasn't working. With each news story about the cost of the building, the numbers showed that our support in the broad, undecided middle was wavering. We still had a hard base of support, sports fans and die-hard San Jose boosters, while questions in the press, radio, and TV eroded the critical swing voter. Something had to give.

It did. Cannons to the left of us and cannons to the right fired away. The editorial support we did enjoy was dwarfed by the torrent of negative, critical, and questioning news stories. All you have to do in any big bond measure, any large municipal expenditure, is raise the big question of cost, and raise it again and again. Reporters did. Their stories, cynical and questioning, witting or unwitting, were enjoying great success in killing our hopes.

Two weeks before the election, the ides of May, I received the late-night call from Richie Ross that I was expecting and dreading. He responded to my casual salutation with "*I'm doing good.*" "How are *we* doing?" I asked. "*Not* good," he intoned in a low-key, ominous way. "The tracking poll is in." The numbers had gone south: for all practical purposes, the election was lost. The news sunk in quickly and with a sickening impact. All I had worked for in building the spirit of pride and confidence in our new city was drifting in the winds.

I decided against suicide and tried a different tack. The action we needed to take was obvious. We had to present to the people of San Jose the stark reality of what a failure to approve the arena would mean. Actually, this was the part of the campaign that I relished more than any other, and I approached it with a new gusto. A round of press conferences and briefings were held in which each and every facet of the project— and the campaign—was discussed. We released our internal tracking poll, an unheard-of thing to do, trumpeting the fact that we were losing. With Munro and the rest, I decided it would take this type of boldness to turn the tide. If our citizens could look beyond the short term and any irritation they might have with me personally or with some municipal screwup to the vision of a better community, we would yet have a chance to turn this around. I eagerly embraced the new strategy and feverishly traveled the city like Diogenes with the lantern, not searching for an honest man but an honest break. I cut one last radio commercial that capsulated the feelings I had after so much work and woe. It featured Olympian Peggy Fleming and me, talking about the arena. It concluded with these lines, which I wrote for us and in which I believed: "I'll never skate in this arena," Peggy said, and I added, "And I won't cut the ribbon. But this is so important to the people of our community."

Everything that could be done had been done. All had had their say. I was hoping that I would not have to join the California political pundit who once said after a galling loss: "The people have spoken, the bastards!" I had never lost an election, for myself or for any major bond initiative that I supported. No council member that I had endorsed had ever lost, either. The election I faced in June 1988 would either secure the new city I had attempted to build or send me into lame-duck status for my remaining two and a half years as mayor. The plane was fueled and waiting, for a one-way trip to Elba.

Primary day in California was very warm, and I tried to take my mind off the balloting. Following my custom on voting days, I took in a movie in the late afternoon with my brother. The melodrama on the screen paled in comparison to the one being enacted in polling places across the ten districts of the city. Michael Dukakis was a sure winner for California's Democratic nod for president, but one issue captured most pundits and community leaders in the Bay Area: an arena or no! I started the evening with Jill and Dean Munro, catching early returns in South San Jose at the headquarters of friend and council ally Judy Stabile. The first results were very bad. Bile welled up in my stomach, a mixture of anxiety and dashed hope. We left after a brief stay, and the twenty-minute car ride back downtown seemed interminable. I have never been very good at losing; thankfully, I never got a chance to get used to it.

The reception for arena supporters was at Eulipia restaurant, a downtown survivor from pre-redevelopment days. We entered, and the assembled supporters gave us a cheer. I needed it. I leaned against a wall; I thought I might have to become very familiar with that position. I prepared for the flock of media. The first question threw me off and delighted me. Robert Handa of KNTV asked, "Mayor McEnery, do you attribute the success of the arena campaign to. . . ." Good news! The follow-up questions from a live hook-up with the anchors at the studio indicated that their exit polls were showing a big win. I am superstitious, but could this turnaround really be happening? I began to feel what Mark Twain described as the calm confidence of a Christian holding four aces.

The entourage widened as we picked up the brain trusters, Pandori, Larson, and campaign director Pat Dando, and headed to the county supervisors' chambers, where official vote counts were posted as soon as they were tabulated. We watched the results come in fast and furious—and clear. It was all over. A real comeback, a big vote for the arena and the future. We had won!

A Shark for San Jose

When the final numbers were counted, it was a convincing victory, with 53 percent voting for the arena. The opponents were dashed, the supporters jubilant. The *Mercury News* next day carried the headline, "Vote Is a Slam Dunk for the Mayor!" Not bad—I always had trouble even touching the rim in my playing days. I enjoyed the basking. Being Irish and attuned to the dark side of the force on occasions, I fought hard to savor this win, but the victory was wider. It was taken as an en-

The Arena from Santa Clara Street.

dorsement of our programs in rebuilding the downtown, the linchpin in our reconstitution of the new start-up company known as San Jose, the Capital of Silicon Valley.

We proceeded quickly with Frank Taylor in the lead to begin the design of the arena, with noted architect Charlie Sink, who had designed two arenas: McNichols in Denver and Thomas & Mack of Las Vegas, which I liked a lot. Both were excellent venues for sports fans, great places to watch a game. In August 1988, the contracts were let for the design. By December of that year, we saw the first drawings. They revealed a square, four-level building with a steel truss and eighty-foot glass atriums on either side, one facing the downtown. The outside would be precast concrete with a polished metallic finish. The design included 69 to 76 luxury boxes. It was perfunctory to some people. To me, it was beautiful. You always call your own baby beautiful, but I was actually convinced.

Now we needed a prime tenant. What I wanted was an NBA basketball team, and the Golden State Warriors were just up the road. Basketball was the marquee sport to my mind, and we could also feature college basketball games with Santa Clara and San Jose State nearby and hopefully a men's or women's NCAA regional championship and high school state championships. The thought of the Celtics and the Lakers being trounced by the "San Jose Warriors" was a dream. Although the Warriors were partially owned by San Jose's old friend Lew Wolff, there was a slight complication: a sweetheart lease in Oakland with seven years left to run.

We decided to focus not on stealing another city's franchise but on creating an all-new one. When ground was broken in the summer of 1990, my top staffer, Dean Munro, took a leave of absence to pursue the elusive goal of an NHL franchise. To me, hockey was a sport played by Canadians and assorted foreign thugs and gave rise to everybody's favorite line: "I went to a fight and a hockey game broke out." Not too many years ago, there was a large fight *before* the national anthem was sung. Some sport, I thought. Wrong. I got a quick education.

I picked the reliable Dan Hancock and former San Francisco 49er attorney, Ed Alvarez, to represent the city in the forthcoming deal. They were the best. Negotiations went well, and in the fall of 1989, the league awarded an expansion franchise to San Jose, marking the beginning of a good relationship with the Gund family (also owners of the NBA Cleveland Cavaliers). Again, as in our work with the Swigs on the

Fairmont Hotel, our choice of a competent, straight-shooting family made the difference. George Gund, his brother Gordon and their main man, Sharks president Art Savage, made for a sound relationship the city could trust. George Gund is the complete honorable owner; Savage the new wave of sports executives, attuned to marketing and efficiency. There were Sharks in Silicon Valley by September 1993, giving us a rink tenant for 41 home games and significant national exposure.

When the Sharks, incredibly, made it to the play-offs their first season in the arena, then on to the second round toward the Stanley Cup, they became national media darlings. Our shining arena, the new sports cathedral, enticed CBS News, the *New York Times*, *Sports Illustrated*, and others to trumpet the "San Jose success story."

The Transit Mall: Sometimes We Hit London

In the middle of our rebuilding boom in the mid-Eighties, local papers were suddenly filled with a saga of historical memory and controversial extradition proceedings.

Arthur Rudolf was a low-key, balding engineer who lived in South San Jose and worked for NASA. Unfortunately for Mr. Rudolf, his résumé had a gap: his employer from 1939 to 1945 was Hitler's Third Reich. Rudolf had been a research scientist with Werner von Braun, using slave labor to manufacture the V-2 rockets that rained down on English cities. When that truth came to light, deportation hearings were begun. It reminded me of an old joke about von Braun's autobiography, which was titled *I Aim for the Stars*. Lenny Bruce suggested a better title: *I Aim for the Stars, but Sometimes I Hit London*.

One redevelopment project in particular suffered the same targeting errors. We intended to reconstruct a transit network to link downtown to our suburbs and outlying industry. The centerpiece would be a magnificent Transit Mall. Well, we learned a few lessons in Murphy's Law on that project. A well-run implementation can go for naught when the project is ill conceived from the beginning; conversely, even the most well-conceived project can be botched in implementation.

The downtown had always been the center of transportation and transit in the entire South Bay. That hegemony was lost as centrifugal forces pushed the city to far-flung geographic lengths. As a new era began, we wished to recapture that role. From 1976 on, our general plan called for the conversion of First Street—San Jose's main north-south arterial—to a right-of-way emphasizing mass transit and pedestrians. We analyzed the preferred highway or rail choices for the entire north-south route of the transportation system, a twenty-mile swath called the Guadalupe Corridor that would link the bedroom community of South San Jose to the industrial lands of North San Jose and the suburbs of Santa Clara, Sunnyvale, and Mountain View. The corridor would cut right through downtown San Jose.

With the help of a $1 billion bond measure in 1984, and with the liberal use of redevelopment dollars, the highway system that was promised but never built by the state of California was taking shape. We could have waited for the state or the cavalry, but it was wiser to do it ourselves, with local money. We would then be able to boast that we had a downtown with off-ramps, a novelty for us. Before 1987, there had been no way to enter downtown directly, just a long, circuitous route on the edge of the city that made a traveler feel like a vulture, slowly circling in on his target.

Palms

They were loved by the early Spanish padres and by nineteenth-century marketers luring families West. They are to California what oranges are to Florida or shamrocks to Ireland. We have always had them in San Jose—well, some of them. In the past decade, we returned nearly 1,000 of these beautiful palm trees to key spots in the new, improved-on-nature downtown.

We have used the stately Washingtonia filifera, *the only palm native to California, and the* Washingtonia robusta, *a Mexican fan palm. The latter may have traveled here first with the padres. The palms have stimulated a lively debate in our city, for people either love them or hate them. "They look too L.A.," some critics say. "They harbor rats," say others. Most believe that they make a pleasant statement along a major street. They may be bastards to trim and maintain, but they are our bastards.*

At the center of the corridor, we planned to return San Jose to the pleasant days of America's yesteryear when the streetcar ruled the byways. The Downtown Transit Mall would be a two-street, twenty-two-block pedestrian and transit-rider preserve of trees and granite, with European-style pavings and amenities. The project had first been envisioned in the Carter administration but had been in the conceptual (no-funding) stages for years. The entire project was supposed to cost approximately $20 million and was to be completed in a hectic two-year schedule, 1986 to 1988. Right down the middle of the Transit Mall would run a new high-tech light-rail line, and the path would accommodate the entire hub of the county bus network as well. It seemed too good to be true. Boy, was it.

Sometimes plans are off the mark. This project was not twice as bad as I had imagined; it was ten times as bad. Think for a moment of the sensitivity: a construction project spanning our two busiest downtown streets, which contained the majority of the small business still surviving in the center city. Every single front door and customer entrance had to be dug out to a depth of twenty feet. All utilities had to be replaced. The dirt and discombobulation of a thousand remodelings were focused into one gigantic mess.

Things went wrong from the inception in 1986. The contract was awarded to the low bidder, a nonunion Philadelphia firm called Weiss Brothers. Only in government work are you forced by law to give a job to people you neither know nor trust. This was a multi-million-dollar project that should have been awarded with due care and diligence, yet the choice of contractors became a brouhaha. The local labor unions weighed in with their opinion that if the contract was not given to a union firm, then we would have hell to pay. A crowd of several hundred showed up at city hall and attempted to sway the council. Because my family owned property in the vicinity, I abstained from the vote awarding the contract to Weiss. The council members bent but did not break, and it passed by a narrow margin.

I did make a phone call to get the opinion of a fellow mayor, Charlotte, North Carolina's Harvey Gantt. (Gantt would become a national media celebrity of sorts four years later when he challenged Jesse Helms, unsuccessfully, for his U.S. Senate seat.) Harvey told me that Weiss Brothers had constructed the Charlotte Mall and had done a fine job. He indicated no concerns, and I had no reason to doubt his accuracy or his judgment. After all, who better than a mayor to know how bad is bad?

Two years later, two years of problems, plagues, and scandals, the contractor David Weiss was indicted in San Jose for bribing city inspectors, one of the few scandals of mendacity in my two terms. The project was wildly over budget and hopelessly behind schedule. Budget, time, and bribes: Weiss wound up 0-for-3. I felt like calling Gantt back and saying, Harvey, that is bad even for government work.

The small merchants of any downtown are those least able to handle the vicissitudes of the seasonal cycles of business, let alone a disaster of this scope at their own front door. Those in the construction zone now called our downtown "Beirut," labeling the tear-up job with the very picture of violent urban deconstruction. Small retailers were in shock. So was I. Though I always kept the long view, I understood the anger. As I walked around the jagged, ripped-up blocks downtown, I felt a smidgen of what Wilson Goode must have felt after he ordered the MOVE bombing in Philadelphia. At least we lost no lives.

When the final analysis was in, the cost was staggering. The city had shouldered the entire legal, and equally important moral, responsibility to see that the small-business people of the downtown were not defined as "acceptable casualties" in the great battle to rebuild. Our partner, the county, could not have cared less. We wound up spending over $2.6 million in restitution—war reparations, essentially, for the Beirut years. Most of the small businesses survived, but the city assistance was vital.

The Transit Mall finally opened in the early summer of 1989, and light-rail vehicles commenced their lengthy journey north and south on the route through the downtown. Sleek, high-tech trains were interspersed with a fleet of rebuilt historic trolley cars, redesigned to fit the new rails. As I watched those delightful anachronisms lumbering on their merry way, it was at once a look at the past and a peek at the future.

During my speech at the mall's dedication ceremony, a police horse tied to a nearby pole broke loose and tore across the light-rail line into an intersection, grazing a pedestrian and knocking another woman to the ground. I guess a malignant fate still haunted the project. The woman was injured, and I added her casualty to the long list of things that could go wrong with one project.

"McEnery's Law" states that in a simple deal, conceived or managed by two or more government agencies, whatever *can* go right *will* go straight to hell. The only thing missing from our Transit Mall was a V-2 rocket dropping on the finished product. If our joint staff and that contractor had been running the war for Germany, they would have missed London and England altogether.

A Tree for Colonel Page

Not every construction project spews trouble in its path. Sometimes, fortune smiles. There was once a tree, the scrawniest and least noticeable of all the trees in Plaza Park (now renamed for Cesar Chavez) in front of the Fairmont. One day in 1989, a construction worker from the Collishaw Company came upon the tree in the course of working on the park grounds. The worker, a man named Curt Elrod, could easily have uprooted the spindly tree in accordance with his instructions. Something stopped him. Call it serendipity, call it luck, or perhaps attribute it to the unseen force I like to think played a role. When Elrod looked at the tree, cowering in the shadow of the massive Fairmont Hotel, he noticed a small plaque at its base. Rusty and tarnished, its inscription could barely be read:

> The Freedom Tree: with the vision of universal freedom for all mankind, this tree is dedicated to Lt. Col. Gordon L. Page and all prisoners of war and missing in action, 1973.

The construction worker stopped like a farmer who had just discovered the relic of a long-dead civilization. He called his supervisor, and the supervisor called the mayor's office.

When Gordon Page was shot down over North Vietnam in 1966, I was attending college at Santa Clara University and did not notice the beginning of the Page saga. When the tree was first dedicated in 1973, I was recently married and a new father, deep in the throes of operating a small business, and again took no notice. When the call came in 1989 to the mayor's office, I noticed. I went immediately to see this souvenir of another time and place and marveled at its survival. I thanked Mr. Elrod. I was going to make sure that the courage and commitment of Gordon Page would not be another part of San Jose history relegated to the trash heap.

The project was thoroughly researched and the family of the downed pilot contacted. The widowed Mrs. Page still lived in the area. It was a great honor on Veterans Day, November 11, 1989, to rededicate the long-forgotten Freedom Tree and to present the Key to the City to Mrs. Page. The choir from Castillero Middle School sang that most lovely of songs from *Les Misérables*, "Take Me Home." The emotion at the ceremony was as palpable as any I ever felt as mayor. As the six-foot tree was dedicated among the towering redwoods of Plaza Park and balloons floated toward the towers of St. Joseph's Cathedral, I was able to look at the colonel's wife and father and children and granddaughter and let them know that in San Jose no one would ever again miss the Freedom Tree or what it means. In a way, it is the tallest tree in the park.

The Color Purple

Even the finishing touches of a building can bring controversy. Another phone call one day got my notice: "It's going to be pink!" I could hardly believe my ears at this news about one of my all-time favorite construction projects.

I am never reluctant to give my opinions to anyone, but I reacted strongly when faced with a pretty-in-pink future for the carefully sculpted Children's Discovery Museum, with its signature architecture, at the bend of the major highway leading into the downtown. The color was a nightmarish thought. The phone calls from museum board members predictably began. They sang a refrain imploring me to reason with the courtly architect Ricardo Legoretta. I inquired of one member what the board's vote had been on the color and received a startling response: 23–2. Assuming that pink had been voted down decisively, I asked why they were proceeding with the hated color. "Oh, no," he replied, "the vote was 23-2 in favor!" He explained sheepishly that, faced with Legoretta's vaunted charm and persuasiveness, the board had sat silent and endorsed a color that many thought ruinous to the museum's viability.

"We'll be a joke," the museum's new director told me. "You have got to do something." Fools rush in, or so the saying goes, and that is exactly what I did. I had a low opinion of even the finest collection of citizens for their inability to say no in a group dynamic. I have watched time and again as the good judgment of the many is overruled by the stridency of the few. Most of us dislike conflict and are only too happy to agree, adjourn, and avoid. That was the story of Legoretta's pink.

Frank Taylor and I went to see the architect, and with all my diplomacy, I notified him that a change was necessary. We used a reference to Carl Sandburg's epigram that "a museum is a place where the community and its artists meet each other." We flattered, and we cajoled. He took it well and did not openly show disdain or the feeling that he was among the philistines. Our little victory was achieved quickly, much more quickly than the arena victory.

Together we looked at the color green, and then settled on another lively color, which will now forever be synonymous with children in our city. It is the color purple.

Part Three

A Manual

9

THINK LIKE A GENERAL

> The streets of this city are safe.
> It's only the people who make them unsafe.
> —Mayor Frank Rizzo of Philadelphia

Before becoming mayor of Philadelphia, Frank Rizzo was a hard-line police chief in the City of Brotherly Love. In 1972, when George McGovern first visited Philadelphia during his campaign against Richard Nixon, McGovern's advisers were afraid that the very liberal Democrat might not receive the best in security protection from Rizzo's ultraconservative police force. Everything went smoothly, though, with no reminders of the Chicago debacle four years before, no trouble of any kind. Though he despised McGovern, Rizzo told his lieutenants: "I'll be damned if I'll have any politician shot in *my* city."

Rizzo later became a popular mayor, talk-show host, and then almost mayor again—he dropped dead on the campaign trail on the verge of a comeback. His understanding of the issue of safety in our cities comes close to providing a broad-brush outline for the leader of a new city-state. Rizzo was right: it *is* the people who make our streets unsafe. It's just not in the way he thought. After all, cities do not need to acquire neutron bombs, which the Pentagon once designed to use on urban European battlefields. The neutron bomb kills by radiation: it kills people and leaves buildings intact. Metropolitan leaders concerned about crime need not go that far.

What they should do instead is think of urban security as a general might. We can learn something from the history of cold war military

197

strategies. The American city developing a crime-fighting plan today stands in much the same situation as the nation did three decades ago. As the Russians developed their own atomic stockpile, our nuclear deterrent became "noncredible," in war game language. In 1961, John Kennedy decided to move away from our massive-retaliation strategy, which only invited mutual destruction. He ordered Pentagon generals to develop a program of "flexible response" instead, designed to meet other challenges and threats in a multipolar world.

The federal government's oft-declared "war on crime" is today noncredible. Mayors and police chiefs around the country have known that for years. The hard-line stance from Washington is no more than a cruel joke on citizens, whose votes are lured and manipulated every election cycle by politicians standing before police union crowds, pledging to "win the war on crime."

It is up to local leaders to learn the lesson Jack Kennedy did more than thirty years ago and stop relying on a federal threat of massive retaliation. No one believes that threat anymore, least of all the criminals. The city-state mayor must begin to think like a general, with his police chief and public safety staff filling other military leadership positions in support of the common defense. The new city-state should consider its police and security resources as a self-reliant defense department, the local equivalent of a Pentagon. The policies those provincial Pentagons develop must, of necessity, be "flexible response" policies. The menaces and dangers on the crime front are varied and not easily attacked head-on.

Understanding the Nature of the Threat

Crime is difficult to understand and therefore difficult to contain. Economic growth has done little to stem the crime wave in the past decade. And you might expect more prosperous cities to have less crime, but that is not necessarily the case. Some cities have higher crime rates than others, much higher, and the reasons are not always perfectly apparent.

Experts tell us that levels of crime are sometimes rooted deep in a community's culture, and general rules may not help in explaining the differences. A San Jose resident is in a particularly strong position to offer some thoughts on the question because of the striking statistics the city generates. Although San Jose is the nation's eleventh-largest city by population, it has the lowest crime rate of the top fifty cities. The FBI's 1991 figures for violent crimes showed Miami ranking first in total number of crimes, with 4,353. Atlanta, which is smaller than San Jose, was a close second, with 4,085. San Jose had only 601. Our low rate of violent crime is put into more remarkable relief when we compare ourselves to our Bay Area neighbors. In 1991, San Francisco had an index of violent crimes per 1,000 residents of 96; Oakland's index was a staggering 126. Yet San Jose, bigger than San Francisco and twice as large as Oakland, witnessed only 55 incidents per 1,000 residents.

The murder rate is the single most feared statistic for a city's population. Despite the shocking individual murder cases I have seen in San Jose, our murder rate is minuscule compared with others around the country. Admittedly, one murder is a terrible tragedy, but San Jose's 1993 murder tally of 41 gave us a rate of only 5.1 homicides per 100,000 residents. New York City's astounding 1,995 murders meant a murder rate of 27.2, and Los Angeles's rate was 29.8 (a total of 1,077 murders). Oakland's 154 murders meant a murder rate of 42 per 100,000. Washington D.C., smaller than San Jose but with the sad title of the nation's murder capital, had 465 murders for a high rate of 78 per 100,000.

We have kept for quite a few years our ranking as the safest big city in America, but as mayor, that never left me satisfied or particularly proud. Instead, I almost obsessively looked to other cities to monitor their own progress and failures, much as a corporate president might look to other companies to observe potential dangers. Take the example of gangs. Gangs are not a new phenomenon in America's cities. We may romanticize the organized-crime cells of the Prohibition era, but urban gangs today are structured similarly and present much the same type of challenge to a city's residents.

The difference is one of scale—massive scale. Los Angeles today has an estimated 1,000 gangs, with 120,000 to 150,000 members, many heavily armed. To put that number in perspective, consider that the Soviets invaded and subdued Afghanistan for almost a decade with 120,000 soldiers. San Jose's gang problem is much smaller, with between 40 and 50 active gangs in the San Jose metro area, totaling perhaps 2,000 members. Our numbers are deceptively small, though, for a number of reasons. The newest gangs are younger and more violent, with increasing recruitment among juveniles, so our problem can only grow. Gang-related violence has increased dramatically in the past decade, and we have seen our first drive-by shootings and car-jackings.[153] I mentioned monitoring the crime situation in other cities. Gangs are the equivalent of invading, rampaging guerrilla armies, and our police department knows that well-worn paths lead directly from Los Angeles and Oakland into San Jose's more peaceful neighborhoods.

Fortify Your First Line of Defense

As a nation, we have tried to make the streets safer by locking up more criminals, particularly during the Reagan era. According to the FBI, in 1980, for every 100,000 people in the United States, there were 134 imprisoned. By 1990, that figure had risen to 290 per 100,000—more than double the proportion. Violent crime, unfortunately, is still rising. Don't get me wrong. I never had one occasion where an incarcerated individual committed a crime in my city; locked-up criminals are safe criminals. Critics of "just locking up more convicts" should keep that in mind. Once a violent crime has been committed, the perpetrator should be kept away from society for a long time.

As important as punishment is, the American city is having to rely more and more on its own ability to prevent crime. That job falls to the city-state's first-line department of defense, its thin-blue-line police force.

It is difficult to develop a national strategy for fighting crime in our cities' streets. There are some 15,000 independent police departments in the United States, each protecting a community with its own particular needs, vulnerabilities, and ability to match the crime problem with resources. Just as the nation got used to paying large Pentagon budgets during the cold war, cities are accustomed to expensive local defense programs. In San Jose, as in most other cities, the largest single budget item in our general fund goes for "public safety"—around 40 percent of our total budget in 1994—paying for over 1,250 police officers and a smaller force in the fire department.

For the 222 police departments in American cities with a population of more than 100,000 people, their total police budgets combined add up to $4.7 billion, according to research by Professor John DiIulio of Princeton University. Some have suggested that we take some of the billions we spend on the drug "war" ($13 billion in 1992 at the federal level) and make the money available instead to local governments for police departments. For a modest diversion of funds, we could perhaps double the number of police officers on duty in the streets of our big cities.[154] That level of commitment, though, seems impossible to elicit from the federal government. It is at the local level that citizens and political leaders are most responsive to the defense needs of the community.

In San Jose, we take our police department, its reputation, and its effectiveness very seriously. Every single officer stands proud in his or her uniform and enjoys the respect of the public. They work hard to earn it. Our department has a national reputation as one of the finest in the country primarily because of its well-trained, professional staff. Our officers are highly educated: while many other cities still require only a high school diploma to qualify as an officer candidate, we require a minimum of sixty units of college credit. More than half our police have four-year college degrees, and many have advanced degrees.

The Ideal Chief

Like Gilbert and Sullivan's "model of a modern major general," Joe McNamara, longtime San Jose police chief until 1991, set a good example for his troops with his Ph.D. from Harvard. McNamara served as chief during both my terms, gaining a national reputation for his competence, crime novels, and public relations flair. He also received some criticism for his outspoken stands on gun control (he's for it) and the war on drugs (he's against it, as it has been defined by administration after administration). Joe had been a beat cop in the Bronx. After he received a Ph.D. in public administration and served as police chief in Kansas City, he came to San Jose in 1976. When he retired a couple of years ago, he was still a relatively young man but had already suffered heart problems, and he wanted to avoid making them worse.

The job of police chief is a tough job in any town. The Police Executive Research Forum, a Washington-based group, pointed out in 1992 that in the five years prior, forty-one of the nation's fifty largest cities had lost their police chiefs to resignation or dismissal. Thirteen of those big cities had replaced their chiefs twice in that period. San Francisco has seen four men occupying the hot seat in the past three years. Gerald Lynch, president of the John Jay College of Criminal Justice in New York City, goes on record to argue that after the mayor's job, "nothing in the city demands more time and energy and total commitment."[155]

A police chief can provide effective crime prevention only with an effective force beneath him. San Jose has fewer officers per 1,000 people than most other cities our size, with only 1.3 per 1,000 for our 800,000 people. Most big cities have at least 2 officers per 1,000 people. Miami has about 3 officers per 1,000 people, in a city of 360,000. Cleveland, with a population of 505,000, has 3.4 officers per 1,000 people, and St. Louis fields 3.8 officers per 1,000, in a population of just under 400,000.

Wealthier communities, of course, are able to field more police officers. Beverly Hills has 4 per 1,000, 127 officers for 31,800 people, policing just 5.5 square miles. The massive city of Los Angeles as a whole is able to put 2.4 officers per 1,000 on the streets—that's 8,500 officers in a population of 3.6 million, spread over 465 square miles. Mayor Dick Riordan has now committed to adding even more. But L.A.'s suburb Compton, a very bad neighborhood chronicled in rap songs and the movie *Boyz N the Hood*, has only 135 officers for 90,500 people over 10 square miles, giving it a ratio of only 1.5 per 1,000, one of the lowest ratios in Los Angeles County. In February 1993, two Compton officers were killed on duty making a routine vehicle stop. One of the slain officers was on his very last day of service in Compton, having already arranged a new job and a family move—to San Jose and a job with our P.D.

It is not simply a numbers game. A police department must have the committed support of the community behind it, and the city administration must provide the department the financial and moral support it needs. In 1989, I proposed and began a new hiring plan to hire forty-five additional officers every year for five years. I made sure to match that with eleven support staff members hired each year to back them up in the stations, so that officers are spending more time in the field and less behind a desk. Susan Hammer has continued that five-year plan, including forty-five new officers for the 1995 budget.

For the police department, a large semiautonomous organization within the city-state, just as important as money is morale. After the 1992 Los Angeles riots and the prosecution of the officers in the Rodney King beating, California's largest police department suffered a sinking esprit de corps. A reporter found that some L.A.P.D. officers were "now reluctant to confront suspects in volatile situations and are more likely to delay responding to urgent calls . . . or they simply let fleeing suspects get away." Some police officers became disenchanted with their career choice. L.A.P.D. retirements were up, jumping 60 percent in 1992.[156]

The People's Army: A Police Force in and of the Community

As mayor, I tried to do something about the twin problems of not enough cops and declining morale on the force. I had always been a strong supporter of the police department as a downtown small-business man. In my first year as mayor, I learned of a proposal by Adam Walinsky, onetime aide to Senator Robert F. Kennedy, who has long argued in favor of community service. Walinsky came up with the idea of a domestic "police corps," using college students. Students' college tuition would be paid by local police departments, on the condition that after graduation, the students would serve three full years on the police force. Their salary and fringe benefits for those three years would be about half those of regular new officers coming out of the police academy.

The plan appealed to me: it used a flexible new approach to address an age-old problem, it saved the city money, it provided more cops for safer streets, and it harnessed the energy and idealism natural to young people. The mayor's office said "Do it" in January 1984, and planning for the program began with eager volunteers and some corporate stipends. Our quick action got the attention of the national media and was featured in *Time* magazine, but it also met local opposition. Members of the San Jose Police Officers Association opposed the plan, predictably enough. They were concerned that lower benefit scales for the police corps recruits might lead to lower benefits for full officers. They were sincere but wrong, yet their opposition ensured that the police corps idea never got a fair trial in San Jose. Nor has it been implemented to any large degree anywhere else in the country; we were to be the first city, and no one has taken that crown yet. In 1991, Congress actually authorized some money for a national police corps, but the Bush administration never got around to implementing it. President Clinton has pledged in the new crime bill to assist in putting 100,000 more cops on city streets, but the police corps model will not be a part of that. This may be a case of a good idea ahead of its time.

Some cities cannot afford to wait for federal help, for they are overwhelmed by crime, unable to respond to the level of threat. In East Palo Alto, a city plagued by murders and drug dealing, the community has been unable to afford the level of policing that would provide an adequate defense against the onslaught of violent dealers. Like a beleaguered small country, the town needed a collective response from allies. Those allies were found in 1993 in a unique arrangement: thirty-eight officers from four neighboring law-enforcement agencies were assigned to patrol East Palo Alto's streets. That effectively meant doubling the city's police force, in a city of 24,000 people packed into 2.5 square miles. The surrounding cities understood the fallacy of the drawbridge mentality and the necessity of joint action.

An idea that is very much in its time is community policing, which aims to restructure the relationship between a police force and community residents in order to prevent high levels of crime. The concept has received much attention across the country and is being implemented in many cities. San Jose had an early commitment to community policing and its mission to get police away from the "911 syndrome"—just responding once a crime has been committed. We have been using our police in ways reminiscent of the old beat cop, sending them back into the neighborhoods to work closely with residents to improve their lives. As our new chief, Lou Cobarruviaz, says, "Community policing demands innovation and decentralization of our services to where they belong—the community and the individual."

Community policing is the most important way we can work to avoid the problems Los Angeles faced with Chief Darryl Gates. His police force was no "people's army." It was seen by many residents in minority communities as practically an alien occupying force.

Crackdown on Gangs

The gang problem is reflected in cities across the country, though gangs are a particularly tenacious presence in Los Angeles. They represent the new kind of specialized threat that cities face. Gangs are organized (tightly or loosely) on ethnic, racial, or neighborhood lines and can have memberships spanning across generations. As the menace becomes more specialized, so must the response. The type of pragmatic defense needed to overcome the gang problem comes best at the local level.

San Jose's history with gangs, like that of many California towns, dates back to the 1950s. Many of our gangs are now Hispanic, and most of them fall under two umbrella categories: the Norteños and the Sureños. Red or blue is the color chosen by these gang families, and they respectively descend from different regional backgrounds and rely on different prison-based gangs for leadership. In California as a whole, there are an estimated 200,000 gang members, according to the state Department of Justice—maybe many more. Meanwhile, the FBI has called young Asian gangs the fastest-growing organized-crime problem in the country. This kind of concentrated threat requires a localized, community-specific response. Only at the city level can effective strategies that reflect a local understanding of the problem and its roots be found and implemented. For example, according to the FBI's organized-crime investigations, Vietnamese gangs are marked by their mobility and high propensity for violence. These loose-knit gangs commute among a network of local gang territories up and down the East and West coasts. Their concern is not turf, but money. They cooperate with one another—albeit with cancerous "shared goals." The San Jose Police Department has found with such gangs that the most important approach is prevention and early intervention. Community policing provides police close contact with the neighborhood and its youth, which can prevent kids from ever getting involved in gangs. Police in many big cities are joining with other groups, public and private, to provide attractive alternatives to gang activity.

Such measures come too late for too many. The shooting death of a twelve-year-old girl gang member brought to light the grip of gang warfare on the neighborhoods of Long Beach. In that city of 430,000, one of Southern California's largest, there are an estimated 10,000 gang members. Long Beach police on gang patrol are pessimistic about the prospects for the area's youth. "It's going to keep getting worse," Detective Norm Sorenson told a reporter. "You have friends, you have families, you have gang members on the victims' side who will never, ever forget this. And who knows what paybacks are to come. There will be hatred in their heart forever."[157] While the police are stretched beyond any reasonable limits on their resources, the problems get worse and worse, and the average kid or adult is afraid to venture on neighborhood streets even in broad daylight. That is an ugly urban reality.

In a very true sense, today's inner-city teenagers are fighting their generation's Vietnam, a bloody conflict with no clear lines dividing friend from enemy and with no real commitment from our leaders to see the combat end. To stretch the analogy just one step further, we are going to have to see the equivalent of "Vietnamization" if this war on our streets is ever to be won. The local community has to be involved, and the fight has to be its own.

In San Jose, we answered the warnings with a workmanlike approach, setting our sights at winning the battle block by block, neighborhood by neighborhood. We said that we would not surrender one neighborhood, one street, one blade of grass to the drug dealers. First, we met the enemy head-on with "Project Crackdown," a multiagency, multiservice effort for direct intervention in areas most affected by crack cocaine. The Crackdown team was like football's "flying wedge," leading with the police department's Narcotics Enforcement Team and following up with intensive enforcement of health and safety codes, improved lighting, removal of abandoned vehicles (often the venue of drug deals), and neighborhood cleanups to remove the visual impact of graffiti and blight. In its first year, 1989, Project Crackdown resulted in an 80 percent reduction in drug-related arrests in targeted areas, but our effort didn't stop there.

I spent many days and nights out in the targeted neighborhoods, but the courage of those who actually lived there was prodigious. We knew that long-term success would come only if local residents were empowered, spurring parents and families to reclaim their streets, their parks, their schools. San Jose hired several full-time bilingual coordinators to organize neighborhood Community Action Teams, which meet monthly to discuss strategies to keep their neighborhoods safe. With police, city services, and neighborhood residents all working together, we have had some remarkable success. We restored playgrounds to students, because we put our faith in the courage of parents and teachers and in the resilience of children. Under the leadership of a remarkable principal named Jennie Collett, O. B. Whalley Elementary—a school in a crackdown area where students used to carry fear instead of homework with them each morning—has received a national presidential education award.

Every city has its version of Crackdown, often under a similarly tough-sounding name. Not all cities back up their rhetoric with attention and commitment over the long haul, so not all cities see results. New York City's "Tactical Narcotics Team," formed in 1988 with a force of 100 or so officers, was designed to come down hard on street dealers. The program cost the city some $60 million a year. While TNT's effort did result in thousands of arrests, the end result was not a decrease in crime or even directly in street drug trafficking. Dealers simply adopted new tactics to stay at arm's length, avoiding arrest. Courts and jails were packed with low-level dealing cases, while the amount of dealing did not drop. Finally, in 1992, the city quietly reduced the TNT program, admitting that it was not having the intended effect.[158] What the city was missing was true community involvement, perhaps a difficult proposition in New York City but one that is an essential prerequisite of success.

Strong mayors are beginning to realize that the federal government's policy emphasizing a "war on drugs" led by a "drug czar" is an ineffective shell game, wasting billions of dollars ($14 billion in 1994) on a largely cynical public relations effort. During the 1992 campaign, the Bush White House and its Office of National Drug Control Policy heavily promoted their Weed and Seed program, designed to "weed" dealers and gangs out of neighborhoods and to "seed" those neighborhoods with social programs. In an internal memo, a staffer admitted that "while the prospects for enactment in 1992 appear dim, there may be some real political value in giving it a high profile (hearings, op-ed pieces, a presidential campaign event, etc.) during the coming months."[159]

Since then, the Clinton administration has begun to change the emphasis of the so-called war on drugs away from the supply side, which tries to decrease the amounts of drugs produced and exported by South America and South Asia. Supply-side drug policies seem just as ephemeral as supply-side economics, and meanwhile the war is lost every day on our city streets. Mayors know this, police chiefs know this, and we are tired of losing the drug war the same way we lost Vietnam. We need to stop our impotent bombing of the equivalent of the Ho Chi Minh supply trail and start winning the war in the cities and in our neighborhoods, with positive alternatives and a dramatic new focus on prevention. We must stop destroying the village to save it.

Nowhere has this lesson been more painfully learned and, now, hopefully applied than in Austin, Texas. Walt Rostow was a key national security adviser to Presidents Kennedy and Johnson and is now leading a civic effort called the Austin Project. It is an attempt to address the problems of urban America in the Texas capital. Rostow was drafted to head the project because of his position at the LBJ Presidential Library in Austin and has taken to the task with the fervor he once felt fighting communism in Vietnam. He proposes massive drug and crime prevention efforts, like school dropout programs and prenatal care for every teenage mother, pointing out that they will require less money over the long run: "You rapidly and drastically increase your prevention efforts with the young until they are equal to the scale of the problem, and in a short time the investment will pay for itself because you'll pay less for damage control."[160] His voice is now echoed by President Clinton himself, who has declared unequivocally some moral truths for our youth: illegitimacy is wrong, children having children is wrong, and Martin Luther King, Jr., did not live so that young black men could slaughter one another on American streets. We have lost an entire generation of urban youth and are in danger of losing another. We cannot ignore the question of moral wrongs and rights.

Don't Make It a Federal Case

When in doubt, it seems that the choice of most members of the U.S. Congress is to avoid dealing with problems directly. In the past, on the issue of crime, Congress prefers not to work with those bearing frontline responsibility for crimefighting in the cities of America, but rather to make more and more crimes "federal offenses." There has been a disturbing trend to attack drug "kingpins," high-profile kidnappers, and other mediagenic types with a zeal and flair for promotion that is singularly unhelpful. This is not a time for an Elliot Ness or J. Edgar Hoover, but a time to deal with our crisis through sober calculation.

Last year, all the federal law enforcement agents together generated fewer than 47,000 felonies and misdemeanors in all the federal courts. Compare this figure to the number of cases handled by the district attorney of my home

county, Santa Clara County, nearly 50,000. *As our very able and succinct
D.A. George Kennedy notes, designating additional crimes as federal does little good because the federal courts are not set up for a high volume of cases,
and lifetime appointees in federal judgeships do not like being bothered with
street crimes. Outside of a Patty Hearst case or a political sting operation, federal resources brought to bear on a single crime are often wasted and counter-
productive to the real safety of most citizens.*

*Kennedy works closely with the mayor's office to minimize processing time
in criminal drug cases, and to prevent long periods of "out-of-bail" time for defendants in violent cases. It is axiomatic to point out that cries of "speedy justice" is the ultimate oxymoron. Delays often mean the punishment is barely
even associated with the crime. Criminal defendants who know ahead of time
that their sentencing judge will not approve a lengthy delay almost always plead
guilty, and do so quietly.*

*A few more district attorneys like Kennedy who push reforms like one-judge
calendarizing and sentencing accountability, could be more beneficial than one
hundred congressional debates. The Clinton initiated Crime Bill of 1994 takes
a notable step toward reflecting the needs of local D.A.'s and Police Chiefs. It
also bans more of the obscene assault weapons. It is a significant achievement
in a difficult field.*

Cities are under siege by violent crime, but as a city becomes more like
a nation-state itself, citizens will come to realize that strong defense for
America means strong defense at home, strong defense of the city-state
against the internal enemy of crime. It is even possible that cities will
prove better able to address violent crime than will federal law enforcement, as our urban police departments become more sophisticated and
experienced in prevention strategies. President Clinton's appointment of
former San Jose cop and New York police commissioner Lee Brown as his
drug policy chief is a hopeful sign. Brown knows city streets. Another
streetwise individual, Mayor Kurt Schmoke of Baltimore, says the drug
war is destroying our trial court system. Now some cities and counties are
completing the self-defense circle, independently experimenting with alternative methods of handling the rising tide of drug-related crimes that
clog the nation's courts and jails. New "drug courts" in Miami and San
Diego are focusing on rehabilitation programs instead of punishment and
incarceration, at a lower cost and with lower long-term recidivism rates.

Coordinated prevention efforts, alternative sentencing, community
policing, all are elements of a larger self-defense approach that the city-

state needs to adopt. Such a broad effort needs leadership, and sometimes a city serendipitously gets new leadership to spark a renewal. Baltimore had the good judgment in 1994 to select as its new police chief San Jose's deputy chief Tom Frazier, who, more than any other officer, led our Project Crackdown successes. The city of Atlanta in the early 1990s indulged in what a reporter called "a self-congratulatory orgy over the success of its professional sports teams," along with euphoria over its selection as the host city for the 1996 Summer Olympics.[161] Yet one of the city's most thoughtful citizens, and certainly our country's finest former president, Jimmy Carter, recently issued a wake-up call to Atlantans, describing the grimmer side of their urban reality and challenging them to address urgent problems. In the spring of 1992, Carter announced the Atlanta Project, a head-on assault against the problems of drugs, crime, substandard housing and teenage pregnancy—the laundry list of urban ills that lie beneath the surface of violence. "Underneath, Atlanta is rotten in many ways," Carter pointed out, "and this needs to be addressed frankly."

Carter is enlisting business leaders from Coca-Cola and IBM, along with thousands of individual volunteers, in his effort. Most refreshing, he's not relying upon, not even calling for, major injections of new federal dollars. In fact, Bill Clinton has invited him to the White House to discuss what the federal government could learn from Atlanta.

Such coordinated and creative efforts are the essence of a flexible response to the multiple threats posed by crime to the city. If we are lucky and prepare prodigiously, we will have the same success the United States military did in Desert Storm, when our sophisticated air attack stealthily destroyed the infrastructure and our land armies swung into action with "maneuver warfare," not a crude frontal assault. Reform-minded military officers had predicted for a decade that modern combat would look less and less like a head-to-head slugfest and that maneuverability and flexible tactics would surprise, outflank, and conquer lead-footed enemies. City-state police can take on criminals in our neighborhoods the same way, establishing a flexible presence with community policing and employing various prevention strategies to preempt and outflank the bad guys.

Some cities will not be up to this challenge. They will duck the hard work, continuing to look the other way and avoiding real solutions to crime. Perhaps we should take account of their failure and warn visitors by adopting the State Department's restrictions on travel to dangerous countries. Someday, driver's licenses for Americans may be stamped with a list of cities that refuse to take their security seriously. The warning: "Avoid this city."

10

CAN'T WE ALL
JUST GET ALONG?

> If we open a quarrel between the past and the present,
> we shall surely find that we've lost the future.
> —Winston Churchill

Rarely does the debate over our country's racial and ethnic divisions stop at Rodney King's plaintive question of why we cannot all live together in peace. The debate instead becomes an argument, a feud, a fistfight, or a riot. Cities witness it all, most often in our schools and in controversial renditions of local history, as we will see. One of the most contentious of all areas in which our divisions are revealed is local politics. I can verify Tip O'Neill's maxim: "All politics are local." The national debate on multiculturalism boils over at the city and neighborhood levels, for any argument over power and representation is loudest on your own doorstep.

I have a particular point of view on multiculturalism, a view reinforced by a decade in power in one of America's most extraordinarily diverse cities. I believe in the unifying vision represented in the founding credo of our immigrant nation: E Pluribus Unum. Out of many, one. That doctrine is not dead, but it lies forgotten like too much of our country's history. Popular definitions of social reality have come to focus only on our differences, no longer on our commonalities. This chapter looks at some successful and unsuccessful definitions in two arenas: local politics and local history. Mayors and elected officials live by the former. Legends, true and false, die by the latter.

211

Choosing Your Constituents

City governments try to incorporate division through the apportionment of political power. Their primary vehicle is the redistricting of city council seats, just like congressional redistricting, to take account of local demographic changes in cities as reflected in the federal census every ten years. The process is complex and highly charged, and sometimes absurd. In New York, the city council was expanded from thirty-five to fifty-one members in 1991 specifically to ensure more minority representation, but redrawing the lines still resulted in squabbles and charges of discrimination. George Will has noted that in the old days, citizens chose their elected officials; now, with computers and erasable maps, elected officials choose their citizens.

Chicago, like most cities, has a shifting population base: while whites and blacks each total about 1 million inhabitants, their numbers have been shrinking from exodus, while the Hispanic population is at 500,000 and growing rapidly. The redistricting that took place after the 1990 census changed many of Chicago's historic wards, resulting in what one political consultant called "grotesqueries" for districts. Gerrymandering has many adherents in the old machine cities, of course, and many fine practitioners. Longtime alderman Burton Natarus, a two-decade veteran, was jimmied out of his 42nd District, which included the Magnificent Mile and Chicago's downtown skyscrapers and penthouses. The new district boundary lay a tantalizing three blocks away from his house under the new lines. Natarus had two options: He could run for office in his new home ward, now the 1st District, featuring the notorious Cabrini-Green housing project and a black-majority population who might not reelect him. (Natarus is white.) Or he could leave office for the private sector.

Natarus did not like those two options, so he found a third. "So I'll move," he announced to reporters. "It's only three or four blocks." Natarus is once again the alderman from the 42nd Ward. This kind of electoral relocation is so common in local politics around the country that entire moving-van lines could be sustained in the early years of a decade following census reapportionment, as frustrated office seekers look for more hospitable neighborhoods. There is one fellow in San Jose who has moved so many times that in his latest failed campaign, for the downtown city council seat, he became popularly known as "Suitcase."

Some cities are introducing fairer systems of reapportionment to minimize the possibility of tampering with district boundaries. Under a new measure passed by voters in 1990, San Jose now requires a Redistricting Advisory Council appointed by the mayor and city council, designed to ensure fairness in drawing district boundaries.

Cities can point to some successes in their efforts to encourage minority representation in politics. By the 1990s, more than 300 blacks were serving as mayors of cities around the country, 10 of them in cities over 400,000 people. In a promising measure, not all have been in cities with African-American majorities: Norman Rice was recently elected mayor of Seattle, which is less than 10 percent black. Los Angeles was only 17 percent black when Tom Bradley was first elected mayor, and Philadelphia only 38 percent under Wilson Goode. New York City does not have a black majority, yet David Dinkins was elected in 1989 as our largest city's first black mayor. By 1990, at least three major American cities had elected Hispanic mayors: San Antonio, Denver, and Miami.

Our progress should be judged not with a passing or failing grade, but with an Incomplete. In the past two decades, the preferred way to increase minority representation in a city power structure has been to design on purpose council districts with demographic concentrations of minority residents. Between a quarter and a third of all cities elect council members by geographic ward or district, as do over half of the big cities over 100,000. But most cities overall still elect their councils with candidates running at large, on a citywide basis. San Jose, like most California cities, has district elections, but I am not convinced that the demographic question alone is sufficient to ensure harmonious ethnic politics. District elections may be more likely to produce minority council members, but will those minority members differ from their white counterparts all that much? Will they be radically divergent in their socioeconomic characteristics, in their political focus or style, or in personal perspectives they bring to city policies? I doubt it, and the academic evidence so far has been very inconclusive.[162] In any case, our attention needs to be focused more on how minority concerns are treated when they are brought to city government for redress. That is where the rubber meets the road.

Battles over political power can be fierce, but local battles over history can be homicidal. Who decides when a note of historical interest deserves the full-blown treatment of controversy? My graduate degree in history did not prepare me for the strife I would see once I entered public life.

The Past Bludgeons the Present

I usually enjoyed my frequent appearances on television and radio talk shows in the course of my duties as mayor. One particular day in early 1986, though, I knew I was in for a bad time. It was one of my monthly visits with the San Francisco–based "Frank and Mike Show," a drive-time potpourri of sports, current events, and madcap satire. They put a premium on lighthearted shots at "Mayor Tom," enjoying most of all that I did not take myself very seriously and enjoyed the ribbing. That morning, an odd little story appeared on the front page of the *Mercury News*. It seems the city had engaged in another dubious venture in multicultural expression. We had unveiled a twenty-foot banner on the front of the Martin Luther King Main Library saluting the diversity of our city by rendering the word "welcome" in two dozen languages. It seemed a nice gesture and a colorful addition to the streetscape, nothing more, until a number of puzzled Filipino visitors to the building pointed out a slight error in the Tagalog translation of "welcome." Instead of saying what it was supposed to say, the huge letters on the banner clearly stated to those familiar with the language: "Circumcision to you." Not quite the connotation we were intending. The banner was quickly, but not quietly, changed.

The radio hosts that morning and a few on-air phone callers had quite a time with the blunder, but no one was seriously injured and the mistake was rather humorous. Our citizens of Philippine extraction might have been discouraged from borrowing books for a few days, but I don't believe this particular incident caused any lasting harm.

There are other issues of multiculturalism, though, that cause pain, personal hurt, and social disruption. In 1989 our city faced an impromptu passion play representing in microcosm the nation's debate over past wrongs and current reparations, symbolized by a public-relations crucifixion of one of the city's founding fathers. I learned many lessons from the episode, but I came up with as many questions as answers.

It began one night in city hall with a debate over a statue. The city council meeting had gone on for quite some time, and the caliber of debate had deteriorated greatly. We first witnessed a lively presentation of an ancient Aztec dance, complete with serpents and multicolored feathers. Next, a number of children read a hastily scripted but earnestly delivered manifesto. Others followed and, quite predictably, the language got progressively more strident. The measure at hand proposed a statue to a man long dead. One speaker raised a shrill voice to denounce him as imperialist Captain Thomas Fallon, the despoiler of all that was good in California. Another railed against a man "worse than Hitler or Stalin." Tempers rose as speaker after speaker denounced the name of this veritable Satan. The statue of Captain Fallon would never sit undisturbed at old Plaza Park, they threatened.

All the while I presided, the subdued council members did their imitation of Muhammad Ali's rope-a-dope strategy in the Foreman fight, but in this case they had no intention of coming off the ropes and engaging. As I listened intently to the pseudohistory, I thought to myself: these people aren't describing the man I once wrote a book about (titled *California Cavalier*, published before I went into government). How different from the way things really were, how completely different. . . .

Fallon's Ghost Rides Again

Let us return to 1846, the controversy's earliest chapter. It was early in the morning when a band of riders approached the center of the town. They numbered about twenty and were well mounted. Most wore the homespuns of the time, but the leader had on a buckskin jacket and held a Hawken rifle across the horn of his saddle. All of them carried themselves with a determination that belied their relatively young ages. Their leader was twenty-nine years old and had already had an eventful life traveling the Western frontier. He had ranged from lower Canada to Texas, finally arriving three years earlier over dangerous and little-known mountains with the early U.S. Army exploring party of Captain John C. Fremont. This leader's name was Fallon, and his 1846 ride over the Santa Cruz mountains to the dusty pueblo of San Jose would be a minor chapter in the brief and successful Mexican War in California. Not even a chapter—it was a footnote.

Awaiting the band of soldiers (Western editions of Minutemen) was the assembled army of General Jose Castro, the military commander of California. San Jose was a critical link in the military and civilian settlements that bound the land of California together. If this key northern settlement fell, the rest of Northern California would certainly follow. The riders of Captain Fallon were men with the names Peckham, Sinclair, Hecox, and Daubenbiss. And they were not exactly entering an unknown region, for most of them had friends and family in the pueblo of San Jose. Others were men of property who maintained business relationships with many of the old Californio families. The war presented the blurry lines and allegiances of a civil war instead of the clear lines of

Captain Thomas Fallon.

a foreign conquest. These northernmost reaches of the Republic of Mexico had endured the mismanagement and exploitation of a colony but had also been rent by internal disagreements, often settled by physical confrontations with foreign "Yankee" interlopers enlisted on one side or the other.

But no shots rang out that day in 1846. There was no confrontation between forces on this morning. General Castro apparently had determined that discretion was the better part of valor and made a strategic withdrawal to the old capital at San Juan Bautista, forty-five miles to the south. In California, the bombastic Castro gave rise to a facetious term: *cuando veulve Castro,* or "when Castro returns." The saying may be apocryphal, but Castro never would return. Fallon's men rode into San Jose from the south, past the plaza that marked the center of the tiny settlement, past the small St. Joseph's Church and on to the *juzgado,* the courthouse. Here was the target: the center of law and civil administration in the valley.

There was very little fanfare as San Jose was "conquered," taken for the United States by a meager force of arms. A few people stood around. Some even greeted the riders by name with friendly salutations. The July day was very hot and dry, one of the hottest days in the memory of even the oldest inhabitants, who had ridden into the valley nearly seventy years before with de Anza the conquistador. There was one problem not anticipated by Fallon's California battalion: they had no flag to raise. One was quickly sent for by dispatch; it was exceedingly difficult to be an arriving hero without one. Two days later, a flag arrived by messenger from U.S. troops in San Francisco.

On July 14, 1846, the Stars and Stripes were raised over the newly American settlement of San Jose. No blows were exchanged, and no one was injured—yet. San Jose was now and forever a part of the United States of America.

A Flag for the Captain

A long while passed before the first shot rang out over the raising of that flag in the dusty streets. In my last year as mayor, the real confrontation began, this time in the city council chambers over the decision to place a statue commemorating the 1846 raising of the flag. San Jose in the intervening years had done little but destroy and desecrate its history, and we were in an embryonic stage of recognition. We had initiated a plan to rectify that with an elaborate series of commemorations, living-history presentations, and local curriculum inserts in the lesson plans of elementary schools. As part of this effort, Captain Fallon and another Californio rider would be captured in larger-than-life bronze, looking up at the rising flag. The statue was to be placed where the original event occurred, on Market Street near the old courthouse and in the shadow of St. Joseph's. The site was old Plaza Park. To me, it was a local equivalent of the Iwo Jima flag raising, an act of photogenic and symbolic import. In that assessment, I was greatly mistaken. It became something much more. This statue became a cause célèbre for both the national press yearning for an ethnic angle and local columnists looking for a clue (to anything) and a rallying point for various groups of activists who, accurately or not, considered themselves wronged by my administration or by the vicissitudes of the century and a half that had intervened, leaving many of them feeling left out. This episode unfolded as one of the most instructive and one of the saddest in my time as mayor. The injustices and historical canards of generations past blazed again on the pages of the *Mercury News* and the *New York Times*.

The statute of Captain Thomas Fallon and an aide, raising the U.S. flag over San Jose.

Back to the council meeting. As the evening droned on, the speakers became more and more strident. I heard a motion to "study the matter," an attempt to satisfy all parties. That prospect was idealistic but woolly-headed. As I sat on the dais, the words of a long-ago television show came to mind: "You are traveling through another dimension, a journey taking truth into a strange land whose boundaries are that of imagination. That's the signpost up ahead, your next stop: the historical twilight zone. . . . " For nearly four hours we had been entertained, serenaded, chastised, and threatened concerning the events of 144 years before—a time so distant that not even the ancestors of most in the room had set foot on the luxurious California firmament.

This story of a statue and a historical brawl had tranquil roots in the development agreement to build the Fairmont Hotel. We had a commitment to spend 2 percent of the total cost of the structure on works of art. The inside of the hotel, designed as the most public part of the building, was decorated with some very pleasing and well-received pieces of art, including some lovely wall-sized paintings of horses. For an outdoor plaza between the Museum of Art and the hotel, and for the area in front surrounding the park, we had the opportunity to place some very large and meaningful pieces. One work, by a sculptor named Scanga, was a multicolored ten-foot futuristic figure holding a sun. It provoked comments but little controversy: nobody could tell what it was, as with most modern art. No harm, no foul. I seized the occasion to put one little piece of history back into the city, suggesting that a topic for another spot be the raising of the flag by Captain Fallon. I had researched Fallon and his Irish roots years before and written a history of his life in the form of a fictionalized journal. I believed he exemplified much about our immigrant culture. Fallon married into one of the state's oldest families, the Castros, becoming yet another assimilated immigrant. He was on the best of terms with many of the old residents of San Jose, and in fact, when he was elected mayor in 1859, one of his first acts cleared up the title to lands long in litigation, a litigation that threatened to ruin many of the old Californio families.

Although Fallon was a man of the nineteenth century and had a variety of personal peccadilloes, on balance he played a significant and positive role in local history. In the gaze of the romantic or the misled, he became a symbol of oppression and conquest, and at this meeting, he was being wielded as a club to bludgeon an acquiescent, guilt-ridden press and a nervous council. The protests accelerated from the thoughtful missives of the Aztlan Academy of Ethnic Heritage (a movement of one single thinker), to the blustering assaults of a couple of council wanna-bes. I could feel the support for the statue wilting in the heat of San Jose's imaginary past and supposed conquest. The rhetoric grew, aided by the cover of a couple of minor and questionable local historians. The head of Mexican-American studies at San Jose State charged that "this statue is like throwing us out of our own town and putting up a statue to our conquerors." I was bemused; when all this had happened, my ancestors were still in Ireland, and I imagine the good professor's were still many miles to the south in Mexico. I was determined to fight such nonsense and pointed out that my recommendation echoed the core values of an excellent report from a commission I had appointed a few years before, dubbed the Committee for the Past.

This citizens' group, working through most of 1988 and 1989, did a marvelous job of resurrecting the meaningful in San Jose's history. If you want something done well, give it to a person who loves what he or she is doing. I found that person in Judy Stabile. As a member of the city council, Stabile had made a reputation protecting the senior citizens and mobile-home-park residents of San Jose. She loved the city's history. With an unerring eye for the jugular, Judy welded the citizens together and devised a list of recommendations that were sure not only to look good but to hold up. The list recognized that our city was a special place with a significant history going back long before the first Europeans arrived in the valley. The very uniqueness of our present community only reflected our past. It also noted, quite accurately, that community character also has a physical dimension and that "our buildings are quiet voices from the past speaking of our heritage, now and in the years to come."[163]

There were three distinct findings from the Committee for the Past:

- The key to developing an effective and successful plan for the past is through the restoration and re-creation of our city's most significant historic structures.
- The city's physical resources, its structures, sites, and facilities, should not only serve as monuments to identify our heritage but also provide centers for activities and public uses.
- Preservation of the past is often inspired by a combination of nostalgia, patriotism, and a sense of pride in community, culture, or ethnic heritage. It is time to move historic preservation in San Jose from a movement by select enthusiastic proponents to a citywide ethic. Events, celebrations, art, and promotions will help to instill a community identity and deliver a message.

There were to be historical representations of the Native American, Spanish, Mexican, Californian, and American periods, honoring significant people in our history: the first *comisionado* Luis Peralta, poet Edwin Markham, writer Jack London, flight pioneer John Montgomery, and the original patron of the city, St. Joseph the builder. Four new gateways would herald the people from around the world who brought their hopes and dreams to this valley. We would build living-history centers and a significant commemoration to honor veterans, as well as my personal favorite, a river-walk commemoration to the immigrants of this valley, from the Indians to Southeast Asian boat people—a monument that could rival the Vietnam Memorial in Washington for meaning and poignancy.

It looked very good on paper, but the plan foundered on the shoals of political correctness and historical invention. The Fallon statue lost its place downtown and still sits today in a shuttered warehouse.

Coming to California

Essayist Lance Morrow believes that "a culture is what it remembers and what it knows." In California we have forgotten so much in our headlong rush to the future. Very often in our society, we invent what we have failed to notice and cherish. The nineteenth-century hagiographers of California sang the paeans of a sun-kissed land of orange groves and missions with a boundless supply of opportunity for all. The man whose coattails Thomas Fallon rode was a perfect example of what we have chosen to forget. His name was John C. Fremont, but contemporaries knew him as "the Pathfinder." He was the illegitimate son of an idiosyncratic French teacher and a Southern belle, and early in life Fremont allied himself to Senator Thomas Hart Benton, the apostle of westward expansion, by marrying his daughter. After a number of expeditions and a part in the Mexican War, he and his scout, Kit Carson, rode into history. Of Fremont it is said, "From the ashes of his campfires, great cities were born." From the eastern slopes of the Rockies to a trail through Wyoming and Utah and along the Snake River into Idaho and Oregon, perhaps 300,000 immigrants followed. First they arrived in covered wagons, then on the iron rail of the steam-driven monsters that bound a continent together, and finally in ships of every kind around the horn or from the swelling continent of Asia.

Always they were driven by the power of the dream. When more tangible items fade or are dispelled, dreams can retain their original strength and even grow stronger. That is their mystery and their magic. My great-grandfather had such a dream when he rode the railroad to San Jose in 1869. That same dream brought my grandmother, a young girl traveling alone to the land of opportunity from the stagnant green fields of County Kerry at the mouth of the Shannon River in Ireland. To them, it was a journey west. They may not have known the words of Whitman, "Westward I go by choice," but they were surely propelled by them. All those who traveled through Ellis Island or were descended from the stock of the Founding Fathers came west, but there were those whose compass had another direction. The Chinese, the Japanese, and the Filipinos, and later immigrants from Southeast Asia, were traveling east toward "Gam San," the fabled gold mountain. To the millions of Mexicans who would come home to California after the turn of the century, it was *La Illusion del Norte*, the Dream of the North. That image that was so powerful that no wall or no army could stop their inexorable journey up to the promised land. Of course, there was another point of reference, and that was the center. The original densely populated valleys of California were known as the center of the earth to the Ohlone tribe that first settled along the banks of the Guadalupe River.

San Jose's residents in this century have mirrored the new arrivals from the past. Between 1900 and 1968, 70 percent of all immigrants were from Europe. Since 1968, more than 75 percent of all American immigrants can trace their ancestry to Latin America and Asia.[164] Immigration is now largely an urban phenomenon. Today, over 90 percent of our immigrants head for the bright lights and familiar relationships of cities. As San Jose and Los Angeles and the other cities of the Golden State feel the impact, there is the same optimism of old California but also a rising fear. In the land of a minority majority, it was easy to see the coming problems. They were captured clearly on the Southern California freeways in the recent movie *Falling Down*, with Michael Douglas as the homicidal nerd. Unable to deal with his crumbling life, he abandons his car on the highway and cuts a bloody path to the sea. Along the way, he pulverizes a Korean grocer, blows away Latino gang members, offs a neo-Nazi slimeball, and generally evens the score for legions of white-collar wimps who are sick and tired of what they see as the insanity of immigration. The character joins the insanity.

Obviously, something is not working. We see no signs of hope and a happy ending. The murderous march of the nerd mirrors the comments of an erstwhile Californian who took a more heralded march to the sea during the Civil War. In 1857 William Tecumseh Sherman wrote, "You see no signs of moral reform in California, though some Vigilantes see it sticking out in every direction. My opinion is the very nature of the country begets speculation, extravagance, failures, and rascality."[165] Some views of California never change. Californians today listen in vain for signals of societal coherence. All we hear is a cacophony of opinions on our multicultural future.

At the turn of the century, a man named Israel Zangwill wrote a popular play titled *The Melting Pot*, enshrining the new national identity as a blending of the many into one American culture. Some sixty years later, Nathan Glazer and Daniel Patrick Moynihan wrote their seminal book *Beyond the Melting Pot*, offering the counterbelief that ethnic attachments may grow more (not less) pronounced as time goes on. As we now approach the dawn of a new century, it is becoming more apparent that the collective memory of our nation is in need of a refresher course. In the past, the crucible of the new American culture was the public school, and the culture and history taught was that of the new country. There is a divisiveness and a social unease about the swirling multiculturalism that is rampant today. Arthur Schlesinger, Jr., said it best: "The U.S. escaped the divisiveness of a multiethnic society by the creation of a brand new national identity. The point of America was not to preserve the old culture but to forge a new, American culture."[166]

No one would quibble with the inclusion in schools of the history and literature of all of the different cultures that have played a part in the building of our country. Most would understand that it is relevant to have role models that speak to all children and not just to white or Anglo kids. Yet on our current course, we flirt with the danger of undermining the positive feeling of becoming an American. Much damage could be done if earnest ideologues and unscrupulous opportunists take advantage of the turmoil to sound their divisive clarion call. Unifying ideals have always been the raison d'être of our nation. If those are lost or muddied, the central organizing principle of the republic could be in peril.

Fallon's Bronze Friends

San Jose was not the first city to have a serious brouhaha over the issue of history. There have been others and the number continues to grow.

To documentary filmmaker Ken Burns, "History is a wonderfully unfolding pageant" and a way to teach and learn. To many others, often members of minorities, history can be construed as an open wound through which the idealized hopes of teeming millions bleed. And of course there are occasionally some leaders who for the sake of their own ego and advancement would force confrontations with the majority culture, as they choose to define it. San Jose State professor Shelby Steele received both a national book critics' award and a storm of criticism by attacking what he calls a "victim-focused identity," one that still sees blacks as victims and keeps them at war with society even as new possibilities for advancement open all around. He argues in *The Content of Our Character* that focusing so exclusively on white racism and black victimization implies that our fate is in society's control rather than our own and that "opportunity itself is given rather than taken."[167] Steele further points out that victimization has been a primary source of black power; it encourages and rewards a vision of the world as filled with victims and oppressors. Steele presents a novel analysis of minorities in contemporary society.

There are many examples of minority leaders carrying the union card of minority status while living lives considerably different from the people they represent. The Latino community has seen a subset of selfish leaders attempt to obtain and maintain power, often denying their constituencies the opportunity to drink of cultural assimilation. Even the best of the Hispanic leaders of the Eighties, Henry Cisneros, trips on his rhetoric when speaking of a "decade of the Hispanic." Idealistic speeches in the ballrooms of Hyatt Hotels cannot supplant real achievement in the classroom, the building block of any minority's success. The future very much lies in the education of the millions of Hispanic youth in the cities and barrios of America. It is necessary to concentrate on the primary goals, not the secondary or tertiary.

We have seen many of these tertiary goals in the recent past. Across America there have been any number of battles over history and its portrayal. In Pittsburgh, a major flap occurred over the "hunky steelworker," a fifteen-foot-tall statue of a steelworker standing near a fountain at a confluence of rivers known as "the Point." On its back is the word "hunky."[168] Several public officials insisted that the term was an insult to the people of Eastern European ancestry who built Pittsburgh. Sculptor Luis Jimenez maintained that he was trying to depict the working-class people who, through their strenuous work in the mills and the mines, created the modern city. Public art is supposed to stimulate dialogue, and in this case, that certainly was accomplished. Differing perceptions led to a vocal clash of wills and egos.

The treatment of Native American peoples, always a hot button for controversy, was the focus of a pitched battle on the placement of the Pioneer Monument at the site of the new San Francisco Library. It showed a Westerner, a hooded priest, and a prone Indian. Debate over the fate of the ninety-five-year-old statue raged on at the local planning commission. A group of activists insisted that this represented "the memorialization of the genocide of a people." Yet it also was the only remaining monument in front of the old City Hall that had not been destroyed in the 1906 earthquake. Should it not be saved?

The city of Palo Alto recently found itself in the middle of a full-fledged controversy over a simple request by a number of firefighters to buy their own leather helmets instead of the standard plastic ones. They fell afoul of a self-appointed Political Correctness in Headgear Society, for the name of the chosen headgear was the "Sam Houston helmet." Houston, like many nineteenth-century heroes, was not exactly a candidate for canonization. He owned slaves (a few) and killed Indians and Mexican soldiers (a lot). But even a local and unfriendly columnist observed that "he wasn't in the same genocidal league as the Spanish conquistadors Hernán Cortés or Francisco Pizarro. Or even his friend, President Andrew Jackson, who nearly destroyed the Cherokee Nation."[169] The mere name on a piece of equipment can stir vitriolic exchanges. The fact that this was a superior helmet, safer and more reliable, should have been the sole factor. Even the hallowed Alamo is not safe from revisionists, who want it to represent "modern" political sensibilities. In the current climate of correctness and timidity, words means little; facts mean less. Abraham Lincoln asked, if you call a dog's tail a leg, how many legs does the dog have? The answer, Lincoln assures us, is still only four. This eternal verity is often lost in the miasma of what passes for political discourse nowadays.

If nihilist historical reinventors were successful, we might indulge in an orgy of name changing in the state of Texas. Houston or Austin might be replaced on the map. Observers of history remember that it has been tried before in the defunct Soviet Union, with short-lived results. Try finding Stalingrad or Leningrad on a current map.

There are, of course, symbols that richly deserve being relegated to the ash bin of history. The inclusion of the Confederate battle flag in the state flag of Georgia leaps to mind. Throughout the South, people "are battling like never before over the symbols that once defined the South and now divide it."[170] This is not a symbol of the bonny blue flag that Robert E. Lee and Stonewall Jackson carried so bravely but a more modern and odious addition attached to the Georgia flag made in the days of the stubborn segregation fights of the 1950s and 1960s. It is the flag that George Wallace placed on the capital dome in Montgomery to protest a visit by Attorney General Robert Kennedy, not a memorial to the Army of Northern Virginia, and it should be treated as such—as an anachronism that has no place in the new South.

Things always seem to go too far, such as the request in New Orleans to rechristen every high school named after a slaveholder, including those named after Washington and Jefferson. This is absurd and a rewriting of history worthy of a Stalin. All history should be told and written and represented, "warts and all," as Oliver Cromwell said to his painter. The statues of Martin Luther King, Jr., and Rosa Parks should take their place on Monument Avenue in Richmond alongside those of Lee and Jeb Stuart—not in place of them. As they have made the history of America, all should be honestly portrayed.

Spin Masters of Elizabethan Times

It has been a time-honored and invidious method of reverse bigotry to attempt to demonize the onetime oppressor and to sacrifice historical truth on the altar of political expediency and correctness. To fully understand the imprisonment of the "Fallon Two" portrayed in the statue I tried to erect, I have since looked back to a series of earlier battles waged by a chorus of California historians and their just as numerous revisionists.

Long-simmering embers of the "Columbus: Saint or Sinner" debate exploded on the pages of national magazines and in op-ed columns in 1992 with a fury hitherto reserved for a presidential scandal or a national emergency. In fact, it was but a continuation of a masterful campaign waged by the spin doctors of England, France, and Holland for centuries. The fact that Columbus was a slightly confused overachiever who did not know where he was going, and did not know where he was when he arrived, is only slightly relevant. He was certainly not even the first to arrive on the shores of the New World. No one painted Columbus in his lifetime, but historians and hagiographers have had a great time coloring him ever since. The native of Genoa was quite easy to mythologize and easier to debunk. He was an enigma and lies in an unmarked grave. European immigrants wishing for an icon elevated him; descendants of the conquered pulled him down. It has a nice symmetry. He was the vanguard of a vastly superior, technologically powerful set of nation-states newly flexing their muscles and looking for new worlds to conquer— "the Enlightenment meets the Benighted" is Professor James Sandos's cynical phrase. Although the new immigrants found a world that surprised them, they nonetheless set out on their task with a zealotry and rapaciousness that leaves a good deal to criticize.

There lies the birth of the Black Legend. With Spain having the most extensive empire in the New World and hegemony in Europe under the aegis of Charles V, the always combative emerging nations of Europe collided. Although the battles waged to and fro, it was in the area of public relations that the Spanish took their hardest shots.

The writers of history had a free field of fire. The English predominantly set our opinions of Spain and its treatment of the Native Americans. As children we saw Errol Flynn swashbuckling his way across the Spanish Main, fighting the perfidious Spaniard. The story of the rape, pillage, and murders perpetrated on the peoples of America became a staple of political warfare that passed for fact in our understanding of the four centuries between 1492 and 1898. The legend had a basis in truth but greatly overemphasized the misdeeds of the Spanish—to the benefit of the other colonial powers. Some observers would even say that the Spanish acted in moderation compared with the English and French, who drove the Indians before them and exterminated them. The Spanish system provided a subservient and lowly place for the Indians; nonetheless, it was a rung in their society, and a chance through conversion of eternal life. Carlos Fuentes in his television documentary *The Buried Mirror: Reflections on Spain and the New World* points out that

Spain was constantly questioning itself: "Am I right, am I wrong? What am I doing with these people?"[171] However subordinated to greed or passion, the Spanish had moral impulse notably absent in other conquerors.

La Leyenda Negra

The Black Legend against Columbus echoed in the twentieth century attempt to canonize the father of the California missions, Junípero Serra. The first efforts to make him a saint were begun in 1934. Serra is one of only two Californians whose statue stands in the great Capital Rotunda in Washington, and he has been called "all in all, the outstanding Spanish pioneer of California."[172] With the missions in total decline, it was only the marketing and entrepreneurial urge of American and largely Protestant boosters beginning late in the nineteenth century that preserved them. They are the only true ruins that the country has. The "Sainthood for Serra" campaign gave the missions a spark of life and spurred a look at the good life in sunny, orange-blossomed California. It gave new impetus to the tale of Father Serra's role as the progenitor of the California myth. This unfolding tale prompted a more demonic counterinterpretation of the Spanish colonization of the Golden State by Carry McWilliams, in which he offered the following damning conclusion: "With the best theological intentions in the world, the Franciscan padres eliminated the Indians with the effectiveness of Nazis operating concentration camps."[173]

In that charge, one can see the historical antecedent of the Fallon affair. According to such a narrow view, every Indian is *enslava de la mission*, or a slave of the mission, inhabiting a charnel house. Father Serra becomes the moral equivalent of Hitler, and the Mission San Jose comparable to Auschwitz. It is amazing and frightening to what lengths history can be perverted by dramatic interpretation.

History must be set straight. Although no one could endorse the effects of the colonization on the Native Americans, the Spanish at least provided a spot for them (however low) in the new world order of the sixteenth century. The spot was enough for them eventually to form the stronger partner in the marriage of races that followed the conquest of what is now Mexico. As Mexican poet Homero Aridhis says, "The Spanish were conquered in turn by those they conquered." It is a piece of historical poetic justice on a monumental scale. The new *la raza* that spreads from Mexico to the Rockies and to the shores of the Pacific in California may speak with a Spanish tongue, but it has more the look, feel, and passion of the Aztlan. Aztlan is the ancient homeland of the Aztec people, and it was originally thought to be the far north of Mexico. Colloquially, modern Chicano ideology refers to all the Southwestern United States as this ancestral area.

San Jose and the Creation of a Chicano Identity

The roots of Mexican-American activism go very deep into the fertile soil of San Jose. You do not have to look very hard to find the first seeds of that plant in the pioneering efforts of Ernesto Galarza.

The Progressive movement in America that helped throw out the old bossism of many a city government was nowhere stronger than in San Jose. Yet this very significant movement also had a dark side. In San Jose, it was manifested in a nativism that champed at the bit when the issue of immigration was discussed. Progressives fumed about the Yellow Peril as large numbers of Chinese arrived in California. No less a proponent of reform than Senator Hiram Johnson, onetime governor and an exemplar of Progressivism, mouthed outrageous attacks on Mexican immigrants as "a mixed breed, low type, and docile people."[174] Mexicans were often compared with Negroes in the South, and Senator Thomas Heflin of Alabama attempted to equate Mexicans with promiscuous peons and filthy squaws.

Into this environment in California, the young and idealistic Galarza entered. As in many a success story, he was heavily influenced by his first school principal, who "warmed knowledge into us and roasted racial hatreds out of us." He was never scolded for speaking Spanish but met many teachers who encouraged him to visit the world outside the barrio.[175] From studies at Occidental College to graduate work at Stanford, Galarza kept in touch with the migrant workers and urban dwellers who fed the need for cheap labor but whose children had a difficult time finishing grammar school. This reality succeeded in shutting them out of any chance at higher education. At Stanford in 1929, Galarza ushered in the era of student activism when he stood up for the rights of immigrant workers. It was the beginning of a promising new age for the Mexican-American.[176]

After college Galarza continued his efforts to improve the lot of the worker and to provide educational opportunities for the young. He waded into an ongoing battle between ties to the mother country and the quest for an assimilated American identity. It was the Hobson's choice of all immigrants: am I what my family left, or am I an American, the product of what we found and what this new land has created? During World War II, the animosities and confusion boiled over in a series of confrontations in Los Angeles resulting in the infamous Zoot Suit riots. Full of liquor and bravado, American servicemen, primarily sailors, attacked the nattily attired young *cholos* of Los Angeles. The press threw gasoline on the fire.

A fascinating intersection in the history of Mexican-Americans then took place in postwar San Jose. Galarza, in his sixties, ensconced himself in the ivy-covered towers of San Jose State. A few miles away, a young organizer was beginning a career in an East side barrio known as *Sal Si Puedes*, "Get Out If You Can." His name was Cesar Chavez. His monumental and heroic attempts to create a union for the farmworkers of California and then America are admired as an act of supreme achievement even by his opponents. His will, along with his placid magnetism, galvanized the new Chicano movement and gave Chavez an international acclaim equivalent to Martin Luther King, Jr. He was undoubtedly the premier Chicano figure of twentieth century America. Beyond that, in the eyes of many, he was a secular saint.

Last Shot from Saigon

One of the unforeseen but positive consequences of the tragic aftermath of the American involvement in Vietnam was the salutary effect that the stream of Vietnamese immigrants to San Jose have had. From our universities to our start-up companies to our mom-and-pop inner-city grocery stores, they have invigorated and excelled, in numbers approaching 70,000 in San Jose alone.

In 1987, their placid new lives were ruptured by the selection of state assemblyman Tom Hayden as the commencement speaker at the San Jose City College graduation ceremony. Hayden, a leading antiwar activist and onetime husband of Jane Fonda, was the devil incarnate to the scores of Vietnamese and their families in the graduating class. His wartime harangues and apparent sympathy for Hanoi caused the largest outpouring of emotion since our new citizens' arrival, and city officials heard their protests. I talked to Hayden and school officials and arranged for another speaking date for Hayden and for a replacement commencement speaker. After all, this was a family event, and while we guaranteed his right to speak, all agreed that this course was prudent.

On the night of the graduation, a call from police to my home let me know that a betrayal was under way: Hayden was surreptitiously to appear on stage, "to make a point." I rushed to the Civic Auditorium, just in time to see him step to the stage to try to speak. When the audience caught sight of him, pan-

demonium erupted, as students and families yelled in dismay. Many fled in tears from the auditorium. The ceremony was destroyed. Livid, I climbed the stairs to the platform and told Hayden what a despicable character I thought he was. I felt like punching him. His cheap stunts had ruined the key moment in the lives of these young immigrants—and written another sorrowful chapter, a final shot, in a war from another time.

Chavez's vision was grounded in a deep Catholic spirituality. Chavez's chief mentor, Father Donald McDonnell, was one of a young band of Spanish-speaking priests sent to minister to migrant workers in the fields of San Jose. A movement eventually coalesced around the United Farm Workers union and the personality of Caesar Chavez. Some of his more talented adherents left his side later when they perceived that the farm-workers did not support Chicano nationalism; Chavez instead pursued a straightforward unionism. It was that simple.

Luis Valdez was one of those who left Chavez, going on to acclaim with El Téatro Campesiño. Valdez drew his strength from his emotional and psychological center in the old Spanish capital of San Juan Bautista. More than any other single individual, Luis helped forge the new Chicano consciousness of the Mexican-American, an identity that harkened to an ancient past and glory. In the theater, he recounts through his plays the great accomplishments of the working people who came north

Cesar Chavez.

to America, the fabled Aztlan of myth and the *Illusion del Norte* of so many impoverished denizens of Michoacan and Guadalajara. The Spanish conquest of Mexico was in fact no conquest at all; although it was traumatic to the ancient Indian culture, Valdez reminds us that "much more of it was left above ground than beans and tortillas."[177]

Textbooks and Tomahawks: Who Decides in History

History is the most interesting of topics. It can range from the "agreed-upon fables" of Napoleon's musings to a trick on the dead, as Voltaire would have us believe. Although there are certain moral verities that translate in any time, a historical figure should be judged by the standards of his time. This ought to be the basis of the historical record. To hold a person to any other test is intellectually dishonest and prevents the objectivity that can most illuminate the true meaning of that individual's role in history. The telling of history in its finest sense should light the way through shadows to an understanding of the currents of our time and how we arrived at certain junctures.

Teddy Roosevelt described Americans as "children of the crucible," and that seems as apt a description as possible. In a recent interview, Arthur Schlesinger, Jr., underlined the importance of history when he compared it with a person's own individual memory. If he loses that memory, Schlesinger mused, he becomes disoriented and doesn't know where he's coming from or where he's going. It can have the same effect on a nation.[178]

As our cities and towns become more and more diverse, we have a choice: we can pull together and emphasize our common values. Or we can emphasize our differences and be pulled apart. Our choice will determine the future for our children, and in many cities that choice is being made for them by default in a decisive setting: the classroom.

A case in point involves the recent battle over a new California history textbook and its treatment of multiculturalism. In California the state board and the state superintendent of public instruction play a considerable role in the selection of textbooks and, even earlier, in their formulation. With a state-approved historical framework in hand, publishers Houghton Mifflin took on the task of producing a suitable work for the gigantic and lucrative California market. The question for the new writers was posed well by Robert Reinhold of the *New York Times:* "Can these students, from the earliest school years, be exposed to the full diversity of cultures and traditions that make up the United States and still arrive at the conclusion that we are united by ideals, bonds and legal instruments that support our national motto *E Pluribus Unum?*"[179]

The writers of the new text confronted the eternal American question of whether our ideals, if not the telling of our history, are a lie. Common ideals propelled so many of our immigrant fathers and mothers to this land, mostly white in the nineteenth and early twentieth century, but now black and brown and yellow. Those ideals are questioned by these writers for their appropriateness to new immigrants, the people of color. The seventh grade book devotes fifty-one pages to the history of sub-Saharan Africa, tracing the Bantu migration in detail. It also covers Asia and the civilizations of pre-Columbian America and takes as a traditional look at the age of Enlightenment and the Reformation in Europe. Although the book's discussion of the Mission era in California details the cruelties suffered by the Indians at the hands of the erstwhile saint Father Serra, still it is seemingly not enough. It has not satisfied the critics who feel the treatment is patronizing and unintentionally racist in many ways. The criticism astounded such academic liberals as Professor Gary Nash of UCLA, one contributor to the new text. "I never heard of the Bantu migration when I received my Ph.D. at Princeton," he complains. This series covers such previously untouched esoterica at length. "If I am the bad guy," says Nash, "who are your allies?"

It would seem that by this stage in the history of America, we should be able to look at the good as well as the bad. There seems to be no shortage of evil portrayals in our popular culture of movies, television, or print to convince all. Only the disingenuous do not know that the winning of the West, in a heavy dose of manifest destiny, was accomplished with a great deal of horror, carnage, and racism. Anyone who offers the opinion that those parts of our history are ignored has been asleep for the last decade. But it is as imperative to point out that the unfortunate and outrageous is not the total history of America. There is much more, much that is good.

Getting Along

We have a choice as a nation. We can give in to the xenophobic cant of political opportunists, exemplified by Governor Pete Wilson's attacks on immigrants or Senator Barbara Boxer's thoughtless appeals for armies on the border. There is a better course.

America can be both a melting pot and a quilt. When Israel Zangwill first wrote of the melting pot as an American crucible, he did not mean that all newcomers must fit a preexisting mold shaped by white Europeans. His concluding comments held that "the real American has not yet arrived. He is only in the crucible, I tell you. He will be the fusion of all the races, perhaps the coming superman."

The historical record that has informed our people, most of all the eagerly arriving immigrants from southwest Ireland or Southeast Asia, must not be changed to suit the purely modern, political needs of anyone or any group. Shelby Foote, award-winning expositor of America's most bloody event, the Civil War, poses the question in a typically interesting way: "Are you willing to dilute the pure stream of history in order to investigate all the creeks that run into it?"[180] Or we could listen to Gary Wills's cautionary note, reminding us that "things that have been accepted in academic history are filtering down into the elementary schools and have become part of a political fight." It is not a fight that Americans of good will and sound judgment should encourage. Many observers have legitimate concerns about the effect of teaching a history in which one group so clearly seems to be the victim and another the oppressor. The fears of creating a victim mentality, as Shelby Steele warns, may be mirrored by a resentment in the group that is singled out as the oppressor. A simmering resentment can reach a low boiling point rather quickly. History in this form is not edifying and can degenerate into maligning worthy individuals or groups with scorn. The authors of our Constitution, and perhaps even the authors of the new textbooks, would be aghast to see such a result.

Every year the San Jose Tomorrow youth foundation sponsors a Young Woman of the Year scholarship competition, honoring outstanding high school girls in Silicon Valley. The event is like thousands of others in schools and cities across the country: a quiet moment of revelry in the positive attributes of youth. It is a small competition in the scheme of things but large in the life of an individual. As the young women showcase their singular talents, we see a kaleidoscope of our citizenry: an Indian girl singing a song celebrating the heritage of her parents, a black girl reciting a moving poem, a native of Guadalajara performing a Mexican ethnic dance, or a Vietnamese pianist binding the audience in a classical spell. The evening begins with the national anthem. I am always struck by the thought that such colorfully diverse talents and cultures can all be showcased in a single forum, reflecting the same aspirations of a better personal future in a common home.

Such a symbol represents the key to our society or, rather, our assembled societies: learning to get along with one another. We must continue to provide unified forums, harmonious settings for expression and advancement. In spite of ongoing controversies over education, I believe schools are the best arena we have for the continuing American experiment, offering a single curriculum with a multitude of diverse elements. In our schools, our homes, and our hearts, we can all support the common goal of achieving a society of tolerance in every American city.

11

THINK LOCALLY, ACT GLOBALLY: FOREIGN POLICY OF THE CITY-STATE

At a moment of crisis, a city which lacks leadership and strength
may be subjugated by some neighboring one which enjoys better rule.
—Niccolò Machiavelli

There we stood, Art Agnos and I, the leaders of two of America's largest cities, personifying the San Francisco Bay Area and the Silicon Valley, representing a combined major economic powerhouse of world scale.

We stood before the foreign crowd of hundreds wearing short Japanese silk jackets and holding comically large wooden mallets. I felt foolish, but it was worth it.

My visit to Asia in May 1989 was more than just the typical junket. Seventy-five people came along for this unprecedented joint San Jose–San Francisco trade mission. We were able to highlight specific Bay Area products for export, and we touted our attractions for investment. We visited Hong Kong, China, and Japan, with stops in San Jose's sister cities of Tainan (Taiwan), Nanjing (China), and Okayama (Japan). Beyond the huckster commercial pitch, our underlying purpose was to practice the global exchange of ideas, values, and resources. Cities need to recognize the reality of the shrinking globe just as American companies have and learn to profit from it.

235

Our final stop was in Osaka, a sister city to San Francisco for thirty years. At the farewell reception, our Japanese hosts gave us the pair of large wooden mallets to smash open a barrel of sake. In my remarks afterward, I acknowledged the need for cities to extend their vision beyond provincial horizons: "Politicians may talk about national boundaries, but very clearly the international economy doesn't operate that way. What the Pacific Rim means to me is a reflection of reality—a one-world economy where national boundaries are becoming less and less meaningful."

We visited in Osaka the massive corporate headquarters of the Matsushita Electric Company, a firm that also has facilities in Silicon Valley. In the company's impressive courtyard, we saw an array of statues, the largest of which was not of a Japanese business pioneer but of an American inventor: Thomas Edison. I think that proves more than any words the tremendous lineage that we share as two peoples and, beyond American-Japanese ties, the links we share with all nations. The statue was indicative of what the entire technological revolution has been about: the best ideas, no matter their origin, are triumphant.

As the capital of Silicon Valley and as a leading international hub for the western United States, San Jose is leading the march into world markets and becoming a center of the globally integrated U.S. economy. We have worked closely with the federal Department of Commerce to strengthen our ties with Europe and Asia, building upon the existing relationships that private industry has built. Silicon Valley companies rely tremendously on exports and on their ability to deal fluidly with global suppliers, markets, and relationships. San Jose is now beginning to learn that lesson.

We in San Jose have reversed a popular political slogan that advises, "Think globally, act locally." We instead think of local priorities but act globally in pursuit of our self-interest.

Practicing Bottom-up Diplomacy

As a city-state becomes more self-reliant and confident in shaping its economic future, international economics will become second nature to mayors. Some mayors are as quick to hop on a jet for a "trade mission" as members of Congress are for a dubious fact-finding jaunt overseas. Many mayors and city council members have faced the embarrassing skepticism and sometimes ridicule of local newspaper watchdogs who expose the junkets paid for from the public purse. In fact, there is a long history of controversy over local involvement abroad.

When the Founding Fathers split responsibility over foreign affairs between the federal legislative and executive branches, they were creating a muddle that would last two centuries and more. Somewhere in that muddied field lies the dispute between two distinct camps on whether or not cities have any role or right of involvement in international matters. The traditional legal-oriented view has been skeptical. Legal scholar John Norton Moore of the University of Virginia School of Law has written, "The United States, to be effective in foreign policy, must speak with but one voice. It cannot have a cacophony of different states and municipalities seeking to speak about foreign policy issues."[181]

As president, Thomas Jefferson tried to stop the cities of New England from trading with Britain or France in 1807 during the Napoleonic Wars, but his efforts were rebuffed when the towns rebelled against the young federal government. With their economies facing ruin under Jefferson's Embargo Act, their state legislatures replied by declaring the right of interposition, the state power to invalidate federal laws that state citizens find unacceptable. Jefferson said that he had "felt the foundation of government shaken under my feet by the New England townships." Of course, the doctrine of interposition was a key states' rights argument during the Civil War and for years afterward. Martin Luther King, Jr., mentioned with disdain the interposition argument of Southern whites in his "I have a dream" speech in 1963.

The opposing view is much more positive and encouraging of cities' involvement abroad. Michael Shuman has written that "there are literally hundreds of examples of municipal foreign policies that have benefited U.S. foreign policy by making it more democratic, more accountable, and more effective."[182] Local officials have had more on their minds than commercial interests as they looked overseas, particularly since World War II. According to Shuman, editor of *Global Communities* newsletter and a scholar who follows cities' foreign policies, political and cultural issues have also come up. Even the fortunes of the cold war had an impact on cities. In the 1950s and early 1960s, many Bible Belt communities, and big cities in the North with substantial Eastern European immigrant populations, passed city ordinances deploring Soviet communism and forbidding any city investment in companies that traded with the Red bloc.

As international politics and the American political scene changed, so did local involvement in foreign affairs. In the 1980s, many cities began protesting Reagan administration policies on defense spending and Central American affairs in particular, responding both to grassroots pressure and to Democratic local leaders. By 1991, more than 900 localities in the

United States had passed resolutions supporting a nuclear arms race freeze, almost 200 had passed resolutions demanding a halt to nuclear testing, and 125 had divested their municipal investments, more than $20 billion worth, in firms doing business in South Africa. Eighty-five cities or towns established sister-city links with Nicaraguan towns during the 1980s and were providing moral support to the Sandinista government's fight against the U.S.-backed contras, while some twenty-seven cities were providing sanctuary for Guatemalan or Salvadoran refugees.

In San Jose, we do not have a long record of that kind of political activism on overseas issues. Our immigrant citizens seem more interested in integrating successfully into their workplaces and neighborhoods. We are also, thankfully, missing the radicalized fringe elements that drive overtly political stands on foreign policy issues in some other cities. Frank Jordan ran for mayor in San Francisco against incumbent Art Agnos with a promise to "veto every foreign policy resolution passed by the board of supervisors." Jordan charged during the 1991 campaign that Agnos had spent too much time on foreign junkets, and that the board (San Francisco's equivalent of a city council) was too consumed with exhibiting political correctness by weighing in on Nicaragua and Central America, apartheid in South Africa, and American nuclear policy.

The first test of Frank's stand as mayor was on an issue that hit the Irishman hard, but he swallowed and kept his campaign promise. He vetoed a supervisors' resolution supporting Irish Republican Army member Joe Doherty, who was fighting extradition to Great Britain. After the mayor's veto, Supervisor Terence Hallinan responded, "Shame on him. This is a minor little resolution. How can anyone object to that?" Hallinan's comment inadvertently revealed why some people did object: city councils too often spend their time and energy on minor little issues far removed from the real concerns of citizens at home. One supervisor who supported Jordan's veto, Tom Hsieh, rightly summed it up: "People in this city are sick and tired of this stuff." (Of course, Hsieh had originally voted in favor of the resolution, but put that down to a mistake— he did not know what he was voting on. He chastised himself, saying, "There is no excuse for that." From the sublime to the ridiculous, one rarely tires of the phrase, "Only in San Francisco. . . . ") Through it all, Frank Jordan kept his word.

In the era of the city-state, I see new and more serious directions for local involvement overseas. The end of the cold war brings the opportunity for a new politics of municipal foreign policy. Some cities will continue to act on their concern for human rights, particularly in countries linked to cities by substantial ethnic populations. Some cities will address emerging problems that respect no borders or clear distinctions between federal and local jurisdictions, like environmental hazards. Cities will be cooperating with one another and with other countries in research and practical efforts.

Most of all, economics will once again drive cities into relationships beyond our shores. New technological and business realities are forcing societies to operate globally, and cities cannot afford to stand apart. The American economy now includes many activities that have been globalized; products are designed to world standards and are produced and marketed globally. Just as major cities have a professional lobbying representative or office in their state capital and often in Washington, D.C., so they take very seriously their new role in the world outside. At least a dozen American cities have formed offices of international affairs, essentially municipal state departments.

The city of San Jose finds itself interacting frequently with multinational corporations, often as an equal or lesser partner. Like every city-state, we are adjusting to that role and seeking comparative advantages by acting in concert with the internationalization of business and commerce. In 1988, I attended the groundbreaking ceremony for the largest computer-chip factory in the world near Dublin. The company was none other than Intel, led by the incomparable Gordon Moore. Its Irish plant proved critical in the 1990s resurgence of American dominance in the international microprocessor industry. Our creation in 1990 of the Center for International Trade and Development, to work beside the Office of Economic Development, was a tangible recognition that our imagination and our enterprise no longer stop at the city limits. The only way for today's cities to survive into the next century is to define our place in a new society before that place is defined for us as obsolescence.

Sister Cities

In the winter of 1990, a sister-city relationship brought me face to face with the past, in a tiny square with a turreted church and a rectangular school. It was called San Joaquin de Flores. The locale was indeed San Jose, but it was a San Jose many miles away in Costa Rica. From behind the clouds the sun peeked out, hovering over the central highlands in this tiny country. A president whom I had grown to know well walked the dusty street to the school opposite the church, and I followed him into a makeshift polling place. Soon he would cast his vote for his suc-

The author with Costa Rican president Oscar Arias, launching the "Bullets to Bytes" educational project.

cessor. Affection from onlookers washed over him and his wife and two children, in waves of kisses and *abrazos*. Mothers held up their babies, and fathers their children, for a look or a touch.

His name was Oscar Arias, and he was participating in the celebration of democracy that occurs regularly in this oasis of peace and the rule of law. Costa Rica always observes its presidential elections with an air of festivity, wonderful testimony to the values contained in a nation of 3 million who face the future, in a dangerous and embattled world, with no tanks, no army, only a constitution.

As Arias spoke of the future that morning, I thought of the past. I thought of the other president who had influenced him so: John Kennedy. "Liberty performs miracles," Arias said. "To free men, everything is possible." I watched this winner of the Nobel Peace Prize (for his role in ending the Nicaraguan civil war) as he continued on his way across the square. The milling and churning crowd would evoke consternation, even panic, if it surrounded one of America's leaders. Here it seemed so good-natured and friendly. On that election day, thousands of miles from

America, I felt very much at home. The power of ideals and the transferred flame could burn very brightly even when the original fires had long since banked.

With the sun now out from behind the clouds, I realized that my look at the past might also be a glimpse of the future. It was only of passing interest that the mayor of an American city was immersed in a political event in a Central American republic. Many mayors have begun to look beyond the fraternal and friendly linkages of the sister-city concept, which originated in the Eisenhower era, to more meaningful and economically rewarding alliances between our citizens, our companies, and their markets. The importance of the world economy to San Jose and to all cities cannot be overestimated, and sister-city relationships are a ready-made channel to expand a city's reach into the world outside.

Returning the Trojan Horse

The Greek poet Homer wrote fanciful tales of Odysseus fighting for the city-state of Sparta around 1300 B.C. to win back the beautiful Helen, the wife of Sparta's ruler who had been kidnapped and taken to Troy. In 1871, a German archaeologist named Schliemann working in western Turkey found the ancient city of Troy, famous for the Trojan Wars. Unfortunately, the modern archaeologist could find only scant evidence of the grand city Homer described, and after Schliemann's discovery, dubious historians scoffed at Homer's account. No epic

wars on the scale described in The Iliad *and* The Odyssey *could have been fought, they believed, by the tiny village found by Schliemann. Homer must have fictionalized Odysseus's ten-year voyage of adventures.*

In a fascinating twist, though, an American sister-city relationship is helping to rescue the reputation of city-state rivalries dating back millennia. Troy, Ohio, has been interested in setting up a linkage with Troy, Turkey, in honor of the historic heritage in its name. Officials in the American Troy have been supporting an archaeological group from the University of Cincinnati that is excavating in the ancient city. In 1993, the group finally found evidence of the larger, grander city.

Homer stands vindicated, Ohio's Troy is proud, and the legend of the Trojan Horse lives on.

By 1993 there were more than 925 U.S. cities and towns with sister-city relationships overseas in some 111 countries. Some cities have only a single relationship with one city they view as a natural partner. Others, like Los Angeles, Seattle, and Atlanta, have accumulated ten or more links over the years, like a charm bracelet.

San Jose was one of the first to establish a sister city, in 1957, just after President Eisenhower set up the sister cities program through the State Department. We began a relationship with Okayama, establishing some of California's first cultural and economic ties with Japan since the end of World War II. After Eisenhower left office, the national program spun off into the nonprofit group Sister Cities International, based in Virginia. San Jose went on to link up with San Jose, Costa Rica, in 1961, and Veracruz, Mexico, and Tainan, Taiwan, in 1975. As mayor in 1986, I established a very successful link with Dublin, Ireland, the only city added during my two terms. In 1992, San Jose added two more: Pune, India, and Ekaterinburg, Russia, also known as the "Russian Silicon Valley" (and more darkly remembered as the place where Czar Nicholas and his family were murdered).

Some ties are more appropriate than others. I am still unsure of the rationale for our link with Pune. On the other hand, I helped the Irish city of Listowel in County Kerry set up an informal relationship with Los Gatos, California, a suburb of San Jose. Both are very cultured towns with literary pasts and famous writers. Los Angeles established another nice and appropriately limited tie in 1979, twinning L.A.'s historic Olivera Street Square—the old pueblo birthplace of the city—with Mexico City's Musical Garibaldi Square, the "heart of folklore" in that capital. The actual benefit has been limited, with periodic exchanges of musical groups and ceremonial visits, but this small tie is a symbolic nod to the continuing vital Mexican contribution to Californian culture.

Regionalism and Rivalries

The flip side of a city reaching out for partnerships with others is the likelihood that the city-state will engage in competition with other cities for economic benefits and other less tangible titles. San Jose has long been said to have a chip on its shoulder about our Bay Area neighbor San Francisco, and vice versa. As we quietly grew to big-city size in the past three decades, mutterings were heard from northern quarters about the sprawling upstart that dared to lay claim to economic predominance in the region. When we passed San Francisco in population for the first time in 1989, its media had a field day at our expense, hyping the rivalry beyond the interest of even the most ardent civic booster in either town.

Rivalries almost always exist between geographically close cities, and there is usually some emotional undercurrent of challenged loyalty or unrequited love. Quite frankly, the best way to battle out these rivalries is on the sports field between neighboring teams. Sometimes, though, the fight to gain a franchise sparks an intense rivalry, spilling over into lawsuits. The San Francisco Giants almost became the San Jose Giants a number of times. When Bob Lurie tried to sell the team to Florida, San Francisco papers instantly developed an intense dislike for St. Petersburg, shown in editorials and slanted stories. Fans in St. Petersburg did not appear to rise to the bait, though. They had their own long-standing feud with Tampa, their neighbor across the bay.

Behind the facade of city rivalries lies an important level of competition over economic resources and political power. Some well-intentioned public-policy buffs have created a regionalism bandwagon partly in response to what they see as the problems of city rivalries and of overlapping authorities. The rationale for regionalism is at odds with the development of powerful city-states. Its advocates are motivated by an attempt to decrease the power of cities by empowering a newly created level of government, awkwardly situated between the state and local level and with no constitutional underpinning to guide its authority. With the new regional bodies crammed in above the municipal level, the average city would be left with greatly diminished autonomy and resources and with a clouded future as an independent actor.

Regional advocates are not shy about their intentions. Brian Dickinson, writing in the *Providence Journal*, argued that "regional governments, reflecting the innumerable links between core cities and their fringe cities, should be given new emphasis. . . . As an effective working unit of governance, the core city, seen in isolation, is obsolete."[183] In 1991, the Bay Vision 2020 Commission, a task force of business leaders, politicians, academics, and environmentalists, submitted a report recommending the creation of a high-powered Bay Area Regional Commission. BARC would combine the powers of a number of authorities: the Association of Bay Area Governments, the Metropolitan Transportation Commission, and the Bay Area Air Quality Management District. The group would have thirty to forty members and would "prepare a comprehensive regional plan by 1995 to handle growth and transit concerns."[184] The idea of BARC may be worse than its bite. Many have opposed the commission's primary intent: to draw lines limiting urban-growth for the Bay Area's cities. Governor Wilson opposed the effort from the state's perspective. His director of planning and research stated that the governor did not "want to let any region of the state, the Bay Area or San Diego, [go] marching off in a way that would be incompatible with the state government."[185] My concern is not protecting state bureaucrats. The real threat of regionalism is that it reduces a city's ability to set its own course, to make its own decisions, to decide its own future. My opposition to the central thrust of regionalism lies in my conviction that cities remain the best forum in which to find solutions to the very problems of economics and quality of life that regionalism addresses. Regional approaches dilute the political accountability that underlies all progress in public policy, and we should never forget that most important principle of democracy: leaders must be held responsible by the people.

The bottom line in this age of city-states is that some cities are always going to prove better able to succeed than others, including neighboring rivals. No San Francisco mayor since Dianne Feinstein has exercised more than diluted power, and I see no changes in the city's political culture by the turn of the century. Even Frank Jordan's middle-of-the-road approach has been thwarted. Power in San Francisco is too diffused among the mayor, the board of supervisors, the professional bureaucracy, and an entire constellation of activist, know-nothing, single-interest groups. "No branch of government has enough authority or power," one civic observer has complained, "to create and implement a comprehensive, citywide strategy."[186]

Cities like that are ripe for the plucking. That lesson should keep mayors on their toes. When Bill Hudnut wanted to put Indianapolis on the map as the country's tenth-largest city, he set out to rob an East Coast city. "Indianapolis pursues economic growth very assiduously," he admitted forthrightly. "If you don't believe me, ask our friends from Baltimore."[187] The municipal boosters of medieval Venice would be pleased: in the middle of the night, Indianapolis stole the Baltimore Colts.

The new city-state is not afraid to dream the great dream and to take its successes where it finds them—at home or abroad.

12

NEW SOURCES
OF LEADERSHIP

Where the populace rise at once against
the never-ending audacity of elected persons, . . .
There the great city stands.
—Walt Whitman

When Clint Eastwood became mayor of the tiny coastal town of Carmel, sixty miles from San Jose, it caused an international stir. From around the world, the paparazzi descended on the quaint bohemian village at the bend of the Monterey Bay. It was considered an amazing event for an established businessman—an international movie star, no less—to set all that aside to become mayor. Those accustomed to politics in the West saw it as entirely ordinary. It was, in fact, a logical evolution in the life and times of so many cities in the western United States. The person who takes the reins of power is rarely a celebrity, and we see more entrepreneurs like L.A.'s interesting Richard Riordan than entertainers like Sonny Bono of Palm Springs. The impulses that propelled Eastwood were as familiar and time-honored in our culture as the stern look and clear motives of one of his own celluloid characters.

I believe that cities, West and East, North and South, are still the greatest platform for leadership in America. At the local level, closest to the people, is where the most change can occur. Perhaps only those who have served as mayor should be elected as president of our country. We would get better government by having a successful former big-city may-

247

or in the White House than someone with a substantial career in legislative corridors.

City officials are better judges of the political mood of the populace. We have our fingers on the pulse of that misnomer, the average American, not with pollsters or focus-group studies as part of an expensive re-election campaign. We keep in touch by living in the very communities in which we serve, and we encounter our constituents and neighbors at high school football games, at the supermarket, or in the line at the movies. To me, that is the key difference between members of Congress (or state legislators) and local city officials: we have to live with the results of our decisions. We take the heat. We have to walk our own streets, send our children to local schools, and live in the neighborhoods that elected us. In short, we are closer to our communities, and that proximity and that bond give us an added responsibility to face the hard decisions of government squarely.

That bond has consistently imbued local politics with a dynamism not seen in anything but presidential elections, and not in many of those. Local politics are good and bad, fun and mysterious, with a range of outcomes from ideal to evil. The juiciest stories of corruption leak from city halls, and yet anyone waiting for real political and ethical reform knows better than to look to Congress. From the smoke-filled rooms of Tammany Hall to any realistic plan for a brighter democracy 2000, cities have always been in the forefront of American politics.

Be an Inside Outsider

A confident city can and should remake itself around a cathedral of an idea. To extend the religious analogy just a bit, you could say that the authoritative mayor of such a city might be seen as the bishop of the cathedral. But a mayor cannot have his eyes turned to some higher political personage, in the way that a bishop defers to an archbishop or pope. In local politics in America, too many mayors have their eyes fixed on Washington or the state capital. Some seek money and resources, but others a shot at the big time—a higher office, "the Show."

The best mayors, the most accomplished and successful municipal chief executives, view themselves as a solitary leader of their modern city-state. They preside in a local democracy, of course, subject to the strict will of the people from whom they spring. They bear no other allegiances, though, no preoccupations with partisan politics or competing national agendas. They act chauvinistically in the best interests of their city, which they know intimately.

Most important, they understand the central paradox of local power in modern American politics: the best leader is an insider but an outsider.

At one end of the Machiavellian scale, the leader of the city-state must master local politics, from academic debates over the nature of influence right down to the folklore of neighborhood histories. Power politics is the lifeblood of leadership in the city, and if that power is not abused, it will flow from city hall outward and accomplish great things for a mayor. (Chapter 13 discusses the inside politics of leadership.)

At the other end of the scale, however, the mayor must be grounded in the people, a reformer with the zealous light of good government burning in his eyes. To guarantee the legitimacy of the cathedral, he has to get the signature of a city's populace on the social contract underwriting a successful administration. He can do that only if he remembers his roots among them and his personal spot in the pecking order of local life. In the eyes of most Americans, politicians are low-life, larcenous lamebrains, and Americans always favor an outsider, Dirty Harry or Ross Perot, over a potentially corrupt career politician. The difficult task for the leader of the city-state is to wield power furiously from city hall but remain an outsider in the halls of power. If he succeeds, the personal reward is not fame and fortune but a return to the streets.

But those streets will be clean and pothole-free.

My father saw the inside of politics from a great vantage point. He was part of the local machine, its leader in fact, and served a term as state chairman of the California Democratic party. For a while he was a consummate back-room operator and was well known as Harry Truman's local connection. One of my favorite old photographs of my dad, John P. McEnery, shows him smiling at Truman's side as the president beams out over a San Jose crowd from the back of his whistle-stop train car in 1948. But my father never held elective office and in his later years was seen by the new inside gang at city hall as a nemesis.

My brother John and I went through our formative years listening to my father's political philosophy, much of it focused on the abuses of power exercised by local elected officials. We developed the all-American distrust of political insiders, an innate suspicion of the swells and a preference for the upstart underdog. My first political skirmish against the entrenched cliques came on the streets of San Jose when I was nineteen years old. Congressman James Roosevelt, son of FDR and a behind-the-scenes national player, came to town speaking on behalf of some local incumbent. My brother and I, motivated almost as much by our po-

John P. McEnery, the author's father, on President Harry Truman's "whistle stop" train with Mayor Al Ruffo (middle).

litical opinions as by a rowdy definition of having fun, decided to disrupt the political meeting. We heckled Roosevelt mercilessly, reminding him of the traitorous time that he deserted Harry Truman in the dark days of 1948. Standing just in front of the platform, waving signs, we heckled and yelled until the police came along and shooed us away. We beat a hasty retreat, laughing all the way.

Stranger on a White Horse

One of our most popular national sports has always been ridiculing the people in power. I heckled Jimmy Roosevelt, and then when I held office, I bore the same burden. That suspicion of political power is our defining national characteristic and has been since the Revolution. Will Rogers gave voice to it when he jocularly defined Congress as "the only native criminal class in America." The spirit that drives that suspicion is alive and well at the local level. California cities and many other Western locales have long had faith in the paradigm of the reformer, the Clint Eastwood who rides into town and cleans up the corruption plaguing the good people.

Progressive reform politics in America was a reaction to notoriously corrupt big-city machine politics. In most post–Civil War industrial cities of the East and Midwest, political machines emerged just as American industry was being mechanized. The old neighborhoods were already hotbeds of highly factionalized politics, and their local officials were the products of turf organizations run by ward bosses. Though the system had its own internal logic and stability, it was expensive, fractious, and downright ugly at times. The trains ran on time, but you had to pay off a conductor to make it happen. Businessmen were frustrated at the common practice of deal making with politicians in order to accomplish anything, and terms depended on the whimsy or greed of the political boss. It had a human face, all right, but the system oozed corruption.

Sure, you could argue for the positive elements of political machines. They helped integrate a generation of newly arrived immigrants into American society and provided an avenue for ambitious young people to find jobs in politics and business. Many local machines in the old Northeast were ethnic powerhouses of Italian, Irish, German, and black Americans. Although the machines did have a human face, I have to come down on the side of an outsider's condemnation of then. The favors machines doled out were usually petty, patronage jobs that failed to improve the overall social conditions of the slums. Immigrant groups were usually crowded out of the important back-room discussions.[188] Most of all, the overwhelming corruption in a machine's hierarchy inevitably created a backlash that led to change.

In California and then in other states across the country, a new coalition of businessmen and citizen reformers finally rebelled against the machine system at the turn of the century. The Progressive movement in California took Hiram Johnson to the governor's mansion, and nationally it almost took Teddy Roosevelt back to the White House for a second term in 1912, on a third-party "Progressive Bull Moose" ticket. The movement's biggest impact was always at the local level, though.

In San Jose, the original Progressive movement convulsed the local machine and left ethical reforms and political innovation in its wake. Just before the turn of the century, the city had a population of 21,000, a city council with four members, and a municipal government dominated by bosses and back-room deals. The ruling machine of the day, according to a 1908 article in the *San Jose Mercury*, kept power through "large contracts. . . . let out to the favored patrons of the machine. . . . Gamblers and saloonkeepers were subjected to monthly 'graft' and school teachers were compelled at the risk of their positions to deal in 'machine' stores." Politically appointed patronage employees, including policemen and firemen, were dunned for kickback contributions to the ward heelers. The city administration was corrupt, and a string of unethical mayors held absolute control over the city purse.

In 1897, the Progressive reform movement arose, composed of leading members of the business community, journalists, and courageous individual citizens, among them my grandfather "Honest Ben" Sellers. They took on the machine, and they won. Acting through a new "Good Government League," they won voter approval of a new city charter that ended "one-man rule" by stripping the mayor of virtually all appointive powers. Over the next decades, the perks and powers of the mayor's office were diminished until another charter revision in 1916 practically abolished the position, making it almost an honorary title hidden among the city council. It was the era of the city manager form of government, and San Jose was a leader. The Good Government League kept close ties with reformist Republicans in Sacramento and across the country and were strong supporters of Teddy Roosevelt's Progressive Bull Moose party.[189]

In so many Western cities, reform enthusiasm led to a new model of city politics, attempting to smash the power of oligarchies and to let the sun shine on the processes that created public policy. Political parties were attacked and a nonpartisan ballot was proposed; at-large elections were created to replace ward or district base elections. Election boards were created to oversee campaigns and voting. Other Progressive era reforms included the primary election system (so important now in presidential campaigns), voter registration requirements, the secret ballot, and the introduction of civil service reform in cities.

I am a maverick Democrat, but I believe the words of Fiorello La Guardia, the legendary New York mayor who once said there is no Democrat or Republican way to clean the streets. As a mayor elected twice without a party label, I can testify to the merit of the nonpartisan ballot on a local level. Smaller cities, where machines were not well entrenched, have introduced reforms more quickly. In 1910, almost no cities had nonpartisan elections. Less than twenty years later, half of all cities with over 25,000 people used them, and today about three-quarters of those cities have nonpartisan ballots. Some cities have been slow to accept them, and there are regional variations in political reform. Most city councils in the Northeast are dominated by Democrats and are strongly partisan down to the old-style "ticket" campaigning, while in the West, there are more Republican-led or entirely nonpartisan councils.

In general, Western cities are most likely to have instituted Progressive reforms. In many East Coast cities, the local machine keeps chugging along, and you can see that in the different kind of people who get involved in local city council races. One academic survey found that council members in Northeastern cities were most likely to view a council seat as a stepping-stone to higher political office, while council members in the West were more likely to list concern about a particular issue as their reason for seeking election. Northeastern and Midwestern councils had the lowest levels of college education, while the West has more college-educated members.[190] All these differences testify to the value of reform.

The Progressive spirit has not died. It is periodically revived in cities around the country as citizens rebel against local concentrations of power gone awry. Chicago's city government is much more open today under Richard Daley than it was under his father in previous decades. New York City recently implemented a commendable campaign finance system for city council elections. It is, unfortunately, only voluntary. Many incumbents simply choose not to participate in its system of contribution limits and disclosure. New York politicians sometimes seem to be channeling the spirit of a former mayor, John F. Hylan, who said in 1918 that "we have had all the reform that we want in this city for some time to come."

Like many elected officials who came of age in the 1960s, I had my radical reformist impulses, boosted by my family's tradition of rabble-rousing. My father was a leader of San Jose's "New Progressives," formed in 1944 as the Progress Committee, a watchdog against City Hall's incompetence and cronyism. During San Jose's modern Progressive era, in the 1970s and 1980s, I introduced a number of measures to city government to keep us in the forefront of cities addressing voter mistrust in public officials. The city enacted strict campaign contribution prohibitions, registration of lobbyists, gift limitations, and conflict-of-interest regulations, which were all quickly approved by the city council. San Jose also added a revolving-door ordinance to keep former officials from profiting off their public service.

Many issues in political ethics are not as easy to control legislatively. The relationship between the lobbyist and the elected official is a gray area; lobbyists like to keep it gray and undefined, and so do some politicians. One of the most influential local lobbyists in the country in the early 1990s, New York City lawyer Sid Davidoff was a tennis partner and close friend of David Dinkins, yet he claimed that his personal relationship with the mayor was not compromised by his representation of such clients as Warner Cable Communications, Philip Morris, McDonald's, and the Building Contractors Association. All have had business before the city, and Davidoff was paid handsomely for his services to them. He defined his success on behalf of his clients in terms of simple access and argued to a reporter that his influence did not prejudice a deal. "Power to me is getting your phone calls returned so that you can make their case. Everything else is on the merits of the case."[191] Left unanswered is the question of access for opposing viewpoints or the fundamental question of why money itself (in the form of campaign contributions and lobbyists' fees) should be the criterion by which a mayor returns calls.

In the mayor's office, I always kept my distance from lobbyists. When I felt even the slightest bit uncomfortable in a discussion, I had a choice: sever the relationship immediately or proceed cautiously now but agonize later about the potential for civic harm. I preferred the former. In fact, I preferred the high drama of kicking someone out of my office. I am not inclined to post hoc agonizing. Henry Stern, president of the civic group Citizens Union in New York City, has advocated the "nose test." He advises mayors and other city officials to ask themselves on any deal, "Does it smell? Is it based on a personal relationship? Was the lobbyist hired for a particular transaction? Does it run contrary to the city's interest?" Excellent questions all, and let the voters damn the mayor who forgets them.

In my bias for cities, I am not suggesting that politicians are historically more clean at the local level—far from it. Power corrupts. "I seen my opportunities, and I took 'em." So said George Washington Plunkitt, a leader in the assorted band of grafters and ne'er-do-wells known to history as Tammany Hall. His type of political animal, which populated the machine politics of New York, Boston, and Chicago, was rarely seen in the cities of the far West except for old San Francisco. We did have an infamous San Jose city councilman in the 1980s who inadvertently paraphrased Plunkett, explaining, "I saw a business opportunity, and I took it." He almost took an indictment as well and did take an electoral pounding.

Usually, though, stories of old-style graft today come from cities with the remnants of a machine. The faces may have changed, but the strings and levers are still attached at one end to the big-money bagmen and at the other to the smiling politician. Jersey City, New Jersey, may not have a strict machine as it did under Frank "I am the law" Hague, who served as mayor for thirty-two years early in this century, but his legacy lives on and the city has recently had a string of mayors convicted or prosecuted on corruption charges.

Sometimes it is difficult to imagine how an official bright enough to be elected could succumb to such a mundane temptation as tainted money. In 1991, Mayor Raul Martinez of Hialeah, Florida, was sentenced to ten years in prison for racketeering and extortion and for selling his vote and influence on zoning matters. Martinez had served ten years as mayor but was only forty-two and was considered a real rising star, a possible candidate for Congress (or even a respectable higher office). Power corrupts, though, drawing money like a magnet. Hialeah is a fast-growing suburb of Miami, and Martinez had no trouble in the boom years of the 1980s extorting almost $1 million from high-flying developers for favors on zoning and real estate matters before city government.

One case in particular in the past decade shocked mayors around the country. Lee Alexander, mayor of Syracuse for sixteen years, served as president of the U.S. Conference of Mayors, a top spokesman for the nation's cities. Although he was from New York State, I always noticed his perpetual Florida tan. This should have been a warning. In 1988, he was sentenced to ten years in prison after pleading guilty to charges of racketeering, conspiracy to obstruct a government investigation, and tax evasion, all centering on a $1.5 million extortion and kickback scheme. The plot grew out of a political fund-raising effort, but Alexander began diverting kickback money to his own personal use. When the judge sentenced him, he mentioned how Alexander's work had made Syracuse shine as an example for other cities, "but your criminal actions have placed national attention on it again in another light, and for that you must pay." Alexander even wound up having to pay $100,000 in restitution to the city of Syracuse.

Such incidents are sad, as lives are ruined and potential contributions to the community are betrayed. One thing they do confirm, though, is the adage that eternal vigilance is the cost of liberty. The light of public scrutiny should never be dimmed, and local groups have the brightest spotlight. At the local level, citizens can gain a more direct handle on the problem and usually more access to the facts of the issue. They also have an easier time effecting the ultimate solution: scaring up an opponent and voting the bum out.

Quite often the local political scandals are the most enjoyable, just for the absurd humor of what jackasses officials can be. In Hawthorne, California, recently, it turned out that the city clerk was living in Hawaii while still drawing his city paycheck. He was an elected official, but the city charter required him only to be a registered voter in the city—not a resident. The mayor noticed the arrangement, since the part-time clerk was spending more and more time in Hawaii. (His Hawaiian shirts must have been the tip-off.) In 1991, after about a year, the mayor tried but failed to persuade the clerk to move back to Hawthorne. Inevitably, the press got hold of the story, and outrage ensued. The clerk finally resigned amid scandal.[192]

New State Motto: Quid Meam en Rem est? (What's in It for Me?)

Local politicians have bad role models in their big brothers and sisters at the state capital. Across the country, state legislatures experienced a wave of corruption in the early 1990s not seen since—well, since the 1980s. Since 1989, at least seventy state legislators in 12 states have been indicted or convicted as a result of federal or state investigations, mostly using sting operations. Dozens more have been investigated, along with aides and lobbyists. In high-profile cases in Arizona, South Carolina, Florida, and California, FBI and local law-enforcement officials have snared corrupt politicians. Citizens often have the educational benefit of legislators captured on hidden-camera videotapes, stuffing their pockets with bribe money and laughing about the gullibility of voters. In Arizona, a state representative was on tape saying, "I don't give a [expletive] about issues. . . . My favorite line is, 'What's in it for me?'" Another told an undercover cop, "We all have our prices."[193]

A few years back, I caught a lot of heat from Sacramento for a grave political sin: pointing out the obvious. In an interview with *West* magazine, I criticized the degree of influence exercised by special interests in California's legislative corridors. I also had a few choice words for our own state political boss, Speaker of the Assembly Willie Brown. I referred to him as "the Manchurian Candidate of the state Democratic party," explaining that, to my mind, the Republican party could not possibly have a better friend buried deep within the Democratic party. Brown was almost acting as a mole by undermining public trust in our party and its capacity for honest leadership and good government. Speaker Brown apparently blew his fuse at my remarks, but his reaction merely underlines my point. Brown symbolizes all the things about politics that voters detest: an affinity for back-room deals and closed-door sessions, a web of personal and professional relationships with special-interest lobbyists, and a propensity for high living on a public salary. While he is glib and charismatic, the Democratic party owes Speaker Brown as much as the Donner party owed its scout.

State legislators respond to such admonition by local officials just as they do to indignant "letters to the editor" in newspapers and to handlettered signs at state capitol protests: with a stony silence. There is too much personally at stake, apparently, for our legislators to clean up their own acts.

Their attempts to avoid responsibility at times border on the ludicrous. After a number of Sacramento legislators were convicted of bribery charges, ethics workshops were scheduled in 1991 for state senators and their staffs. Some legislators bristled at anyone daring to question their righteousness. One irritable reaction came from Senator Diane Watson, a Los Angeles Democrat. Watson was perhaps smarting from her own ethical investigations by the Sacramento district attorney's office or from her previous $21,075 penalty for using campaign funds to pay for personal expenses (credit card charges, a family reunion, airline tickets, personal parties). Watson seemed to find insult in the very idea of being forced to participate in a workshop on better ethical decision making. She was particularly incensed at the discussion of taking gifts and cash from lobbyists. "We're not ordinary people, and I think that's what is throwing this discussion off," she protested. "Ordinary people are not required to travel twice a week to and from their work. . . . Ordinary people are not required to live in two different places." When the workshop leader replied that lawmakers are paid an additional $17,000 allowance to cover living expenses, Watson was not satisfied. Later she told a reporter, "This person is an expert in ethics. He knows nothing about the political arena. A guy whose expertise is ethics isn't very realistic to me. . . . I didn't need an ethics workshop."[194]

By the end of the 1980s, I was fed up with such a morass of loose morals in our state capital. A book published in 1988 by San Jose authors Lee Brandenburg and Lewis Shepherd was a factor in my thinking. *The Captive American* lays out a modern argument for an age-old idea: limitations on the amount of time served in office by our state and federal officials. The authors describe how ordinary individuals and voters feel further removed from government because it is dominated so invincibly by career politicians. Long-term incumbency, in both Washington and any state capital, tends to produce both gridlock and corruption.

I have always credited much of my success to having served under a two-term limitation as mayor. The fixed term actually afforded me greater flexibility and focus in problem solving. Although I was reelected in something of a landslide, when my second term ended in 1990, I declined to run for office. I took some pride in the distinction of being a "citizen-politician."

I was convinced that a reasonable limit on the terms of our state legislators would add an incredibly valuable perspective on their political and governmental responsibilities. In 1989, with an election year approaching, I began discussing with state attorney general John Van de Kamp the possibility of passing such a term limit. We were convinced that we could do so through a vehicle provided us by the Progressive reforms decades before: the citizen-sponsored initiative. I chaired the statewide campaign for the 1990 "Clean Government Initiative," Proposition 131. It was an omnibus measure, encompassing term limits for elected officials and limits on campaign contributions and spending, along with a moderate program to finance campaigns with public funds. Van de Kamp was in the midst of a hard-fought but unsuccessful campaign of his own against Dianne Feinstein for the Democratic gubernatorial nomination, and the issue was a staple of his campaign. We received endorsements from Ralph Nader, Common Cause, the state chapter of the National Organization for Women and the Sierra Club, among many other groups. The measure qualified for the November 1990 state ballot faster than any other initiative in history, with a record 1.2 million signatures of citizens throughout California. We had the support of the people, but we knew we were up against the entrenched interests of Sacramento—the iron triangle of incumbents, bureaucrats, and lobbyists.

One group we had not counted on fighting was a quartet of Hollywood stars, world famous and well liked. We walked right into their buzz saw, and I learned something about the difference between local government and the big-money world of state politics.

David versus Goliath: Slings against Money

Thucydides said it first: Victory has a thousand fathers, while defeat is an orphan. Proposition 131, a real model for good government, was orphaned by a pauper's campaign, unable to raise the money to be competitive against the very interests it sought to control. In the end, we were done in by a tidal wave of negative TV commercials featuring of all people Angela Lansbury, Walter Matthau, Sharon Gless and Jack Lemmon.

I was no novice in politics by any means, but this lineup came as a shock. They were on the wrong side. Political reform is a fuzzy, noble cause too easily misunderstood and caricatured to withstand a concerted onslaught.

Proposition 131 did not. Poll results throughout the long campaign year showed the measure winning substantially, including a final poll released the week before the election. The last month before the election, though, proved to be critical. In this game, only the fourth quarter counted. We marveled in the face of a massive avalanche of attack materials, from misleading "voter-slate" cards to negative direct-mail letters to slashing television ads, all paid for with lobbyists' and incumbents' war chests, both Republican and Democrat. After a frustrating campaign in which the good guys never had enough money to counter the bad guys, we lost. The initiative was defeated on election day by a large margin, losing 62 percent to 38 percent. Proposition 140, a much harsher initiative that ignored campaign finance reforms and ethical measures altogether but imposed shorter term limits, narrowly passed 51.9 percent to 48.1 percent.

I was surprised in one sense on election night: it was the first time I had witnessed the defeat of any measure I had ever supported in a vote of the people. I actually felt more disappointment than surprise, though, for I realized that I shared the blame. Looking back, I believe that our array of high-minded reformers across California had misjudged the voters. They were much angrier at the system than all of us had believed, and their verdict that November day in 1990 holds lessons for political reformers at all levels of American government.

Overall, I think that the Clean Government Initiative was a victim of a generally hostile electorate. Voters were angry not only at politicians, not only at "the system," but at a political process that handed them a long, crowded ballot crammed with confusing measures. As the longest, most confusing measure on that year's ballot, ours was inevitably fated to receive some of the voters' anger in the form of "no" votes.

Most striking was the distinction voters could make between Propositions 131 and 140. Ours would have imposed a twelve-year limit on legislators, while Proposition 140 set a six-year limit for the assembly, eight for the state senate. Ours also included an entire campaign financing scheme, while 140 ignored the issue.

The Clean Government Initiative campaign suffered from a fascinating paradox. Where newspaper editorial boards were concerned, having shorter term limits to point to as the more "draconian" measure was a dream. We practically wrote the editorials ourselves, as paper after paper accepted our measure as "the reasonable approach to reform." If the other measure had not existed, we would have had to invent its specter to sway some of the boards, notoriously populated with do-gooders.

But winning over the *San Jose Mercury News*, the *Los Angeles Times*, the *San Francisco Examiner*, the *Oakland Tribune*, the *San Diego Tribune*, and others, as we did, was not the same as winning votes. That is where the paradox appears. Voters thought almost in reverse: given two approaches to throwing the bums out, let's take the more radical.

The bottom line in the entire campaign, though, was the money raised and spent by the Sacramento opponents of both measures, the entrenched incumbents who saw danger in either term-limits measure. Together, from special-interest donations and personal campaign war chests, the machine was able to put together more than $5 million, dwarfing our efforts.

The Power of Television in a Political Campaign

When the Sacramento political machine decided to defeat the Clean Government Initiative, Assembly Speaker Willie Brown launched a statewide airborne assault via television. The campaign was a textbook case in how to throw an election, deserving study in classes on applied politics.

Our opponents aired five negative attack ads. Individual spots featured celebrities: Angela Lansbury, Sharon Gless, Jack Lemmon, and Walter Matthau. All the actors read from an identical script attacking our measure. With the utmost sincerity and credibility, the actors intoned their concern: "Don't fall into the term-limits trap." The spots were personal, impressively slick, and devastatingly effective.

We also were mugged with another very powerful commercial: the infamous KKK ad. The concept was recycled from a spot broadcast the last time public financing had been before the voters, in 1988. The short advertisement showed a hooded, white-robed figure flanked by neo-Nazis, speaking to a crowd of people. His sneering message was that his campaign would be funded with taxpayers' dollars, and his followers cheered.

The ad was dishonest but effective. While our proposition had built-in safeguards to prevent any such misuse of public funds, it proved impossible in the short time that the spot aired (just a week or so) to counter the message effectively. We impotently issued angry press releases and were able to get some newspapers to notice the disreputable claim in the commercial, but their stories were hidden amid other political "he said, she said" reportage. We even pro-

duced our own television response ad but had no money to air it widely. Meanwhile, night after night, the Brown machine paid to broadcast its ads on stations throughout the state. Just as with most negative campaigning in any political race, if you can sow enough doubt in voters' minds without creating an overwhelming backlash, you win. The voters have a lot of common sense, but they rarely have enough independent information about an issue to make a decent interpretation of the facts and half-truths they are given.

The commercials worked. The ads began airing just after a poll had been released showing the Clean Government Initiative passing 66 percent to 18 percent. A poll one week before the election showed that support had dropped to 51percent. After that last poll, the ads continued, and we wound up in the dumps. Proposition 140 passed by a razor's edge.

Winston Churchill loved the tug-of-war of politics, but he had no taste for noble defeat. After listening to a Labour member harangue the House of Commons while sponsoring some inane and doomed bill, Churchill rose and pronounced, "I have seen many men beat their heads against brick walls. This is the first time I have ever seen a man erect such a wall specifically for that purpose." I ruefully recalled the anecdote on election night 1990, having tried and failed to do the right thing with a long and complex initiative tailor-made for defeat. We fought the good fight and lost.

The Future of Reform

At least fifteen states have passed or plan to vote on term limitations for their state representatives and, in some cases, members of Congress. Some limits are better than others. California's government will be profoundly affected by the very short term limits imposed by Proposition 140. From now on, new incumbents operate under the six- and eight-year limits. We do not yet have the idyllic scenario of Cincinnatus and his plow. These guys are not Cincinnatus, and most would not recognize a plow. What they hope to return to is likely a lobbyist's desk. Term limits that are too short may not encourage participation in the system by motivated individuals who wish to devote a career to public service. Six-year terms may attract primarily individuals who figure that legislative service will enhance their résumé, in a sense, giving them access to a more lucrative world of lobbying and consulting. The bottom line is, with too-short limits and absolutely no campaign-finance reform, we now risk even worse government.

In any case, I have analyzed my foray into state politics for what it says about political reform as a whole. The goal of reform must be to sponsor new leadership for our cities, states, and nation. That new leadership should, I believe, represent the highest and most positive aspirations of the voters. The term-limits bandwagon is essentially a negative movement, requiring negative arguments and widespread dissatisfaction for its success. Conservative and antitax groups are now in the forefront of a congressional term-limits movement and are fanning the flames of disenchantment with the federal government. That is not tough to accomplish. Yet if and when the economy picks up again, as it surely must, then the economic component of public anger will be gone, and perhaps people will begin thinking positively about their state and federal elected officials again. I believe that would be good for local government as well, for most of us at the level closest to the people work hard to convince citizens that they have a real stake in the success of government.

I am not suggesting that the issue of term limits itself, with which I have been personally associated, is dead. I endorse it gladly. I have lived by that sword and let my term die by it as well. In December 1990, a month after our defeat, I hosted the first National Conference on Term Limitations in San Jose, which drew political activists and national media from across the country and the political spectrum.

I have to admit, though, that I have grown uncomfortable with a political reform movement that is based so firmly on a negative zeitgeist.

There have to be other ways of changing our political system for the better that go beyond a primitive and populist appeal to the anger of the crowd. When Bill Clinton was elected to the presidency, I felt somewhat reassured in my conviction that the Nineties might be a decade waiting for a positive vision of our commonwealth and its future. Political reformers should focus on affirmative proposals, with an uplifting message to inspire Americans and recapture our confidence in government from the White House to city hall.

Whatever path our reform drive may take, we must ensure that citizens retain the reins. Marshall McLuhan's analysis is often correct: the medium can be as important as the message itself. In the case of political reform, you must weigh the value of the message by paying attention to the messenger; the message he bears may be nothing more than a sound bite.

I have a bias for political dynamics that genuinely move from the bottom up. I believe that from the grassroots of local politics in cities across America will come the leaders and voters of a new American politics, a more responsive and more responsible generation who will understand the true nature of leadership practiced in the new city-state.

13

HOW TO BE MR. INSIDE

Anarchy, anarchy! Show me a greater evil!
This is why cities tumble, and the great houses rain down.
—Sophocles, *Oedipus Rex*

After a chapter-long discussion of my outsider reformist inclinations, I suppose I should come clean. For more than a decade, I was inside the halls of big-city power. I guess in a way I still am. More than that, I am not afraid to accumulate political power or to use it to change things. I actually enjoy it.

In 1980, before I became mayor, San Jose's governmental structure was of the weak-mayor/strong-city-council variety, with a strong city manager. The form is common in many cities and is a remnant of the Progressive era's reforms. I ran for a mayor's position that featured a staff of two and a half, no budgetary power over the city administration, and a legacy of ineffectual occupancy. A decade later, near the end of my second term, the *Mercury News* ran a cover story on power and leadership in the city and Silicon Valley. Things had changed. The paper's long-time political editor, Phil Trounstine, wrote of me "brandishing the iron fist and the velvet glove."[195]

I had not changed—the mayor's job had, dramatically. At the same time, though, I believe Trounstine caught the essence of a particular philosophy of government. It is an old one. The quote that begins this chapter sums up my feelings about the need for effective government: I have a great aversion to disorder. I was elected to office on a platform, with certain promises to keep. They were promises on important policies and problems, and my constituents had a right to expect me to keep them. I needed more power to do so and I acquired it by thoroughly legal means. I then used it, without relish but with a certain pride of authorship.

The point is, I attempted to lead, not to maintain. I wanted a level of dynamic energy in our city government to match the momentum of the Silicon Valley miracle occurring around us. My idea of governing involves something more than a static notion of performance indicators. Policy wonks would do better to peruse David Osborne and Ted Gabler's *Reinventing Government*, a book so often quoted by administrators and so rarely read. Their concern is with the nuts and bolts of technobureaucrats. My concern is with vision and leadership.

Politics is central to leadership. Government can't always be run more like a business, as the old bromide goes. Government is not a business. People often talk about gathering the smartest people in the room and getting them to agree. They misunderstand: government is not only about achieving consensus. Consensus is *always* possible in business, for all within a company can agree that the shared goal is the bottom line, a quantifiable, objective target. In public affairs, in real life, there are few quantifiable goals beyond a rhetorical flourish. There are differing opinions about what government's priorities should be, about what our society should look like. People do not always agree with one another.

Somehow, not only do the decisions need to be made, they need to be explained to the public, to the bureaucracy, and to everybody down the line. Therefore politics is key: the art of pursuing an idea in the face of opposing ideas and winning. You have to push and push again. I had a vision for our new city. Some in San Jose did not agree. I pushed harder. It so happened, at the end of the day, that most people agreed with me.

The Tripod of Power

I have analyzed the nature of political power in the urban arena, both retrospectively over the course of my terms in office and by casting an eye across the country to successful mayors and administrators. The power of a city's leader, particularly of a strong mayor, rests on a tripod of three interconnected legs:

- *First, the leader must have a rationale, or practical theory, of power.*
- *Second, he or she must have the tools of power, and if they are not available, they must be procured.*
- *Third, and just as critical, the leader of the city-state must rely on the concentric circles of power that surround the mayor's office.*

You may get elected without a rationale of power or find yourself in an office with no tools and resources. If so, you won't be an effective insider, you'll flounder in office, and you may be sadly retired at an upcoming election. I prescribe a radical attempt to change. Politically, all three legs of the tripod are necessary to lead the larger community from inside city hall.

A Rationale of Power: Understanding How Things Get Done

Tom Bradley, former mayor of Los Angeles, revealed to a reporter his guiding theory of mayoral power after twenty years in office in the country's second-largest city: "The influence you have, the ability to get things done, is not so much a matter of law as it is a matter of your being able to persuade people to join with you to do something you set out as a goal."[196]

Bradley was speaking for himself and inadvertently explaining just why his mayoralty received mixed reviews from knowledgeable political observers. His theory of power was abstract, reflecting the hemmed-in, isolated position of his mayor's office in relation to a powerful fifteen-member Los Angeles City Council. Affable as he was, like many other mayors around the country, Bradley sat in the hot seat unarmed: he did not always have a *practical* theory of power. Particularly in an activist city-state that intends to take on new responsibilities and to create new opportunities, the leader needs to have an explicit rationale of power, an understanding of the way his political world works and the ways to move its levers. Contrary to Bradley's belief, the most important of those levers are real, definable institutions, not wispy bands of influence. Their operation is defined, yes, by law. But the law can be changed.

By the 1960s, the traditional models of how cities governed themselves were falling apart. In so-called unreformed cities, political machines still controlled everything, with local parties collaborating with business elites to keep the behemoth alive. Many more cities had reformed but were missing a vital center to the city's leadership. Business interests had played a prominent part in enacting Progressive reforms and distributing power away from back rooms at city hall, and business leaders now often worked directly with local candidates, sometimes recruiting them from within the business community. Political parties were dead or ignored, and ethnic changes were weakening cities' accepted patterns of power. Pluralism reigned, as the dichotomy grew between city hall and neighborhoods, between downtown and popular interests, between progrowth and antigrowth coalitions.[197]

Things are changing. In the past decade, some mayors have taken the bull by the horns and replaced these centrifugal forces with a new rationale of power, focusing on a strong center. I had learned something from the excesses of Progressive-era reforms. In my analysis, San Jose, like some other cities, had swung its own pendulum too far away from the elected mayor over to the power of the appointed city manager. My rationale was going to be progressive in a different way.

Academic theorists of urban power have forever studied the various arrangements featured in modern American cities and have focused on the key distinction between the "strong-mayor" system and the "strong-manager" alternative. They are not exact opposites, and many cities have a hybrid, but there are significant distinctions. An administration centering on a strong mayor creates an executive operating in counterbalance to a city council, but the system provides the mayor with executive powers and prerogatives and at least some formal tools to strengthen his hand. A strong-manager system is inherently weaker. The manager, though often a power unto himself, is hired and fired by the city council. The mayor under that system is at most a facilitator for the council, a presider. The mayor's seat is often rotated among council members, with no salary, office, or practical distinction.[198]

My rationale of power, which I needed to underwrite a transformation of our city from sleepy town to city of the future, depended on a beefed-up mayor's position. One can never minimize the ex cathedra power of the mayor to verbalize city goals—even to personify the city. Early in my tenure, I had recruited Greg Larson, a brilliant Stanford University graduate who combined an academic understanding of political science with a real interest in the practical exercise of power. Greg and David

Pandori, my longtime aide, worked with me on the task of transforming San Jose's city administration from a strong-manager to a strong-mayor system.

To give life to this new rationale of power, we made three main structural changes and one change of emphasis. First, we moved to a council "committee" and "vice-mayor" system. This change made council members individually and corporately beholden to the mayor for influence and favor, for the mayor holds committee assignment power. I am still surprised at how eager the council members are to wear the crown of the vice-mayor, a position that carries no real weight or power. Second and very important, we increased the mayor's staff. By the time I left office, my staff had grown from two full-time aides to almost thirty. I make no apologies for the increase, for my office was by that time handling a vastly increased workload of city responsibilities. (We reduced staff positions elsewhere in exchange.)

The third and perhaps most significant change was to transfer the budget authority from the city manager's office to the mayor's office. This move was an essential change reflecting the power of the purse. Additionally, in what was more a change of emphasis underscoring my rationale of power, as mayor I paid more attention to elections than my predecessors had, choosing my issues and candidates well. I made sure that I won every local race I touched.

The administrative changes were accomplished with amendments to the city charter, which required voters' approval. In the 1985 debate over Measure H, the campaign was intense. We took criticism for a supposed aggrandizement and arrogance in our grab for power. My response was simple: the voters elected me to accomplish a particular set of goals, and the task required a new, more modern look to our city government. The people passed the measure.

By the end of the 1980s, other cities were taking the cue of city-states like San Jose. A *Sacramento Bee* analysis in 1989 concluded that "the council-manager system of nonpartisan municipal government lies on its deathbed in California. . . . Among local government officials, the model for the new type of mayor is Tom McEnery of San Jose, who put his personal brand on every major project undertaken in his city for the past seven years. He's the new breed of strong mayor in a high-growth California community."[199]

The quote is flattering, but do not confuse the personal issue of power with a mayor's necessary rationale of practical power. The distinction to keep in mind is between a governable city and an ungovernable city.

The city without a strong mayor is not going to be able to compete in the world of the confident city-state, for it will be flirting with anarchy. In an academic's words, it will suffer "hyperpluralism," a bundle of "highly variable fragmented and unstable problem and policy contexts," so fragmented as to resist rational governing.[200] As citizens, we call it the dying city. I wanted the tools to reverse the process.

A Mayor's Toolbox of Power

My predecessor in the mayor's office once showed a particularly absurd degree of attention to the perks of office. When San Jose's city council fired a city manager in 1978, the mayor took the opportunity immediately to have the designated parking spots behind city hall rearranged. A painting crew blotted out the manager's spot, placing the mayor's spot in its preeminent place. To my predecessor, such was the exercise of power. When I was sworn in four years later, I had a more disciplined awareness of authority. In assessing the political effectiveness of a city's leadership, you have to identify the specific tools of power.

A mayor has both formal and informal tools at hand. The formal powers are the most important, a fact that escapes the attention of too many wheeler-dealer types in mayor's offices across the country. They spend their days negotiating and worship only "the art of the deal." Under their noses, missed entirely, are formal powers of the office that can make or break an administration beyond any single deal.

- The most important formal tool is *control over the city's budget* formulation, which gives the mayor not only the ability to set priorities for government, but the political ability to induce and reward support on the council.
- The second most valuable tool is the *hiring of mayoral staff*, which extends the mayor's power directly.
- Third is the *power of appointments to positions* within the administration and to boards and commissions. In many cities, the decision to name a new police chief can be a crucial turning point in "thinking like a general" on public safety.
- A fourth formal tool is the mayor's ex officio *membership on official boards*. In San Jose, the position as chairman of the Redevelopment Agency board has been critical to the mayor's ability to guide the downtown renewal.

- Fifth in my list of tools is the varying ability held by most mayors to *issue executive orders* and fill vacancies in elected offices.
- Sixth, the mayor bears organizational *authority over most city departments*.
- Seventh, many mayors have *veto power over city council* measures (which can be overturned in most cities).[201]

The *informal* tools of power do not lend themselves to a list. Most are the indefinable equipment of the natural politician, the born leader who intuitively handles the reins of a complex city government affecting the lives of thousands of citizens every day. Perhaps the single most important informal tool of power, one favored by high-profile big-city mayors in the Ed Koch mold, is visibility. As political parties become less dominant, the mass media and voters alike are paying more attention to the individual, and as mayors become more visible, they become more powerful in affecting legislation at the state or federal level. They also become better at attracting national attention.

Dealing with the Media

A mayor of one of America's big cities knows the media can serve as an informal tool of power. Politicians in general, though, have an irregular view of the media.

Some are hostages to good press, pursuing coverage for coverage's sake. When Dave Dinkins became mayor of New York, he quickly began the practice of holding press conferences several times a day. A reporter who regularly covered Mayor Dinkins wrote, "The term 'clinical depression' has also been applied to City Hall reporters, whose job description requires them to drag themselves several times a day from Room 9, the pressroom, across the rotunda to a mayoral press conference, which will very often turn out to be nothing more than a photo opportunity."[202]

At the other extreme is the politician who distrusts the media and identifies the press as an enemy. When Progressive leader Hiram Johnson ran for governor of California in 1910, he had some choice words about Los Angeles Times publisher Harrison Gray Otis: "In the city of San Francisco, we have drunk to the very dregs of infamy, we have had vile officials, we have had rotten newspapers. But we have nothing so low, nothing so debased, nothing so infamous as Harrison Gray Otis. He sits there in senile dementia, with gangrened heart and rotting brain, grimacing at every reform, chattering impotently at all things that are decent, frothing, fuming, violent, gibbering, going down to his grave in snarling infamy."[203]

Needless to say, Johnson did not get the paper's endorsement, though he won the race for governor. Politicians should find a better medium between the two extremes of sycophancy and hatred.

Popularity is the Holy Grail of politicians, and the popular mayor can replace party or elite support with the good will of the population. Charisma does much to shape the political power of an insider; dull folks never claim the title "Mr. Inside." A real leader can inspire a wave of followers and partners who join the fight to provide a new generation of leadership for the community. When a young John Lindsay ran for mayor of New York in 1965, he won with a slogan borrowed from a newspaper columnist: "He is fresh, and everyone else is tired." His election seemed like a harbinger of a better future, and he collected around him a team of motivated young people eager to be agents of change. They played important roles during his two terms, and all were motivated by Lindsay's charismatic appeal.

The most surprising informal tool I would suggest is, quite simply, information. A sitting mayor, like a governor or president, has a tremendous advantage over all other centers of governmental power in controlling the information flow from city departments and individuals scattered throughout the community. Knowledge is power, and the benefits to a well-informed leader are obvious. Yet that power must be used fairly. Be honest. Even a tough leader—viewed as a bastard by opponents—can simultaneously be up-front with allies, rivals and voters. Yes, it is possible to thrive as an honest politician. In the event of scandal, crisis, or personal failure, honesty will serve you as the best political policy. I take Mark Twain's advice: "Always do right. This will gratify some people and astonish the rest."

Any political official should also keep in mind that not all the tools of power are vested in the individual office. Some are resources of the city itself but can be wielded by a smart mayor. For example, in the city-state environment, a leader can plan economic regeneration only through a strategy exploiting all public and private resources, including the very geographical or environmental assets of the city. I gained an unexpected boost in the power corridors of San Jose when outsiders began to describe me as the "mayor of Silicon Valley." I turned their convenient labeling instinct to my advantage.

Perhaps the most important thing to remember in any discussion of the tools of power is that their necessity is a political reality. *Reinventing*

Government became the bible of the postliberal crowd and of the new Clinton administration in 1993, but disappointingly, it downplays the political mechanisms and resolve needed to implement reforms. Like reformers everywhere, the authors paint interesting ideas proposed around the country as if they were proven solutions. Most of the battle-scarred mayors and administrators I have spoken with regard the book with some skepticism, born of wariness at the book's boosterish endorsement of marginal programs in small, homogeneous cities. Most of their proposals have little to do with the major issues faced in America's big cities. Worse, there is great danger in launching a reform scheme with no understanding of the practical political tools needed to make it successful. When President-elect Clinton dropped his campaign pledge to seek the line-item veto, he undercut severely his ability to attack the federal deficit or to "reinvent" the balance of power with a spendthrift and ossified Congress.

The Circles of Power

At the core of the city-state sits the mayor. Radiating out from the mayor's office are concentric circles of power, from the innermost group of advisers and allied council members to important elite groups. Further outward, surrounding them all, are the citizens as a whole. A city without a strong mayor may experience a power vacuum as the conflicting interests of the various circles degenerate into anarchy.

I never had cause to worry about the effectiveness of my staff, in large part because of my excellent chief of staff, Dean Munro, who kept tabs on the ever-larger office. He kept his eye on the ball. My efforts were focused more on keeping the city council in line and dealing with the permanent bureaucracy. If a mayor is not exercising strong control over the innermost circle, a city council can stray off into uncharted territory and can practice individualistic, reactive policy that may be good for a day's headline but no good for the city.

Here is an example in which a mayor did not control the inner circle: The Los Angeles City Council enacted an ethics law in 1991, with fanfare from incumbent council members billing it as "the toughest in the nation." Within a year, after an outcry from reform groups and local political activists, the council had to concede that the measure had been hastily conceived and poorly drafted. It was a bomb. Major provisions on financial disclosures and lobbying prohibitions had to be dropped from the package. The measure's flaws came from its hasty birth in a publicity-hungry council. The public had been outraged over Mayor Bradley's legal troubles, as he faced several investigations into his personal finances and conduct of city affairs. Voters were also angry at a city council pay raise. Public outcry can often lead to meaningful change, but only if there is some sense of accountability in the process. Not so in Los Angeles. Mayor Bradley was out of touch, and the ethics law was drafted in back rooms and rushed past the council.

Council president John Ferraro admitted later that the council's haste was attributable to an attempted public relations coup at the expense of the mayor: "That is the mistake we made here. We didn't look at it closely enough. We were too anxious to do something so that it didn't look like we were dragging our feet."[204] Nothing like that would have been attempted in modern San Jose. The city-state leader must control the innermost circle. My approach with the San Jose City Council was a bit more forceful. Six months after I left office, one council member told me privately that the council was continuing to support Susan Hammer with the accustomed unanimous votes I had engineered. She had learned well. As the council member put it, "They still think the seats are hooked up for your electrical shocks. Turn the wrong way, and the electricity goes on, like mice in a maze."

The next closest circle of power around the mayor is the collection of powerful interests throughout the city: business, labor, neighborhood associations, and many other entities. On a given policy, they may be on your side or against you, but they must be taken into account. San Francisco is perhaps the nation's most anarchic city politically, and its array of interest groups makes the label "hyperpluralist" seem inadequate. Its traditional labor and business groups are supplemented by a panoply of special interests unrivaled in the rest of urban America—indeed, in the rest of the world. One mayor in a different era who had a real handle on the dizzying circles of San Francisco elite politics was "Old Joe" Alioto, a friend of my father's in the early days and now a patriarchal lawyer. Of his successors, Dianne Feinstein approached Joe's success at consolidating influence among a wide and unlikely coalition of groups. Others, from the martyred Moscone to Agnos and now the courtly Jordan, have not fared as well.

When the elites squabble, a city loses. Los Angeles was in true political gridlock for a year after the 1991 Rodney King beating. The gridlock at first had little to do with the racial aspect to the case but centered on the political question of who ran the city. Was it Mayor Bradley, who impotently called for Chief Gates's resignation? The city council, with a pack of mayoral wanna-bes all jealous of Bradley and one another? Or was it (in a perversely negative sense) Gates himself, who ran the police department for thirteen years with apparent impunity and commanded a broad and vocal level of public support. The Gates affair lingered for months, long before the trial of the police officers that led to the riots of 1992. Mayor Bradley's inability to fire Gates in the scandal tied the city government up in knots. The *Los Angeles Times* reported in a front-page news analysis that "disappointment in Mayor Tom Bradley and the City Council has bred a nostalgia for a time when a corporate elite . . . virtually hand-picked public officials and dictated city policies in Los Angeles." The June 1991 article quoted "lawyer and investor Richard Riordan" as saying, "The perception is of an almost total lack of leadership coming out of City Hall right now. The question is whether the private sector could get itself organized and play a beneficial role."[205] Two years later, almost to the day, Riordan was sworn in as mayor, succeeding the retired Bradley after promising in a hard-fought campaign to restore a bond between the people of Los Angeles and city hall.

Our Silicon Valley business community has been an interesting case study in how to affect the political arena. The young, fast-growing electronics companies have little inclination to play footsie with politicians. Few of them make political contributions or play the traditional games of currying favor with elected officials and their handmaidens. They are goal-oriented and apolitical. As the industry grows more economically powerful and more politically mature, the captains of the computer industry have begun to realize that their stake in local government is an important one, affecting their bottom line directly. I have found an increasing willingness on the part of computer-industry CEOs to participate in the political process. Quite honestly, they usually tend to play fair. When contrasted to the traditional commercial powerhouse of San Jose, real estate developers, the high-tech business community has been a paragon of virtue. Its members pursue their interests in generally the same logical, methodical, and intellectual manner they use in designing the next generation of microprocessors. They generally respect that San Jose has attempted to strike a balance for both trees and technology, our local version of the "guns versus butter" argument, and I find that representatives of vibrant new industries have been honest and straightforward.

We live in a democracy, and the most important circle of power must be the broadest: the people, each and every resident. A mayor can draw political power from the people, but only if he respects a genuine notion of two-way communication.

Machiavelli, who was more of a populist than his reputation reflects, wrote that "all cities must have devices by which the people can demonstrate their concern and interest, especially those cities which intend to engage the people in important undertakings." Many mayors like to have an open-door policy, whereby the average citizen can walk into the office and speak with their mayor on a topic of personal concern. The practice dates back many years and was immortalized in Edwin O'Connor's novel *The Last Hurrah*, as Frank Skeffington pays audience to a never-ending succession of cranks, do-gooders and "his people," who may want a moment of his time, a pat on the back, or a pothole filled. It is a good system. It gives an interested mayor what someone once called "a street-sized perspective on a high-rise job."

I always found even more valuable the simple act of getting out of the office into the neighborhoods, where I could actually see the crack houses and neighborhood schools, the well-kept parks and the street corners out of control. Sitting in an office all day, even with an open door, is sometimes just an invitation to frustrated office seekers. In the days of President Garfield, "frustrated office seeker" was a description of the typical political assassin. Today, it is more likely to be a synonym for "lobbyist."

Role Models for the Successful Mayor

Like any professional, a mayor should ponder what role models to emulate. There are two categories for mayors to consider. First are other successful mayors from around the country. Second are local heroes.

A local hero I always admired was Silicon Valley pioneer Robert Noyce, who died in 1991. Bob and his principal collaborator, Gordon Moore, both brilliant, were part of the original "Traitorous Eight" engineers who in 1957 bolted from William Shockley's pioneering semiconducting company (Shockley had invented the transistor). Noyce, Moore, and the six others formed Fairchild Semiconductor in Mountain View, the granddaddy of them all in chips. Noyce was then just twenty-seven years old with a doctorate from MIT in physics.

In 1958, he coinvented the integrated circuit, or chip, easily stamped out in mass quantity. Some called him the Henry Ford of the semiconductor industry. Noyce and Moore struck out on their own in 1968, forming Intel Corporation and mass-producing memory chips. The company's remarkable growth made Noyce a wealthy man, but he always supported charity efforts in his new community home. He came out of retirement in the late 1980s to head Sematech, the company that attempted to reclaim U.S. dominance in semiconductor production.

Today, Intel is the world's most profitable electronics company, having re-taken the lead from Japan in chips. Bob Noyce is remembered as a remarkable man of vision, enormous energy, and a determination to rewrite the future. He was a true American hero.

A Career in Politics

Will Rogers once said, "Politics is the best show in America. I love animals and I love politicians and I love to watch both of 'em play, either back home in their native state or after they have been captured and sent to the zoo or to Washington." I believe citizens consider politics a spectator sport not so much because it is fun to watch but because they feel they must be watchdogs, keeping an eye on the hyenas, monkeys, and snakes in charge of their tax money.

As someone who has been around politics all my life, I consider it a spectator sport, too. But there are more serious moments. Someone once said that I have Irish Alzheimer's disease: I forget everything but the grudges. But I remember lighter moments, too, the old anecdotes, the war stories, and the personal triumphs and tragedies of others before me, all of which make up my impression of local politics as something worthy of a life's cause.

That life is less worthy if it is spent in pursuit only of the next rung on a political ladder. I spoke those same words in office, but I believe them even more strongly now that I am just a former "Mr. Inside," looking in from the outside. It took me almost four years out of office before I even considered running for another position, and I am glad I never considered the prospect while I was mayor.

Some of the best moments in local politics seem worthy of a special episode of *Bloopers and Practical Jokes,* and they usually seem to involve politicians whose focus was on their career path to national power. Mayor Sharon Pratt Kelly of Washington, D.C., was eager to speak at the 1992 Democratic National Convention. Advised by organizers that she would face the two-minute limit placed on all "minor" speakers, she tried to bargain for ten minutes but was rebuffed. What would any mayor do under such circumstances, with the bright lights shining? Mayor Kelly simply kept talking after the officially approved two-minute text had slipped by on the TelePrompTer, ad-libbing for another eleven minutes.

It is tempting for a mayor's eyes to stray from the official task at hand and to look to higher office when incumbents up the ladder seem to be doing a worse job. In 1991, when only Paul Tsongas was an announced Democratic presidential candidate, some big-city mayors considered running for president. Ray Flynn of Boston was foremost among them. At a June meeting of the annual Conference of Mayors, a private caucus of Democratic mayors discussed the idea openly, with some like Atlanta's Maynard Jackson arguing in favor of it, so fed up were local officials with the Bush administration and the apparent lack of any real Democratic challenge. Flynn decided not to make the run. It is difficult to imagine a more qualified background for the Oval Office than one steeped in the byzantine lanes of a city like Boston.

It is also difficult to imagine just how mayors might move up the po-

litical ladder in any case, when incumbents in state legislatures and
Congress sit so heavily on their thrones. I advocate campaign finance reform to help dislodge them, but I sometimes believe a crowbar might be
required. After reapportionment was finalized across the country in
1992, local and state politicians began scrambling around, looking for offices and districts to run in. David Roberti, president pro tem of the state
senate in California and one of the most powerful politicians in the
state, found himself without a district to run in and had to change his
residency to find a new venue—and then lost his attempt at the state
controller's job. In the old days, that was called carpetbagging. Tom
Hayden, who ran successfully for a new seat in the state senate after
being chucked from his old seat in the assembly, said, "It's a Darwinian
process. It's unfortunate, but no secret, that everyone is looking at everyone else's seat." (He considered races for the assembly, the senate, and
even a new congressional district.) "I don't know what else we can do
but get used to it." I guess the idea of finding a job in the private sector
never occurred to Hayden. In 1994, he ran a distant third in a Democratic primary for governor.

Veteran Los Angeles city councilwoman Joy Picus recently considered
running for a new seat in Congress, for county supervisor, for mayor of
Los Angeles, and for reelection to her council seat. She first decided on
the congressional race, admitting to a reporter that Congress "is just the
first streetcar to come along, so I'm jumping on."[206] The streetcar broke
down, though, when a congressional incumbent in another redistricted
district decided to run for the seat. Picus retreated to the city council
and remains there, presumably checking streetcar schedules regularly.

Paying the Toll, Reaping the Rewards

Senator Phil Gramm of Texas recently defended his White House aspirations as perfectly natural. "Anybody who's been elected to a city
council, much less the U.S. Senate, thinks about being president," he
told a reporter. "Anybody who says they don't is a liar." That may be
true, but the personal toll that a political life takes on individuals still
can drive the best of them out of the business, long before they get out of
the boondocks to Washington.

Bud Clark served as mayor of Portland from 1984 to 1992 and was
known as the "comedian politician," infamous for his unconventional
approach to office. To raise money for a local museum, he once posed for
a poster as a flasher in a raincoat standing before a public statue; the cap-

tion read, "Expose Yourself to Art." Clark announced he was leaving office to serve as a handyman at the Goose Hollow Inn, which he owns, but all joking aside, the job wore him down. "Most of the feedback you get from a job like this is negative," said Clark. "It's like being a cop: you see and hear all the bad things." Small-town mayors are no exception, and they may even be worse off, since the job is generally part-time and you are expected to make a real living elsewhere. Neal Coonerty of Santa Cruz hoped at first to compress his time in city hall into two days a week, devoting the rest to his bookstore downtown. No such luck. "You can spend sixteen hours a day dealing with mayoral issues," he notes, and that in a small seaside town of just 50,000 people.

The biggest drawback to a career in politics at any level may be the level of personal scrutiny and scorn heaped on elected officials, not always undeserved but always unwanted. Bruce Babbitt once told a convention of city planners, "You almost want to deny that you're in public service. It's looked upon as such a lowdown, inadequate occupation for misfits and for people who can't go out and be real estate developers." The image of a mayor sometimes gets tarnished even after he leaves office but rarely so oddly as in Chicago, where in 1988 the recently deceased mayor Harold Washington was depicted in a painting dressed in a white bra, panties, garter belt and stockings. Outraged Washington loyalists on the board of aldermen stormed into the exhibition at the School of the Art Institute and demanded that the painting be taken down because it disgraced the former mayor, but a judge returned the portrait and chastised the aldermen.

No mayor should be exempt from the indignities of the average citizen, either. Former mayor Sidney Barthelemy of New Orleans probably suffered the ultimate indignity, short of being led away from city hall in handcuffs (which happens to a mayor every now and then). Barthelemy's official city car got the Denver boot locked on its wheel while he was attending a hotel luncheon. The mayor's driver had parked legally, but the car had three outstanding tickets on it, and an officer did the right thing: booted it. I don't know how the officer's career has progressed since that incident, but I would place no bets on his likelihood of ever reaching captain.

Sure, it is a rough life, but our political campaigns would be mighty short if no one wanted to run for office. My feeling is that those who complain about the indignities are those most in need of being taken down a peg or two. The rewards of local service on the inside can be overwhelmingly positive. Sophie Masloff, born in Pittsburgh in 1917 to

Rumanian immigrants, began working as a volunteer for the local Democratic party in the 1930s and was rewarded with a succession of local patronage office jobs in the county clerk's office and so on, until in 1976 she was nominated for a seat on the city council. She sat on the council for twelve years before serving for a year as interim mayor when Mayor Richard Caliguiri died in office. In 1989, not endorsed by her party, she surprised every pundit with an upset victory over five male candidates in the mayoral primary, running unopposed in the general election and becoming mayor at the age of seventy-two. She was called "Grandma Mayor" and remained popular and effective by lowering taxes and streamlining government. One can only conclude that she was a better mayor because of her career devotion to local government. Some in her city would call it requited love.

The temptation to move up the ladder is best avoided for some. Donald Schaefer served fifteen very successful, activist years as mayor of Baltimore, then went on to a much less successful stretch in the Maryland's governor's mansion. One state senator confessed that the legislators in Annapolis were probably tougher to deal with than city council members: "He ran Baltimore with an iron hand, had everybody and everything in his pocket, but when he got to Annapolis, he found he couldn't control us, couldn't put us in his pocket. He's had a hard and frustrating time getting used to that cold fact, and it shows. It's a constant tug of war with him."[207] Some people even speculate that Schaefer may decide after his second term in the statehouse to run for mayor of Baltimore, where he could once again find a hospitable arena for his can-do style. I know his old slogan from his city days, "Do It Now!" is one that deserves to be dusted off for copying in many cities.

Meanwhile the battle goes on, fought in many small towns and big cities by a colorful "Mr. Inside" against entrenched special interests. In the Minneapolis suburb of Brooklyn Park, Jesse "the Body" Ventura, one of the biggest names in big-time TV professional wrestling, was elected mayor in 1990. Just as in a good-versus-evil ring clash, he ran promising to fight the old-boy network of chummy relationships between town council members and local developers. Ventura said he enjoyed the job just as much as his old days of banging heads in the ring; he took it seriously.

When most of us on the inside look at the quality of our leaders, we get depressed. Our problems seem so much worse than in the old days, and yet our political class seems so inadequate to the job. John Lindsay, now in his seventies and an outside observer of the urban political scene, wonders how—and whether—New York City can attack its problems.

Having served for eight years in what he called "the second-toughest job in the nation," Lindsay blames leadership. "Mediocrity is everywhere," he told a reporter recently, despairing of the chance of finding a fresh new politician with solutions for our cities, and hope for our future.

But things are not getting worse through historical inevitability. Imagining a new city-state requires a bit of historical perspective, and with that perspective comes hope for the American capacity to reform. Just over a century ago, writing in an 1892 issue of *The Atlantic Monthly*, Moorfield Storey concluded: "We all recognize a steady decadence in our politics. The men in public life today are, with few exceptions, intellectually and morally inferior to the great statesmen of the war and the years which preceded it. Political preferment is less and less tempting to good men. The conditions of public life are more and more repellent. The tendency is dangerous, and it is our duty to arrest it." It all sounds familiar.

A century later, at the dawn of the 1990s, Robert Putnam and William Parent of Harvard's Kennedy School of Government wrote of their belief that this country was on the verge of "a period of sweeping reform and improvement, a return to the American spirit." They judged as political scientists that a "convergence of forces" was leading to "a new era of political activity and reform." They compared our era to the turn of the past century (just as Storey was writing in *The Atlantic*), when public disgust with political corruption and gridlock produced the era of the Progressives.[208] I also am optimistic, but this change can occur only if more of us take the responsibility to become involved in our cities.

It is sometimes difficult to square a personal choice of a "career in public service," as political professionals like to say, with the general low opinion of politics. Not all politicians are deaf to the public mood; some of us hear quite clearly the remarks our neighbors and friends make behind our backs. In *Time* magazine, Charles Krauthammer examines "Why Americans Hate Politicians," while E. J. Dionne writes an entire book titled, *Why Americans Hate Politics*. Dionne's analysis: politicians divide us against ourselves on phony ideological lines, making cooperative, commonsense solutions impossible. Krauthammer's diagnosis: "a decade or two of negative advertising has finally had its cumulative effect. We have really come to believe that politicians are as bad as their opponents have been telling us in a thousand 30-second spots."

Both are right, and yet neither provides an answer to the real dilemma of American democracy. We have allowed the gulf between the governed and the governing classes to widen to its broadest, most alarming chasm in our nation's history. Strip away the photo-op "brush-with-power" moments when a president mingles and shakes hands while the cameras are on, then hustles back to the idling Air Force One. Put aside the staged visits paid to local community centers "back in the district" by members of Congress who return only to wing back to Washington for another reception. Ignore the ritualistic service-club luncheon speech delivered by a state legislator who may not even own a home in his hometown anymore. George Will has called them "rented electors."

Americans have lost touch. Not with reality—our grip there is firm. We have literally lost touch with members of our political class, who have reacted like college freshmen away from home for the first time. They never call, they never write (except in the mass newsletters), and we know darn well they're up to no good at their parties. Are they cracking the books, burning the midnight oil? When the report cards come in with Ds in public policy and Fs in economics, we simply shake our heads, wondering what ever happened to that bright idealistic kid we sent away to the big city? We are reminded of the immortal words of Forrest Gump: "Some people, like me, are born idiots, but many more become stupider as they go along."

Only at the local level can we recapture stewardship of elected officials and with it control over our own destiny. Local politics is the gateway to higher office, and therefore it is and must be the citizen's gateway to an upper hand on the affairs of state. As cities become more independent and self-reliant, with broader horizons on the policies they command, our local officials become more important. With that importance climbs the voters' ability and motivation to exercise reasonable authority over a greater set of issues than ever before considered at the local level. The local voter has the opportunity, and the responsibility, to provide direction for local officials. From that mandate in the new city-state will come reasonable change, responsible policy making, and good government for a more promising future.

For my part, I hope to live up to an editorial in the local paper that spoke kindly of my "premature political retirement." With good humor, the editorial writer mirrored my determination to remain an outside insider in the city I love: "In another twenty years, McEnery could be the kind of aging character who gives a city local color." Thanks, I think.

14

THE TWENTY-FIRST-CENTURY CITY: IMAGINING THE FUTURE

I dreamed a dream I saw a city invincible
to the attacks of the whole of the rest of the earth.
—Walt Whitman

Bill Clinton stared intently into the gigantic microprocessor. A slight grin came to his face. It morphed into a big smile. After two or three attempts at programming a ten- by eight-foot whirling, buzzing, twisting model of the very heart of most personal computers in the world, we had our answer. August 19, 1946, fell on a Monday. Through a rather circuitous route using a mock-up of an Intel 486 chip, we had arrived at the day of the week that Clinton was born.

The governor of Arkansas was quite happy, and he had reason to be. In the center of the Tech Museum of Innovation in downtown San Jose, the wizards of Silicon Valley gathered on a day late in September 1992. John Sculley of Apple joined John Young of Hewlett-Packard, Ed Mc-Cracken of Silicon Graphics, and other CEOs of established firms and start-up companies. Venture capitalist Sandy Robertson of Robertson Stephens was there. Jimmy Treybig of Tandem and Larry Ellison of Oracle were in the group. It was as impressive an assembly as this ever-overachieving Valley could muster, and it had been in the making for

285

Presidential candidate Clinton checks out The Tech Museum's Giant Microchip with
Dave Barram of Apple Computer (middle) and the author (right).

some time. As with many things in Silicon Valley, it seemed to happen
only by chance.

The group gathered around in a large circle. The centerpiece of the
impromptu symposium was the 486 model, the invention that had made
Intel Corporation America's last, best hope against the economic onslaught of Japan.

The conversation began quickly and got quicker. While we were discussing a new technology policy for America, in a corner of the room
the FMC Mars Rover explored the valleys of the red planet on a large
screen with software developed by Apple. The effect of a lowered capital
gains tax was debated over the simulated collapse of a ten-story building
in the 1906 earthquake, presented on a Silicon Graphics monitor. The
people who brought us Forrest Gump were always full of surprises.

The conversation raged on. Within a few feet of a model clean room
fabricating a silicon wafer, we debated free-trade policy with Mexico.
Jimmy Treybig, the peripatetic and friendly genius at the helm of super-
star Tandem, was particularly interested in the trade issue. Before the
meeting began, Treybig had pulled me aside to say that without learning
Clinton's position on that issue, he would not endorse him. Treybig was

The author introduces Silicon Valley CEO's to Bill Clinton (far right). Their endorsement was a key to victory in the 1992 election.

not disappointed by what he heard. Clinton's smile widened; he knew he was making legitimate converts if not outright friends.

After forty-five minutes, the group crossed to a small auditorium where 100 members of the national press corps waited. I took the first shot at the podium, flanked by the future president and the assembled brainpower of technology in America. In a paraphrase of President Kennedy's comments on Thomas Jefferson and Nobel laureates, I noted that this was the greatest convocation of energy and entrepreneurial power at the Tech since the afternoon when Bill Hewlett wandered in alone! It got a knowing laugh from Clinton. I introduced Sculley, who had done more than any single person in the industry to make this day happen. He delivered a pointed and succinct exposition of current national policy and future economic opportunities. Then on behalf of the twenty-two others, mainly rock-ribbed Republicans and willful Independents, Sculley endorsed the candidacy of Bill Clinton for the presidency of the United States. It was clear, unambiguous, and a mortal shot at the solar plexus of the lumbering, out-of-control Bush campaign.

As the limousines and campaign buses rolled out of the Tech's parking lot, I wandered out the front door, hardly pausing on the sidewalk at the gigantic "Imaginary Chip," a sixteen-foot audio-kinetic microchip sculpture by Richard Rhodes that serves as both focal point and entrance way to the museum. This had been a remarkable and historic day, a day that some chroniclers of Election '92 have designated as one of the three or four critical turning points in the entire campaign. Clinton gained a lot of mileage from the Silicon Valley endorsement.

My mind, though, was no longer on politics. I gazed from the Tech Museum of Innovation across the street to the new Convention Center, and beyond to the new Children's Discovery Museum. I had my eyes on the horizon. I was imagining the future.

Optimism in Our Town

I am an inveterate optimist on the future of the city, though I try to ground my hopes in reason. Conditions are bad in cities around the world, certainly, and unfolding prospects are often dismaying. Janice Perlman, director of the Mega-cities Project in New York City, says she can no longer distinguish the cities of the rich, industrialized First World from the left-behind cities of the Third World. "In every Third World city, there is a First World city of high tech, high finance and high fashion," she acknowledges, but "in every First World city, there is a Third World city of malnutrition, infant mortality, unemployment, homelessness."[209] Trend lines that show continuous population growth bear no hidden rays of sunlight, either. As the next century begins, there will be twenty-three city-state areas with populations over 10 million, including New York and Los Angeles. These megacities will dominate their regions and countries and present the world with challenges unlike any we have ever faced.

For a bleak conclusion, though, look elsewhere. Historical perspective should convince us that conditions are auspicious. The city-state plans strategically for the future, but the future as such is unknowable beyond a demographer's chart. We must also have a sense of the past. If we do remember the past, then—just perhaps—we may no longer be condemned to repeat it. We can liberate ourselves to imagine and work toward a better future, one building on a realistic appraisal of our strengths today. After all, we have technological advantages, economic wealth, and human resources unheard of in history, all at our command in every inner city in America. Focus on our "blighted" areas for a moment: are they worse than ever before, worse than yesterday's Five Points in New York? The first use of the word "slum" was not even in this century. It dates back to the 1820s, when the leading edge of the Industrial Revolution was creating urban sprawl, vast traffic jams, and even pollution in cities like London and Edinburgh. People used to joke that you could smoke ham by hanging it out the window.

Some of our supposed liabilities may in fact be turned to our advantage. California will grow by another 6 million during the 1990s nd we should hit the 40 million population mark by the year 2006. Most of that growth will be in cities, some in new inland cities created along the suburbs and valleys, but the majority of immigrants and new births will be counted in our existing cities: Los Angeles, San Diego, and San Jose.

I believe that dynamic central cities could actually fare better in the future than suburbs, the "edge cities" of America. Suburban communities will suffer all the problems of cities—traffic gridlock, crowded schools, crime—but none of the benefits that come from a shared sense of community and a leadership cadre for action. Insular neighborhoods built around people trying to escape people are not really neighborhoods at all. An edge city is no city.

We can sketch the outline of the successful twenty-first-century city. Cities and towns used to be real city-states, independent and ignored by a less activist Washington, left to their own devices. We must return to that kind of self-reliance. Citizens must realize that any city really is "our town." More than just a Thornton Wilder title, the phrase embodies notions of ownership, pride, confidence, and neighborly interdependence. Tonight in any town in America, a community association or neighborhood group could assert its resolve to attack one immediate problem degrading the quality of life. Tomorrow and next week, such groups and their individual members can rise through the local political process to exercise real influence on vital decisions. Next month and next year, all of us acting together in our towns can actually imagine the future by envisioning an entirely new kind of city for ourselves, a new cathedral that only the citizens of each town can define and foresee.

Then they will go out and create it.

Crucial roles will of course be delegated to the mayors of America, working with the state governors and other officials of goodwill. City-state mayors will become a new kind of creature: a mixture of Republican disdain for Washington and its federal solutions imposed from above and an activist Democratic zeal for creative solutions bubbling up from below, from the grassroots of the community. Independence will be the guiding principle. Mayors in a city-state will be more powerful but will recognize the additional leverage they can wield by freeing citizens to provide independent solutions and programs. Leaders and citizens could together produce a burst of energy and civic innovation in the next decade at levels unknown in recent times.

Who Will Fight the Battle with Us?

This book recommends self-reliance for cities, but self-reliance within realistic bounds. The patient undergoing cardiac arrest cannot be expected to perform CPR on himself. One Upper West Side resident wrote a pleading op-ed piece in *The New York Times* in 1991, describing the siege of his Broadway neighborhood by violent panhandlers and street criminals. Only a midnight assault on the homeless by four vigilante residents had cleaned up the area, destroying the shanties and scaring away the rough street people. The writer asked, "Is this what it takes to clean up our neighborhoods? Has New York turned into such a war zone that each block needs a militia to maintain social order? Is that what New York is about these days: armed civility?"[210]

We cannot expect our citizens to take on alone the task of turning our cities around. We must all line up together and seek allies.

In California, we have found no ally in Sacramento. The state is now no partner at all. State legislatures across the country are taking a dastardly attitude toward urban America: NIMBY. They look the other way, pass the buck, and roll down their shutters at night, all to avoid any role in helping cities in need. Daniel Patrick Moynihan used a much-repeated phrase in the 1960s: the policy of "benign neglect." Moynihan, however, had a positive plan that was never implemented. Those words prescribed a course for the federal government, one of procrastination and disregard for the problems of the inner cities. This neglect led only to violence and further hardship. Today's neglect of the problems we face in our communities is not so benign. No-Nothing legislators, both state and congressional, have little understanding of local realities. They don't know what they don't know. Most incumbent congressmen have never served in local government positions.

Within that environment of a hermetically sealed jar, the very real problems faced by our communities are ignored and trivialized. They dither while we work. They delay while we decide where cuts must come. They run for reelection while we run city services on shoestring budgets. Their failures have real consequences for us. Their dawdling puts immense strain on city coffers. Tight budgets cannot expand to meet the responsibilities of a true city-state and certainly cannot underwrite the visionary requirements of the next century.

On notable projects as well as the more mundane issues of municipal policy and services, the cities have to take back the baton of responsibility. It stands to us now to assert the leading role in any partnership with the state and federal governments. Leadership on the most crucial issues facing the United States in the 1990s will have to come from within, from the population centers that give us our vitality and our energy. The leading role of cities in these partnerships is a natural extension of our place on the front line in the struggle with the issues of today—the pernicious scourge of drugs, the challenge of educating our youth, the goal of sustaining growth in an era of decline.

It is only natural that leadership come not from detached colonies of legislators, those oligarchies of incumbents, but from each of us, citizens and leaders of our towns and cities. We are fighting the daily battles. Teddy Roosevelt said that it is not the critic who counts: the credit belongs to the man and woman who are actually in the arena, whose faces are marred by dust and sweat and blood, who strive valiantly and spend themselves in a worthy cause.

Corporate America must join in this partnership to remake our cities, in coalitions with all who depend upon metropolitan vitality—and that criterion is so broad as to be all inclusive. In the business world of the 1990s, we witness daily the creation of new partnerships and alliances in the communications and technology industries. Joint ventures spring up overnight involving billions of dollars in research-and-development investment. The result of these alliances, their participants expect, will be products that we cannot even envision today. That is how we must view public-private partnerships attacking the problems in our cities. The efforts may not fit in a neat municipal box and may not comfortably wear a label that covered something done before. These new partnerships among government, public- and private-sector groups, and individuals will operate creatively, with imagination and daring. The nature of our problems requires imagination; our nature as Americans ensures it.

Good Ideas, Bad Ideas

New York is no longer the face of the American city. The day is past when E. B. White could write, "New York is to the nation what the white church spire is to the village—the visible symbol of aspiration and faith, the white plume saying the way is up!" Presidential candidates still tour the South Bronx or Los Angeles's South Central but only to show concern before the ugliest face a city can present. Today we can look to all sorts of creative cities, suburbs, and towns for more positive examples that will make all our cities more livable.

There is certainly a gulf between those city-states that take seriously their new responsibilities for the next century and those cities that fail to do so. The latter group is falling behind. Some cities seem comatose. But new leadership could emerge in any American city, at any moment, and is likely percolating up today. During the Vietnam War, many young U.S. military officers in the field chafed at the way that war was fought and lost while lowly troops fought and died in jungle firefights. Those young officers who stayed in the military learned some important lessons. They advanced in two decades to become Colin Powell, Norman Schwarzkopf, and all their lieutenants during the Persian Gulf War, exhibiting a quiet competence and high professionalism in no small way due to their different style of leadership and management. Today, some may see only a flickering light at the end of the tunnel for urban America. I see more, and I am not alone. I am confident that there exist young professionals in city, county, and state governments—yes, even in the federal bureaucracy—who are learning the same alternative lessons about government and its problems today. In our country's worst-run cities, there are undoubtedly vibrant cohorts of youthful reformers just itching for the opportunity to turn their cities around. They will do so, to our astonishment and applause.

In the 1980s, there was a cadre of young mayors around the country who sought to change the way the American city worked. Our informal club included Terry Goddard of Phoenix, Roger Hedgecock of San Diego, Henry Cisneros of San Antonio, Federico Peña of Denver and others. Frustrated with the U.S. Conference of Mayors and its stodgy, Washington-centric viewpoint, we even toyed with the idea of starting our own rump group of Sun Belt cities to push our new agenda of change. Back then, we set ourselves apart. No longer. Now maturing, the young Sun Belt cities have taken on a bit more wisdom with age about our proper role in the life of urban America. Today, those cities realize that we can and should be a part of the debate on policy. We intend both to teach and to learn: learn from other cities about their successes and perhaps teach them a bit about ours. The American city, each city, is too important to lose.

Each city will define its own cathedral. Paris already has its Eiffel Tower and Notre Dame, Venice its canals and gondolas (and, yes, its St. Mark), Hong Kong its financial towers attracting the world's attention. We must rival them. Many American cities have a jump start on the cathedral strategy. Dallas began planning in 1965 with a "Goals for Dallas" project, highlighting its position as an international business center. The strategy has succeeded in establishing a first-rate international airport and an educational infrastructure for high-technology industry. At the other end of the spectrum, much smaller Eugene, Oregon, has focused not on economic development but on the performing arts and on the cultural amenities to support a highly educated population. American cities of all sizes must refocus their sights on their cathedrals, the characteristic feature, natural or man-made, that defines their heart and soul.

City leaders will have to be active, not passive, to make these transformations occur. No longer can mayors observe dormantly as their cities change around them. Michael McGreevy, head of NASA's Ames Research Center in Silicon Valley, explains the difference that the new technology known as virtual reality has brought to the computer industry: "Television is like a window. Virtual reality is like a door you can walk through." The shift in governmental styles will be just as radical. Cities will dump their couch-potato slackers in city hall and choose leaders impatient to walk through new doors. We might borrow one concept from industry; that is, the idea of "speed to market," the amount of time it takes to develop a concept into a product and sell it, which is crucially important in Silicon Valley and the high-technology sector. Mayors should also think in terms of speed to market for their ideas on how to improve local government and the quality of life. After all, mayors have only one term or two, if they are lucky.

If a mayor gets the big picture right, the city can confidently turn to less overarching issues affecting the quality of life. Sometimes the little things can make or break a city's atmosphere and livability. In October 1991, *Metropolis* magazine asked architects, civic planners, and urban dwellers for ideas on fixing one thing about city life that drives them crazy and published the results in a "repair manual for the great American city." The remedies ranged from the serious to the absurd, including disappearing dog doo and car horns that sound as loud inside the car as outside. A better source of ideas for mayors and civic activists is the Taubman Center at Harvard's Kennedy School of Government, which annually gives awards for innovations in state and local government, honoring public-sector creativity and excellence. Some ideas do translate well from city to city. Both New York and San Francisco, cities that have had problems with sidewalks being used as human toilets by the homeless, have looked to Paris for a solution. New from France comes the computerized, coin-operated, self-cleaning "toilet kiosk," installed on the sidewalk and available for just a quarter. The new toilets have been tested, the public is enthusiastic, and city officials, God bless them, are flush with pride.

Not all the ideas adopted in San Jose or in any city can be transferred successfully to others. The Mega-cities Project tries to foster the exchange of good programs and once presented two dozen pollution-control innovations from around the world to a New York City interagency task force. Mayor Dinkins was quite taken with a São Paolo, Brazil, program that displayed pollution monitors to discourage driving in the central city during high-pollution days. The program also used an extensive public education campaign: student volunteers in the street approached drivers stopped at the most congested intersections, encouraging them to leave their cars at home on "alert" days. Cynical observers with a little knowledge of the frustration of gridlocked driver might wonder if the volunteers should be armed. I doubt that this particular effort will translate smoothly to most American city streets, let alone New York's.

Even ideas that seem to hold much promise can have holes that wily urbanites exploit. Mexico City once tried a one-day-a-week car ban, with people leaving their cars at home on a day determined by the last digit of their license plate. While the ban worked well at first, reducing measured pollution, drivers began using or buying a second car for the single day they were not allowed to use the first car.

San Jose's focus on its downtown is of little interest to an entire class of new subcities: suburbs that grew linearly along highways. They must find their own ways to make their city relevant to its population. Some small cities do so quite creatively. In 1990, the city of Everett, Washington, outside Seattle, opened a satellite city hall in a local shopping mall on the edge of town, thinking that more people would be able to take advantage of city services. It worked. The "City Hall at the Mall" has been registering voters at four times the rate of the old city hall downtown because of the much greater foot traffic.

Likewise, a city cannot rely solely on economic prosperity as its guiding dream. Singapore, a world capital known more for caning juvenile delinquents than for multinational investment, has performed its economic miracle by using what some call 'the world's most finely honed economic incentives.' That focus has brought short-term success at the expense of a long-term, balanced vision of the community's health. City officials are now very concerned as the next century approaches that rival city-states will strip them of their financial edge, leaving Singapore with no community focus.[211]

San Jose Tomorrow

Since I left the mayor's office, I have concentrated my community efforts in three specific areas: education, citizenship, and technology's role in our lives. By forming the San Jose Tomorrow Youth Foundation, Executive Director Lewis Shepherd and I had a vehicle to channel our energy and the good ideas of others into projects for the future of a metropolis.

We have worked with Elias Chamorro, principal of Overfelt High School, one of the city's largest, to improve the educational opportunities of immigrant students. San Jose Tomorrow set up an after-school mentoring program known as "Overfelt University," with local college students tutoring children who came to this country not speaking English—along the way introducing them to study habits, American values, and shared ways of life. It is a remarkably successful model.

At the initiative of city councilman David Pandori, my former aide, we began "Kids Voting San Jose" to make students of every age aware of the culture, tradition, and importance of voting in our democratic system. Kids Voting is a nationwide program inspired by a youth mock-ballot tradition in Costa Rica, a nation that boasts 95 percent turnout in its elections. In 1992, Kids Voting involved 15,000 San Jose kids in areas of low voter turnout and in 1994 included all 144,000 students in every school, public and private, across the city. Their enthusiasm is overwhelming as they go to actual polling booths on Election Day, dragging sheepish parents along, to cast their own proud ballot and register a new voice.

San Jose Tomorrow is also using technology to draw together two once-segregated urban communities, Catholic and Protestant, in Northern Ireland. Modeled on the Bullets to Bytes program I discussed in Central America with Oscar Arias, Belfast Bytes uses new computer technologies to expand the social and economic opportunities open to the inner-city youth of Belfast. The program is already a success at four community centers in Protestant, Catholic, and "shared" areas, and we hope to apply it to other cities north and south of the border. What we learn of new methods to reach and attract young people can be translated back to America's inner cities.

In any reach outward for good ideas, a city must be sure to maintain a sense of balance and a historical perspective. Great change can often leave important lessons in the dust. After the great Chicago flood of 1992, historian William Cronon noted that the entire city had been rebuilt at the turn of the century above a new system of underground tunnels used by freight cars and locomotives to haul mail and coal around the Loop.[212] By the 1990s, though, the tunnels had long since been forgotten, abandoned over time as Chicago turned to the streetcar and above-ground urban freeways. "People are willing to concentrate extraordinary energy and talent on solving problems," Cronon observed. "Once those problems are solved, however, the artificial systems we erect to protect ourselves recede into the background, becoming second nature for us. As the flood so powerfully demonstrated, the perils of such forgetfulness can be grave, and seem to be an increasing problem of modern life."

Mindful of the past, the city-state aims its sights at the horizon. It may be distant, but sometimes you just need a booster. A *New York Times* editorial titled "Climbing Back" once tried to blast the defeatism out of city residents and elites. Put aside pessimism, New Yorkers were told, and attack problems with a new determination and with new ideas to fit new realities. "Great cities don't die," the paper said, "they adapt." That is a thought for the ages.

The Glittering Future City

"There are three rules to writing a novel," Somerset Maugham once remarked. "Unfortunately, no one remembers what they are." The future of cities, and whether they succeed or fail, is an enigma. Will "Silicon Bayou" in Louisiana or "Silicon Beach" in Dade County, Florida, be the shining cities of the future? We have some clues. In the future, not everything is going to look dramatically different; we should not throw up our hands and assume that we can't even foresee what the city will look like. Change is inevitable and is already here. We need to have the ambition and intelligence to guide that change.

I think often of San Jose beyond the year 2000. There are still a few little things I think we need to get right. I would like to see city hall moved back downtown. Luis Valdez's world-renowned El Téatro Campesiño may help restore the soul and history of San Jose by moving its theater company into our downtown. I would like to see artists' lofts, homes for young couples, and affordable housing for all segments of society. I would like to see scores of children playing safely in parks near their homes. I would like to see jobs for all people who want them. These dreams and many others should happen.

Our cathedral will still be the virtual city, that shining holograph on the hill. The high-tech historian Michael Malone has said that "the Silicon Valley which you see is always obsolete," arguing that what counts instead is the company building going on in the back booth of a local all-night diner as a start-up team energetically plans the next technological revolution. Just as in Valley labs the new technologies of communication are now being invented that will dramatically change, into the next century, the way all of us interact, so are we witnessing in many city-states the fluid re-creation of our concept of "community."

I described earlier San Jose's Project Mindstorm, located in the Gardner neighborhood, a district that in 1960 was 27 percent Hispanic and is now 85 percent Hispanic. A news article not so long ago described the neighborhood as a place "where immigrants' dreams are broken" by the poverty and lack of hope or opportunity. I see a different place. Hope, an optimism more familiar to new Americans, is exactly what Silicon Valley's Mindstorm now gives to immigrant children and many others at Gardner School.

Not everyone understands the promise of the future. George Bush quickly visited Silicon Valley during the 1988 campaign, stopping in at Applied Materials, a local firm. He did not "get it." Bush had brought no real policy, support, or vision to the Valley, and he certainly did not take a page from our CEOs, who have never been without a vision. Bush was turned out of office four years later precisely because he did not learn the lesson of Silicon Valley, as Bill Clinton explicitly did, that change is welcome and can indeed drive the future in a better direction.

The new breed of mayor must learn to thrive in the era of change and metamorphosis, not shrink from it. He must also persevere in chaos. Art Agnos can testify to that. He served as mayor of San Francisco during an earthquake and a homeless invasion of biblical proportions. Art once advised a newly elected mayor of the pressures of the job: "One day you'll be running through an airport late for a plane. You'll look across the concourse and see a man with fear in his eyes. And you'll know that man is also a mayor." This advice is sincere, coming from a man who rode in on a populist crest of nearly 70 percent of the vote and was unceremoniously dumped four years later.

Change is endemic here in San Jose, and in the next decade, other cities are going to make the same discoveries we have. These will be fascinating times. Silicon Valley is a place where Ed McCracken, CEO of Silicon Graphics, could tell President Clinton that all his company's products had been developed in the last eighteen months, and all would be obsolete in the next eighteen. Silicon Graphics computers are now being used in Los Angeles to help city planners, community activists and architects simulate the rebuilding effort in south-central L.A. New software on the 3-D graphics workstations is allowing the question of "what if" to be explored in a more real, dramatic, and exciting way than ever before possible.

One of the greatest living poets, Seamus Heaney, writes of the old bardic schools of Ireland, where poets and artists sat in the dark and stared at a wall until inspiration arrived. Try doing the same exercise in full day's light with a computer! Allow a child the freedom to explore, and the adventures taken will paint in that child's mind a very different image of the future from the one he or she sees on television. I described the nightmare image of our urban future at the beginning of this book: cities aflame and violence overtaking us all. It shall not be.

Our students in Project Mindstorm and at the Tech Museum are already imagining the future, using their own computers to aid them. The next great poet, architect, or scientist may well be in that class. We can

The new San Jose.

all learn from their quiet hope and their calm determination to prosper in the future. After 1991 witnessed the collapse of the Soviet Union and the American victory in the Gulf War, writer Richard Reeves observed that, in the wake of such an unusual year, he hoped for a calm and common year, one devoted to "lesser" concerns like commonsense and community. We still have not had that common year at the national level, and given the multitudinous demands on a president and other federal officials, we may never get it.

But we can get just that from our city, our common hometown. An old Italian proverb holds that *"tutto il mondo e paese"*—the whole world is hometown. Architect Daniel Soloman has written that "the real American frontier is the metropolis," especially those "many sad places at its edges" on the verge of abandonment.[213] Sad edges and all, the new city is the most exciting frontier since the opening of the West; and unlike the final frontier of space, this is one trip we are all going to make.

We approach the year 2000 like the traveler who finds himself walking along a city street toward an unfamiliar destination. He does not know the best route, which road to take, which corner to turn. Along some sidewalks, he may find pleasant shops whose windows entice him momentarily. On a wrong turn into an alley, he may feel afraid of the shadows in the dark. Yet he walks on, certain that all roads lead to the same place: the city. The city-state is more than the sum of its parts, and the traveler pieces together a better image with each new facet he sees. Each step, each sight along the way contributes to his knowledge about his community, his world, his home. Everyone he encounters on his journey becomes his neighbor, and every neighbor becomes a friend.

We are all residents of the American city-state, and we all have a stake in its success.

NOTES

1. Some of these figures on urban growth come from G. Gappert and R. V. Knight, eds., *Cities in a Global Society* (Newbury Park, CA: SAGE Publications, 1989), pp. 224–225. Probably the best book on the subject is Erik H. Monkkonen, *America Becomes Urban: The Development of U.S. Cities and Towns 1780–1980* (Berkeley: University of California, 1988).

2. Figures are from the U.S. Census Bureau, *Report of the 1990 Census*; *New York Times*, December 18, 1991.

3. Aleksandr Solzhenitsyn, *Letter to the Soviet Leaders*. New York: Harper & Row, 1974.

4. Speaking on NBC's *Meet the Press*, March 7, 1992.

5. *New York Times*, June 9, 1992.

6. *Los Angeles Times*, January 22, 1992.

7. Charles Millard, "Why I'm Not Marching in Washington," *New York Times*, May 16, 1992. For academic discussions of old versus new approaches, see Gappert and Knight, *Cities in a Global Society*, pp. 12, 16.

8. *New York Times*, May 17, 1991.

9. *San Jose Mercury News*, April 15, 1993.

10. *Los Angeles Times*, January 25, 1992.

11. Quoted in "Leaders: Bradley, Council Accused of Neglect," *Los Angeles Times*, August 30, 1992.

12. Neal Peirce, "Restoring San Jose's 'Murdered' Downtown," *Washington Post*, March 1, 1987.

13. *City & State*, December 1991.

14. *New York Times*, April 15, 1993.

15. Christopher Byron, "The Monster That Devoured New York," *New York*, January 27, 1992.

16. *New York Times*, February 21, 1992; *Wall Street Journal*, February 22, 1993.

17. Study by Vertex, Inc., and KPMG Peat Marwick; findings printed in *San Francisco Chronicle*, June 8, 1992.

18. William Hudnut, "The Entrepreneurial American City," *Princeton Alumni Weekly*, March 12, 1986.

19. Franklin James and Marshall Kaplan, eds., *The Future of National Urban Policy* (Durham, NC: Duke University Press, 1990), p. 355.

20. *San Francisco Chronicle*, June 3, 1991.

21. *New York Times*, June 16, 1991.

22. *San Francisco Chronicle*, June 3, 1991.

23. *New York Times*, April 22, 1992.

24. Hudnut, "The Entrepreneurial American City."

25. Quoted in "Leaders: Out of Touch," *Los Angeles Times*, August 30, 1992.

26. John W. Gardner, "Constituents and Followers," *Leadership Papers*, no. 8, (Stanford, CA: Stanford University Graduate School of Business, November 1987), pp. 21–23.

27. "A Vietnam Hawk's Battle Plan for a City's Mean Streets," *New York Times*, January 31, 1993.

28. John Markoff, writing in the *New York Times*, October 20, 1991.

29. Niccolò Machiavelli, *The Prince* (New York: Bantam, 1981).

30. "Quoted in *New York Times*," June 15, 1991.

31. *Time*, May 18, 1992.

32. See the table on page 242 of H. V. Savitch and John Clayton Thomas, *Big City Politics in Transition* (Newbury Park, CA: SAGE Publications, 1991).

33. National Institute of Justice/Drug Use Forecasting Program; East Side Union High School District; cited in San Jose Together Implementation Plan (Mayor's Office, City of San Jose, 1992).

34. *New York Times*, September 3, 1992.

35. *New York Times*, August 28, 1992.

36. Leith Mullings, *Cities of the United States* (New York: Columbia University Press, 1987), p. 10.

37. Bernard J. Frieden and Lynne B. Sagalyn, *Downtown, Inc.: How America Rebuilds Cities* (Cambridge, MA: MIT Press, 1990), p. 289.

38. *Time*, May 18, 1992, p. 32.

39. Joel Garreau, *Edge City: Life on the New Frontier* (New York: Doubleday, 1991).

40. Savitch and Thomas, *Big City Politics*, pp. 2–5.

41. John V. Lindsay, *The City* (New York: W.W. Norton and Company, 1968), p. 47.

42. *New York Times*, October 1, 1992.

43. Jean Gottmann, *Megalopolis: The Urbanized Northeastern Seaboard of the United States* (New York: Twentieth Century Fund, 1961).

44. J.K. Galbraith, *The New Industrial State* (Boston: Houghton Mifflin Company, 1967), p. 347.

45. Quoted in Steven Hall, "Standing On Those Corners, Watching All the Folks Go By," *Smithsonian*, September 1989, p. 121.

46. Quoted in *Advantages of the City of San Jose as a Manufacturing Center* (San Jose: Society for the Promotion of Manufactures, 1884; reprinted by the San Jose Historical Museum Association, 1991), pp. 3–4.

47. Harvey Molotch, "The City as a Growth Machine," *American Journal of Sociology* 82 (2), pp. 309–330.

48. John R. Logan and Harvey L. Molotch, *Urban Fortunes: The Political Economy of Place* (Los Angeles: University of California Press, 1987), p. 54.

49. Quoted in Logan and Molotch, *Urban Fortunes*, p. 57.

50. Logan and Molotch, *Urban Fortunes*, p. 151.

51. Joanne Grant, "Annexation Wars Not New to San Jose," *San Jose Mercury News*, October 26, 1992.

52. Peirce, "Restoring San Jose's 'Murdered' Downtown."

53. Professor Elisabeth Plater-Zyberk, quoted in Barbara Flanagan, "A Massachusetts Mall Is Just Disappeared," *New York Times*, March 14, 1991.

54. William H. Whyte, *City: Rediscovering the Center* (New York: Doubleday, 1988), pp. 128–130.

55. Peirce, "Restoring San Jose's 'Murdered' Downtown."

56. *San Francisco Examiner*, January 21, 1992.

57. Edward Gibbon, *The Decline and Fall of the Roman Empire*, vol. VI (New York: The Cooperative Publication Society, 1905), p. 651.

58. Hoefler admits that Ralph Vaerst, a local entrepreneur, suggested the name to him.

59. Michael Malone, "Why San Jose Is Still Second-Rate," *San Jose Mercury News West Magazine*, April 5, 1992.

60. Gene Bylinski, *High Tech: Window to the Future* (Hong Kong: Intercontinental Publishing Corporation, 1985), p. 12.

61. John F. D'Aprix, *The Role of the Research Park in the Future Develop-*

ment of San Antonio (San Antonio: Center for Entrepreneurial Studies, 1987).

62. Quoted in *Fortune*, April 22, 1991 (Fortune 500 issue).

63. A somewhat comprehensive but deeply flawed look at the area's future prospects is laid out in Joint Venture/Silicon Valley, "Progress Report," Winter 1993.

64. *New York Times*, August 13, 1991.

65. Frieden and Sagalyn, *Downtown, Inc.*, p. 162.

66. Guy Kawasaki, *Selling the Dream* (New York: Harper Collins, 1991).

67. Endorsement for the American Association of Advertising Agencies, appearing in *Bay Area Computer Currents*, March 9, 1993.

68. *New York Times*, February 9, 1993.

69. *New York Times*, May 15, 1992.

70. *New York Times*, November 22, 1992.

71. *New York Times*, October 12, 1992.

72. Gappert and Knight, *Cities in a Global Society*, p. 239.

73. *New York Times*, July 5, 1992.

74. Quoted in *Fortune*, April 22, 1991 (Fortune 500 issue).

75. Tom Rudolph, chief executive officer of StarNine Technologies, quoted in the *San Francisco Chronicle*, June 22, 1991.

76. Dale Whittington, *High Hopes for High-Tech*, ix. (Chapel Hill, NC: University of North Carolina Press, 1985). My understanding of the facts of North Carolina's MCNC program is largely based on Whittington's work.

77. Sheridan Tatsuno, *The Technopolis Strategy: Japan, High Technology, and the Control of the 21st Century* (New York: Prentice Hall Press, 1986).

78. Bylinski, *High Tech: Window to the Future*, p. 26.

79. Knight-Ridder News Service story, *San Jose Mercury News*, February 21, 1993.

80. Logan and Molotch, *Urban Fortunes*, pp. 19–20.

81. Anna Lee Saxenian, "The Urban Contradiction of Silicon Valley: Regional Growth and the Restructuring of the Semiconductor Industry," *Sunbelt/Snowbelt*, p. 190.

82. *San Jose Mercury News*, November 8, 1992.

83. Quoted in Bylinski, *High Tech: Window to the Future*, p. 45.

84. Jane Jacobs, *The Death and Life of Great American Cities* (New York: The Modern Library, 1961), p. 4.

85. Frieden and Sagalyn, *Downtown, Inc.*, p. 36.

86. Heywood T. Sanders, "Urban Renewal and the Revitalized City: A Reconsideration of Recent History," in Donald B. Rosenthal, ed., *Urban Revitalization* (Beverly Hills, CA: SAGE Publications, 1980), p. 103.

87. Frieden and Sagalyn, *Downtown, Inc.*, pp. 15–34.

88. Sanders, Donald B. Rosenthal, ed. *Urban Revitalizaton* (Beverly Hills, CA: Sage Publications, 1980), p. 108.

89. Dennis Judd and Michale Parkinson, *Leadership and Urban Regeneration* (Newbury Park, CA: Sage Publications, 1990), p. 18.

90. Herbert Muschamp, "Barcelona Breaks the Record for Inspired Urbanism," *New York Times*, August 2, 1992.

91. Whyte, *City: Rediscovering the Center*, p. 230.

92. Quoted in *San Jose Mercury News*, December 27, 1983.

93. See "The Sun Rises: A Report on the San Jose Water Pollution Control Plant and Land Use," by Tom McEnery, 1980 (personal collection).

94. Daniel Solomon, *Rebuilding* (Princeton, NJ: Princeton Architectural Press, 1992), p. 7.

95. Tom Bradley, quoted in *California Business*, July 1990.

96. Gappert and Knight, *Cities in a Global Society*, p. 239.

97. Spiro Kostof, *The City Shaped: Urban Patterns and Meanings Through History* (New York: Little, Brown & Company, 1992).

98. San Jose Office of Economic Development, "Market Profile" (1990).

99. Frieden and Sagalyn, *Downtown, Inc.*, p. 84.

100. Letter from the Director, in San Jose Redevelopment Agency "Annual Report" (1989).

101. John Schwada, "Politics Mires City Planners," *Los Angeles Times*, August 7, 1991.

102. Quoted in *San Jose Mercury News*, October 28, 1992.

103. Solomon, *Rebuilding*, p. 26.

104. Solomon, *Rebuilding*, p. 5.

105. *New York Times*, October 30, 1991.

106. Quoted in a series on "What's in the Future for L.A.," *Los Angeles Times*, February 9, 1991.

107. San Jose Office of Economic Development, "Market Profile" (1990).

108. Whyte, *City: Rediscovering the Center*.

109. Frieden and Sagalyn, *Downtown, Inc.*, pp. 7–59.

110. Robert Wood, "Cities in Trouble," *Domestic Affairs*, Summer 1991, p. 226.

111. *San Diego Union*, March 21, 1990.

112. Whyte, *City: Rediscovering the Center*, p. 241.

113. Stephen L. Elkin, *City and Regime in the American Republic* (Chicago: University of Chicago Press, 1987), p. 100.

114. Kevin Brass made the pun in, "San Diego Looks Northward to a 12,000 Acre Tract," *New York Times*, August 30, 1992.

115. Ray Tessler, "Do They Know the Way in San Jose?" *Planning*, October 1988, p. 15.

116. Bert Robinson, "His Words Shape Leaders' Opinions," *San Jose Mercury News*, April 5, 1990.

117. *USA Today*, September 20, 1990.

118. Martin Halstuk, "Downtown Concord Trying to Develop a Life after 5," *San Francisco Chronicle*, July 1, 1991.

119. *San Francisco Chronicle*, March 2, 1993.

120. "The shape and tone of San Jose as it moves into the twenty-first century is largely the work of McEnery, who made an indelible stamp on the city's evolution during his two terms as mayor. . . . McEnery determined what the modern look of San Jose would be." Jean Dietz Sexton, *Silicon Valley: Inventing the Future* (Chatsworth, CA: Windsor Publications, 1992).

121. Wood, "Cities in Trouble," p. 223.

122. See, for example, Gregory D. Squires, ed., *Unequal Partnerships: The Political Economy of Urban Redevelopment in Postwar America* (New Brunswick, NJ: Rutgers University Press, 1989), and Judd and Parkinson, *Leadership and Urban Regeneration*, p. 14.

123. Frieden and Sagalyn, *Downtown, Inc.*, p. 133

124. Gary Schoennauer et al., "Paying for Growth: Community Approaches to Development Impact Fees," *American Planning Association Journal*, Winter 1988.

125. David Osborne, "Government That Means Business," *New York Times Magazine*, March 15, 1992.

126. *New York Times*, January 19, 1992.

127. Savitch and Thomas, *Big City Politics*, p. 3.

128. Carl Nolte writing in *San Francisco Chronicle*, March 16, 1992.

129. Frieden and Sagalyn, *Downtown, Inc.*, p. 296.

130. Information supplied to the author by the Connecticut Department of Economic Development.

131. Kevin Coyle, "The Free-Enterprise Plan to Revitalize Depressed Cities," *California Journal*, December 1981.

132. San Jose Office of Economic Development, "News Bytes" (February 1993, no. 4).

133. Louis Trager, "Enterprise Zone Hazy," *San Francisco Examiner*, June 20, 1991.

134. My calculations, based on figures provided by the U.S. Department of Housing and Urban Development. See also John S. DeMott, "Recasting Enterprise Zones," *Nation's Business*, February 1993.

135. Jonathan Glater, "Enterprise Zones Snub California," *San Francisco Chronicle*, August 19, 1993.

136. *Los Angeles Times*, September 26, 1992; *New York Times*, November 27, 1992.

137. Letters to the editor, *New York Times*, July 21, 1992.

138. Quoted in DeMott, "Recasting Enterprise Zones."

139. "Enterprise Zones Plan in Flux," *Daily Report for Executives* (Washington, DC: Bureau of National Affairs, March 9, 1993.)

140. San Jose Office of Economic Development, "Economic Update" (January 1993).

141. "The Redevelopment Agency of the City of San Jose," (agency fact sheet, 1993).

142. Deborah Larson, "Voters of Seattle Should Learn from San Jose's Past," *Seattle Times*, October 28, 1991.

143. *New York Times*, January 29, 1993.

144. Dr. Durand Jacobs, quoted in John Wildermuth, "Lawmakers Turning to Lady Luck," *San Francisco Chronicle*, August 12, 1991.

145. Rev. Gilbert Horn, of the Colorado Council of Churches, quoted in *Los Angeles Times*, August 11, 1991.

146. "Top Gaming Experts to Address Gambling Meeting," *U.S. Mayor*, March 22, 1993.

147. Sarah Bartlett, "A Tax Boon, or Boondoggle?" *New York Times*, March 1, 1992.

148. San Jose Redevelopment Agency, "Focus on San Jose" (Winter 1992); "The Redevelopment Agency of the City of San Jose" (agency fact sheet, 1993).

149. See the description in "The Product of Faith, Hope, and Charity," *Progressive Architecture*, July 1991.

150. Story told to Noah Griffin and recounted in the *San Francisco Examiner*, March 19, 1993.

151. *Los Angeles Times*, November 29, 1984.

152. *San Jose Mercury News*, December 19, 1984.

153. "San Jose Together Implementation Plan Against Substance Abuse and Violence" (Mayor's Office, City of San Jose, 1992).

154. *San Jose Mercury News*, April 23, 1993.

155. Quoted in the *New York Times*, August 8, 1992.

156. *San Francisco Chronicle*, May 4, 1993.

157. *Los Angeles Times*, August 10, 1991.

158. "Why T.N.T. Fizzled," *New York Times*, August 28, 1992.

159. Michael Franc, "Thoughts on Operation Weed and Seed," reprinted

in *Harper's*, July 1992. The memo was originally printed in the *Washington Post*.

160. "A Vietnam Hawk's Battle Plan for a City's Mean Streets," *New York Times*, January 31, 1993.

161. Reuters story in *San Francisco Chronicle*, March 30, 1992.

162. Timothy Bledsoe and Susan Welch, *Urban Reform and Its Consequences* (Chicago: University of Chicago Press, 1988), pp. 1–17.

163. Report of the Committee on the Past, San Jose, 1989.

164. M. Gottdiener and Chris G. Pickvance, *Urban Life in Transition* (Newbury Park, CA: SAGE Publications, 1991), p. 36.

165. Stephen Ives, "Myth and Discovery in the West," keynote speech to California Historical Society, September 18, 1992.

166. Arthur Schlesinger, Jr., "The Cult of Ethnicity, Good and Bad," *Time*, July 8, 1991.

167. Shelby Steele, *The Content of Our Character*, (New York: St. Martin's Press, 1990), pp. 69–170.

168. *Pittsburgh Post-Gazette*, May 25, 1990.

169. Joseph Rodriguez, "Headgear, Heroes, and Heavies," opinion column, *San Jose Mercury News*, July 19, 1992.

170. *New York Times*, January 27, 1993.

171. The series aired on PBS in the fall of 1991.

172. Herbert Bolton, *The Spanish Borderlands: A Chronicle of Old Florida and the Southwest* (New Haven, CT: 1921), p. 379.

173. Carry McWilliams, *Southern California Country: An Island on the Land* (New York: Books for Libraries, 1946), p. 29.

174. U.S. Congress, House Committee on Immigration and Naturalization, *Western Hemisphere Immigration*, 71st Cong., 2nd Sess., (Washington, DC: GPO, 1930), p. 436.

175. Ernesto Galarza, *Barrio Boy* (Notre Dame, IN: University of Notre Dame Press, 1971).

176. Carlos Munoz, Jr., ed. *Youth, Identity, Power: The Chicano Movement*, (New York: Verso, 1989), p. 21.

177. Luis Valdez, "The Tale of La Raza," *Bronze* vol. 1, no. 1 (1968).

178. Interview, *Parade*, July 12, 1992.

179. *New York Times Magazine*, September 29, 1991.

180. *Time*, July 8, 1993.

181. Quoted in Michael H. Shuman, "Dateline Main Street: Courts v. Local Foreign Policies," *Foreign Policy* 86 (Spring 1992), p. 167.

182. Shuman, "Dateline Main Street."

183. Brian Dickinson, "Saving the Cities," *Providence Journal*; reprinted in the *San Jose Mercury News*, October 8, 1991.

184. "Report of the Bay Vision 2020 Commission," (San Francisco, June 1991).

185. *San Francisco Chronicle*, November 1, 1991.

186. Paul Fussell, director of the San Francisco Planning and Urban Research Association, quoted in *San Francisco Chronicle*, January 8, 1992.

187. William Hudnut, "The Entrepreneurial American City."

188. Pro and con views of political machines and the reforms that killed them are given in Bledsoe and Welch, *Urban Reform and Its Consequences*.

189. David W. Eakins, ed. *Businessmen and Municipal Reform: A Study of Ideals and Practice in San Jose and Santa Cruz, 1896–1916* (San Jose, CA: San Jose State University, 1976).

190. Bledsoe and Welch, *Urban Reform and Its Consequences*, pp. 28–31.

191. *New York Times*, March 26, 1991.

192. Information provided by the city clerk's office, Hawthorne, California. Also see "Official's Residency in Hawaii Assailed," *Los Angeles Times*, February 14, 1992.

193. "Civics 101 on Tape in Arizona," *New York Times*, February 10, 1991.

194. "Lawmakers squirm at ethics workshop," *San Jose Mercury News*, February 17, 1991.

195. Phil Trounstine, "Mayor Uses Power Plays," *San Jose Mercury News*, April 8, 1990.

196. William Fulton, "The Reconstruction of Tom Bradley," *California Business*, July 1990, p. 50.

197. Savitch and Thomas, *Big City Politics*, pp. 10–11.

198. James H. Svara, *Official Leadership in the City: Patterns of Conflict and Cooperation* (New York: Oxford University Press, 1990), pp. 95–117.

199. Ed Salzman, "Enter Strong Mayors—Exit City Managers," *Sacramento Bee*, April 23, 1989.

200. D. Yates, *The Ungovernable City: The Politics of Urban Problems and Policy-making* (Cambridge, MA: MIT Press, 1977), p. 85.

201. This list was drawn up from Svara, *Official Leadership in the City*, p. 88, and supplemented from my own experiences and observations.

202. "Around City Hall: Waiting," *The New Yorker*, December 30, 1991.

203. Quoted by Herb Caen in *San Francisco Chronicle*, December 11, 1991.

204. *Los Angeles Times*, November 2, 1991.

205. *Los Angeles Times*, June 2, 1991.

206. Quoted in "Reapportionment Shuffles the Political Deck," *Los Angeles Times*, January 3, 1992.

207. B. Drummond Ayres, "Surprising Governor Keeps State Guessing," *New York Times*, February 1, 1993.

208. Robert Putnam and William B. Parent, "Is America on Path to Major Reforms?" *The Washington Post*; reprinted in the *San Jose Mercury News*, June 23, 1991.

209. Quoted in the *Philadelphia Inquirer*, November 11, 1991.

210. Peter Knobler, "Hell on Upper Broadway," *New York Times*, August 9, 1991.

211. David Sanger, "In Singapore, a Search for a Second Act," *New York Times*, October 13, 1991.

212. William Cronon, "Mud, Memory and the Loop," *New York Times*, May 2, 1992.

213. Soloman, *Rebuilding*, in his "Afterthought" at the book's conclusion.

Photo Credits

For assistance with photographs, the publishers would like to thank the cities of San Jose, Atlanta, Indianapolis, and Memphis; the redevelopment agency of San Jose and the Santa Fe Historical Museum. The offices of Chicago Mayor Richard Daley, Jr. and New York Mayor Rudy Guiliani were also helpful, as were the offices of Intel Corporation, Apple Computer, Hewlett Packard, and Time-Warner, Inc. Greg Perloff of Bill Graham Presents supplied a much needed photo, as did Fernando Chavez, who provided a fine personal photo of his father Cesar Chavez. Elias Chamorro, principal of Overfelt High School in San Jose, helped with several photographs, as did historian Leonard McKay. Christopher Ayers, as always, was invaluable in securing the best shots of the highest quality—quickly. The Tech Museum of Innovation and its president, Peter Giles, provided key elements of that institution's history.

Lastly, the front cover image, the unique and wonderful portrait of Plaza de Cesar Chavez—spiritual and geographic center of San Jose—was painted by Jim LaMarche and hangs in the San Jose McEnery Convention Center.

Index

313